D1193009

The Land Lies Open

Over the roofs of the pioneers
Gathers the moss of a hundred years;
On man and his works has passed the change
Which needs must be in a century's range.
The land lies open and warm in the sun,
Anvils clamor and mill-wheels run,—
Flocks on the hillside, herds on the plain,
The wilderness gladdened with fruit and grain.

WHITTIER

The
LAND
LIES OPEN

by Theodore C. Blegen

UNIVERSITY OF MINNESOTA PRESS, MINNEAPOLIS

LONDON · GEOFFREY CUMBERLEGE · OXFORD UNIVERSITY PRESS

Copyright 1949 by the

UNIVERSITY OF MINNESOTA

PRINTED AT THE LUND PRESS, INC., MINNEAPOLIS

The lines from "Conquistador" on page three are quoted
from page 203 of Archibald MacLeish, *Poems, 1924–1933*,
edition of 1933, published by the Houghton Mifflin
Company, Boston, Massachusetts. Copyright 1925, 1926,
1928, 1932, and 1933 by Archibald MacLeish.

To

MARGARET JANE BLEGEN

To the Reader

THE Midwest may not be precisely at noon, the spot on the clock assigned to it by an English observer and critic, but its hour is no longer early morning or even mid-morning.

This most American of American regions, after some three centuries of change and development since it was first seen by European eyes, has come of age. Its mood today is one of self-appraisal, and that self-appraisal is taking advantage of perspective and retrospect.

Centennials, and other anniversaries reaching still farther into the American past, are the order of the day. These observances may seem to some to be merely affairs of pageantry, of beauty queens, of official pomp and ceremony, of winter carnivals and summer "aquatennials." But such an interpretation misses their meaning.

Actually, they are being conducted in a spirit of sincere self-discovery. Attics are being ransacked in search of unused historical records. Books and articles on the history of the region are being written in increasing numbers. The creative arts — fiction, poetry, music, painting, sculpture — are linking their efforts with those of history and biography to interpret past and present. Museums, aided by the storekeepers on Main Street, are using "visual aids" in getting at the reality of the past. Programs of democratic, popular education, drawing upon radio and picture as well as upon the printed and spoken word, are reaching out to an entire people.

I think it is not too much to say that the Midwest in its maturity is becoming more historical-minded than it has ever been in the past. It has a growing awareness of the fact that history is an avenue to understanding of the present. That awareness embraces, I believe, a concept of history that gives significant place not only to the great and spectacular events in the past — to the giants and captains and leaders — but also to the changing and developing life of the people at the grass roots of their existence and to the influences radiating out from that life to the major acts and forces that so often pre-occupy the writers of the American saga.

If the "land lies open," if the wilderness is "gladdened with fruit and grain," it is the people who have accomplished that opening and gladdening. And their achievement reaches far back into the history of the land.

This book has been written in the framework of the concept of the American past that I set forth in *Grass Roots History*. I have tried to bring to life — and into focus — some of the many scenes in the long record of human achievement symbolized in Whittier's picture of the open land and the gladdened wilderness. These scenes are drawn from two major themes in American history: the saga of channels to the land, which includes some famous names but is mainly the story of people who are little known to present-day Americans, and the all-embracing saga of people on the land, with a few of the thousands of pictures that illustrate the human interest and significance in the striving of generations of American folk to gladden the wilderness.

THEODORE C. BLEGEN

Contents

THE LAND LIES OPEN

Part I. Channels to the Land

Conquistador

In Archibald MacLeish's "Conquistador" the central story is told by Bernal Díaz, a poor and ignorant man, more than eighty years old, and at the outset he compares himself with the learned professor Gomara — young, scholarly, a delver in records, a lover of big names, imperial decorations, and pompous Latin. But Díaz has one advantage over the professor. As he puts it,

> I am an ignorant old sick man: blind with the
> Shadow of death on my face and my hands to lead me:
> And he not ignorant: not sick —
> > but I
> Fought in those battles! These were my own deeds! . . .
> These were my friends: these dead my companions.

Díaz unquestionably strikes an authentic note, but Gomara somehow suggests a caricature. Granted that the historian may not have "fought in those battles," does it follow that he therefore worships big names and imperial decorations or affects pompous speech?

Not the "dates of empire: the dry skull of fame," cries the impatient poet. "No but our lives: the days of our lives." Agreed, but are not our lives the very stuff of history? How can we recapture their days save by going to the records of those who lived? True enough, we cannot say with Díaz that

3

these figures were comrades in the flesh, these deeds our very own, but we can read and study the records of those who took part in events, who told their stories, knew the actors, journeyed with them, fought at their side, and were with them when they died.

Only by so doing can we reconstruct some of the many scenes in that panoramic story of the greatest of all channels to the land — the Mississippi, from its mouth to the pine-fringed lake in northern Minnesota from which it issues.

ONE of those scenes centers in a conquistador, a proud son of Spain in the adventurous sixteenth century, a gentleman "by all four descents," Hernando de Soto. He was nineteen when, in 1519, only twenty-seven years after Columbus sailed out on the "ocean sea," he arrived at Darien from Spain, equipped with "nothing more than blade and buckler." He plunged into adventures incredible alike to Gomaras and Díazes. As a commander of dragoons he went with Córdoba into Nicaragua. He won fame as an Indian fighter and wealth as a slave trader. He joined Pizarro in the conquest of Peru. He was the first Christian to look upon the Inca chieftain Atahualpa. As Theodore Maynard says, he was the first to see the "temple of the sun, gorgeous in gold"; the first to climb the mountains of Peru; the first to walk the "frail trembling bridges of ozier" across the chasms of the Andes.

De Soto came to know the perils of Indian attack, the torture of glaring sun, the fury of sandstorm, the menace of dissension among the Spanish soldiers — and the dangerous delights of fabulous golden treasures. In 1535, wearied by the fratricidal strife of the conquistadors, he set sail for Spain with a fortune — more than a hundred thousand pesos.

A boy had gone out to the New World; a hard-bitten man returned. What manner of man was he? These things jump out at the student of the records: he was shrewd; he had staying power; he was proud; he was engaging and eager; he had a stubborn will; he had self-confidence. He would not admit a mistake. He was toughened by his experience as a soldier and a conqueror. An old soldier of Darien, he was, in the words addressed to Pope Julius II by Peter Martyr, one of those "hardened to abide all sorrows, and exceedingly tollerable of labour, heate, hunger and watching, in so much that they make their boast that they have observed a longer and sharper Lent than ever your Holliness enjoyed: for they say that for the space of foure whole yeere they eate none other than herbes and fruits, except now and then perhappes fysshe, and very seldom flesshe; yea, and that sometime they lack of all these, they have not abhorred from mangie dogs and filthie toads."

De Soto enjoyed wealth and high status in Spain after his return from the treasure land of the Incas. He lived in splendor, flattered by the courtiers of the royal household. The Emperor made him a knight of the order of Santiago. He married Doña Isabel, a daughter of the commander under whom he had served in Nicaragua, and this marriage made him a brother-in-law of Balboa, the discoverer of the Pacific. Soon he was himself dreaming of new worlds to conquer. A conquistador could not be content to remain idle amid the luxury of the Spanish court. And in 1537 he was appointed governor of Cuba and *adelantado* of Florida — the title *adelantado* derived from a word meaning "to advance and to surpass." De Soto meant to advance and to surpass, for he secured permission to explore the unknown land that stretched away to the north from the Gulf of Mexico.

Was Florida another Peru, with treasures comparable to those of the Incas? The wandering Cabeza de Vaca, just back from the New World, told of Florida as the wealthiest of all regions in America. The nobles of Spain were thrilled at the prospect of a Florida conquest, and hundreds sold their estates and flocked to join De Soto. He picked six hundred of the best for his expedition, and on an April morning in 1538, in of nine vessels, with artillery roaring and trumpets ...ding, they sailed from Spain for Santiago de Cuba.

The crossing was uneventful, and the expedition arrived safely at Santiago, where the don and his wife Doña Isabel rode into the city followed by the six hundred. Havana was made the port of departure for the expedition to Florida, and, leaving his wife at Havana, De Soto set out in the spring of 1539 for Tampa Bay.

The odyssey of Hernando de Soto from this point on runs for a period of three years, and it is this odyssey that gives the man a secure place in the history of the United States. It is a confused odyssey, difficult to follow with clearness, but one thing stands out at once. This was no mere exploring expedition; it was an expedition of conquest. In dealing with Indians, the don's policy was to get local chiefs in his hands and then hold them as hostages until he was well out of their territory. He met the chiefs with pretenses of friendship, then made captives of them and compelled them to furnish him with baggage carriers, cooks, and servants.

This deceitful policy had worked well in Peru, but among the fierce and warlike savages of the South it was less successful. De Soto had brought with him packs of bloodhounds and Irish greyhounds, and they were used to bring in fugitives and also as executioners, to tear them to pieces. Make no mistake: the Spanish don was cruel. His experiences as a slave trader in Nicaragua and Panama had bred in him an utter callousness toward Indian life and in his conduct toward the red men he displayed a ruthlessness rarely equaled even by Spaniards, masters of the art. Las Casas wrote of him shortly after he landed in Florida: "This we are sure of, that at the beginning he carried himself very cruelly; and if he is alive most assuredly he hath destroyed an infinite number of people; for he among all those who have done the most mischiefe in ruining both Provinces and Kingdoms, is famous for his savage fury."

The Spaniards were also interested in getting slaves for their Cuban estates. The master of De Soto's camp, when he landed in Florida, was chiefly concerned with securing a supply of Indian slaves, but when he learned how intractable the Seminoles were, he took the first opportunity to return to Cuba.

De Soto — impetuous, fearless, stern — was a better leader of troops in an advance guard than he was a commander of an expedition. But he was dogged, and this quality enabled him to push his way for three years through the swamps and bogs of Florida, the pine forests of Georgia, the canebreaks and sloughs of Mississippi, and the flooded lowlands of Arkansas. Good land he found, and hundreds of pounds of imperfect pearls, but not fabulous treasures of gold. And he would not admit defeat. "It was his object," said one of his companions, "to find another treasure like that of Atahualpa, lord of Peru." He "would not be content with good lands or pearls." Somewhere there was a land of gold, where the people wore "golden hats like casques," and he would not give up until he found that land. So he pressed on. He had a big expedition: 550 lancers, crossbowmen, and arquebusiers, 200 horses, priests, friars, a physician, a carpenter, a calker, a cooper, armorers, and smiths. And his own will to search out the land of the golden hats!

In the autumn of 1540 De Soto learned that his lieutenant Maldonaldo was at Pensacola with ships that had been sent back to Cuba for supplies. De Soto himself by that time had traveled as far northeast as the Savanna River, crossed the Smoky Mountains, gone into Tennessee, and then marched southward to the head of Mobile Bay. He had taken the Indian village of Mabilla, near the head of the bay, after desperate fighting. His supplies were lost; twenty of his men were killed and 150 wounded; twelve of his horses were killed and seventy wounded. His men were in rags. Even the priests' chalices and the wine for Mass had been destroyed. One might suppose that common sense would have dictated a return to the ships.

But De Soto was a conquistador. He swore his informant to secrecy, said nothing about the ships of Maldonaldo, and turned northward into the wilderness!

Is it strange that the historian Oviedo exclaimed: "I have wondered many times at the venturesomeness, stubbornness, and persistency or firmness, to use a better word for the way these baffled conquerors kept on from one toil to another, and then to another still greater; from one danger to many others, here losing one companion, there three and again still more, going from bad to worse without learning from experience. Oh wonderful God! that they should have been so blinded and dazed by a greed so uncertain and by such vain courses as Hernando de Soto was able to utter to these deluded soldiers."

For twenty-eight days after the battle of Mabilla De Soto and his men rested, dressing their wounds with the fat of slain Indians. Then they took up their wanderings again. They reached Chicaça, somewhere in the present state of Mississippi, before winter set in and stayed until the spring of 1541, but before they left this place they suffered another fierce, almost disastrous, Indian attack. Houses were set afire, horses stampeded. In the midst of the clamor De Soto charged the Indians alone, sword in hand, and they fled. More men killed, horses destroyed, and, worst of all, weapons lost! The soldiers must retemper swords and lance heads and shape new shafts. The Indians did not attack again, however, until these things had been done. Wrote one of the chroniclers, "God, who chastiseth his own as he pleaseth, and in the greatest wants and perils hath them in hand, shut the eyes of the Indians, so that they could not discern what they had done."

The wilderness march was resumed April 26, 1541. About the first of May De Soto reached a village where he learned that he was near a great river. That river, the great channel to the American interior, was the Mississippi. De Soto crossed it in June on barges that his men had built.

8

Then began a maze of wanderings west of the river, with tragedy hovering nearer and nearer. Toward the end of August the Spaniards came to a place called Quigate, probably an arm of the Rio Grande, possibly the Arkansas. From there they pushed on to Coligua, in the gorge of the Arkansas, or perhaps one of the tributaries of the Washíta, then turned southeast, following the Washíta and entering Louisiana, a land of fierce Indians. Here, on the Washíta, at Autiamque, they wintered. Then it was spring again, and on March 6, 1542, they crossed the Washíta, hunting for Nilco, which was reported by Indians to be near the Great River. On April 15 they reached Guachoya — perhaps at the junction of the Red and the Mississippi, though some scholars say at the mouth of the Arkansas. Now De Soto sent a party to find a land way to the Gulf — a way of escape, for his situation was desperate.

A hostile land, no trace of the treasures he had hoped to find, more than a third of his men killed, surrounded by the fiercest warriors he had yet encountered, horses gone, weapons worn, hunger, sickness, death striking his followers: that was the plight of the conquistador. And when his reconnoitering party returned, after eight days, to tell only of swamps, mud, and canebreaks, even the stout heart of De Soto failed him. His spirit did not know retreat — yet retreat he must if his men were to escape destruction. Did he, one wonders, admit failure? We know that he fell ill, and one of his men said, "The Governor sank into a deep despondency at sight of the difficulties that presented themselves to his reaching the sea; and, what was worse, from the way in which his men and horses were diminishing in numbers, he could not sustain himself in the country without succour. Of that reflection he pined. . . ." But not without a last effort: he sent a detachment of men to Nilco with orders to destroy every man in the village.

And then, on May 21, 1542, the end came. Calling his officers and men to his side, he gave thanks to God, then thanked

9

his followers for "their great qualities, their love and loyalty to his person"; he asked their prayers, their forgiveness for wrongs done; and he chose a successor: Luís de Moscoso. And then "departed this life," says one chronicle, "the magnanimous, the virtuous, the intrepid captain, Don Hernando de Soto, Governor of Cuba and adelantado of Florida. He was advanced by fortune, in the way she is wont to lead others, that he might fall the greater depth."

His officers buried him between the posts of the gates of the encampment, and his death was kept secret from the Indians. They were told that the Child of the Sun had ascended to the sun. But the red men were suspicious, and so the officers dug up the body, packed it with sand, wrapped it in shawls, took it out to the middle of the Mississippi, and there, under the stars, dropped it into the Father of Waters.

Luís de Moscoso and his men now had but one thought — to get to Cuba or Mexico as quickly as possible. Yet it was fifteen months before this purpose was accomplished. What happened? In the summer and fall a march toward Mexico that took them out on the plains of Texas — then, with food supplies low, a return to the Great River — and finally, in July 1543, in seven brigantines built by the soldiers, a seventeen-day journey down to the sea. When the men after skirting the Texas coast landed on the shore of Panúco, many, we are told, "kissed the ground; and all, on bended knees, with hands raised above them, and their eyes to heaven, remained untiring in giving thanks to God."

Poor Doña Isabel in Havana at last learned of the loss of her husband. She had tried desperately to reach him by letter, but had failed. Now, grief-stricken, she collapsed, and a few days later she died.

These are the main elements in the saga of the conquistador, but a few questions remain. At what point did De Soto reach the Mississippi? Some maintain that the spot was the Fourth Chickasaw Bluff in Memphis, and the Memphis partisans have even named a park in his honor at that place. Others contend that the point was either Council Bend or Walnut Bend in Tunica County, Mississippi. The records seem to lean toward Tunica County rather than Memphis, but unless new historical evidence comes to light, the controversy is likely to continue. As in the Radisson problem in the Upper Mississippi Valley, the records, vague as to identifiable geographic points, do not offer clear-cut answers.

More fundamental is the question, Did De Soto indeed discover the Mississippi River? Discovery, one must insist, means more than finding; it means making known, revealing, reporting to the world.

In 1519, the year De Soto as a youth came to Darien, a Spanish sailor named De Pineda learned that a river disgorged its mighty current into the Gulf of Mexico. He called it the Rio del Espíritu Santo. This may have been the Mississippi; it may have been the Mobile; but in any event soon thereafter the Rio del Espíritu began to appear on maps, and the name itself became associated with the Mississippi. Another Spaniard, Pánfilo de Narváez, touched the mouth of the Mississippi in 1528. Though he did not survive to report his discovery to the world, his companion, Cabeza de Vaca, made the story known. But these explorations were limited indeed. Where did the mighty river come from? What were its sources? What were its relations to other rivers? To these questions De Pineda and Narváez could give no answer.

It is certain that De Soto found the Mississippi, but it is equally clear that to him it was merely a great river, a Rio Grande, an obstacle in the path of his soldiers, something to be crossed. The chroniclers of his expedition dismiss it with only a few words. The anonymous Portuguese Gentleman of Elvas, whose narrative was published at Lisbon in 1557, speaks of it casually: "There was a little maize in the place, and the Governor moved to another town, half a league from the great river, where it was found in sufficiency. He went to look at the river, and saw that near it was much timber where piraguas might be made, and a good situation in which the camp might be placed." The "stream was swift and very deep" and the water flowed "turbidly." De Soto's private secretary, Ranjel, whose narrative comes to us through the Spanish historian Oviedo, has little to say: "There they saw the great river. Saturday, May 21, the force went along to a plain between the river and a small village, and set up quarters and began to build four barges to cross over to the other side." Biedma, whose report was presented to the Spanish king in 1544, is the only one of the chroniclers who calls the river the Espíritu Santo, but he too has little to say: "We left that place and went to camp by the river side, to put ourselves in order for crossing."

This is all casual enough, though it seems significant that these chroniclers say *the* great river. It was not until the time of the French in the seventeenth century that "a correct map was made of that portion of Florida through which the expedition of De Soto travelled." If we think of the De Soto expedition as a whole, we must concede that it did something definitely more than merely *find* the river. To the minds of the survivors of De Soto's party, the Great River turned in the Memphis region, heading east. They carried with them a geographical picture that corresponds, somewhat roughly, to the lower Mississippi and Tennessee rivers. And this picture began to appear in maps. We may therefore justly call De Soto's work, in combination with that of Pineda and Narváez, a partial discovery of the river.

Nor should we forget that De Soto's explorations were of importance to Spanish colonial policy. That importance, shared with Coronado — searcher for El Dorado and man of "unconquerable hope" — was negative, but not the less real for that. These grim and persistent marauders proved to Spain that the American Southwest was not another Peru. The mountains of gold and priceless treasures of jewels were mirages. Great wealth there was indeed, but the eyes of the conquistadors were closed to the sheen of furs and the promise of soil and rain and sun. The river itself did not excite the imagination of the Spaniards.

The Mississippi was too majestic for one man or one group of men to have the glory of its full discovery. France shares that glory with Spain, and the United States with both, for it was not until the nineteenth century that the mystery of the river's source was unlocked. And it is a circumstance that befits the greatness of the river that it was discovered both from north and from south over a period of nearly three centuries. Not until that long task was completed did the land truly lie open.

With Thunder in Both Hands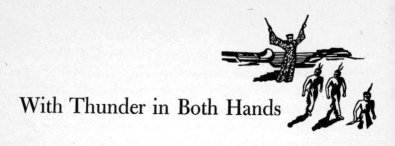

Nearly a century after De Soto's body was buried at night in the lower Mississippi, a white man carrying thunder in both hands stepped ashore from a canoe in Green Bay, on the western side of Lake Michigan, facing the domain of the Rio del Espíritu in northern reaches that the conquistador never saw.

Indian squaws with papooses on their backs and black-haired children scampering after them took to their heels with yells of fear. To see a man with a white face was terrifying enough in this kingdom of red men, but when the strange visitor, dressed in a flowered silk robe, shot thunder from his hands, terror turned to panic.

Jean Nicolet, coasting down Lake Michigan to the shores of Green Bay in a great canoe paddled by seven men, had the Frenchman's love of dramatic effect, and as he landed he could not resist pointing his pistols skyward and pulling the triggers. Civilization met the stone age with a flash of gunpowder.

The Winnebago Indians, seeing a white man for the first time in the hinterland beyond Lake Michigan, soon recovered from their fright. He himself reassured them. They had nothing to fear from him; his errand was one of peace, not of war. He was no Spanish don equipped with an army of soldiers — and bloodhounds. Presently the squaws and children crept back again; the men squatted around a campfire; with Nicolet an honored guest, a feast was held, and the cooked meat of more than a hundred beavers served as a delicacy for this wilderness banquet of East and West.

Who was Jean Nicolet, and why had he come to visit the Indians on Lake Michigan fourteen years after the Pilgrims landed at Plymouth Rock? And why was he armed with long pistols and wearing a Chinese robe? These questions have intrigued historians from the day of Francis Parkman to the present.

Nicolet was a Frenchman. He had pushed his way from the settlements of his countrymen on the St. Lawrence River through a wilderness of land and water a thousand miles into the West. He came looking for a nation known as the "People of the Sea," about whom he had heard from friendly Indians in eastern America. Possibly these western people were different from the red men. Possibly the long-hunted but elusive route to the Orient could be found by going beyond the Great Lakes.

Like many another French explorer, Nicolet seems to have hoped that by paddling his way over lakes and streams into the West he might discover the way to the land of silks, spices, and incredible riches that the Venetian, Ser Marco Polo, had seen with astounded eyes in the thirteenth century and that had stirred European curiosity — and greed — ever since. Nicolet took with him on his travels the gay damask robe he was wearing when he landed at Green Bay in order to be properly dressed for meeting the Khan of Cathay himself, or the people of an outlying Asiatic colony. A true son of old France, he did not forget that he represented the proud court of one of the leading countries of the seventeenth-century world.

In his large canoe Nicolet had crossed Lake Huron, gone through the straits, and passed the towering island of Michilimackinac far in the West. The "People of the Sea," he had learned, lived on a bay on the west side of a mighty lake to the southward. Over Lake Michigan's unexplored stretches and along its wooded shores he pressed. When he met strange Indians he landed, fastened two sticks in the earth, and hung gifts on them, so the red men would understand that he was not an enemy, but their friend. At last he reached the entrance to the bay of which he had heard, and after landing on an island he sent messengers ahead to tell the natives he was coming. So it happened that the Indians, excited by reports that a Manitourinion, or "wonderful man," was coming, were gathered to meet him when he stepped ashore at Green Bay.

Nicolet must surely have been greatly disappointed, if he believed he was nearing the provinces of Cathay. Instead of the silk-clad courtiers of the Khan he found the Green Bay Indians clothed in skins of animals; instead of gold and silver, the Winnebago used implements of chipped stone and dishes of shells and bark and hand-shaped clay. They lived in skin or bark-covered lodges built of poles, and their only tame animals were dogs. Nicolet soon made friends with them, and they agreed to a treaty of peace — one of the objectives the Frenchman had in mind.

So Jean Nicolet came to Green Bay — one white man in the region west of the Great Lakes inhabited today by millions. Did he have any conception of the imperial sweep of the wilderness he faced? To the north, an inland sea with pine-fringed shores — far in the interior, streams flowing toward the icy Arctic, emptying into the bowl of Hudson Bay — off toward the west, forests, lakes, rivers, rapids and falls, hills and prairies. Somewhere in the far distance a jagged range of Rocky Mountains, and yet farther away toward the sunset the slopes of the Pacific Coast. Of the vastness of this western country Nicolet knew only what little he himself saw and what he could learn from his Winnebago friends. Yet one of the things they told him was that a great river flowed out of the north and that on its waters one might float down to the sea — a channel to the sea and from the sea to the land.

The story of this French discoverer of the Middle West

takes one across the sea, for he was a Norman, with Viking blood in his veins. He was born in 1598 at Cherbourg, to which, when he was a boy, came vessels with cargoes of fish and furs from the New World. In Cherbourg were to be seen seamen who had sailed with famous mariners in western waters. The smell of salt is in the air of Cherbourg; its wharves in the days of Henry of Navarre and Louis XIII were crowded with ships from many parts of the world; and among the sailors who lounged about the old town were many who could stir the imagination of a boy with their tales of adventure. There Jean grew up; and there, when he was twenty years old, he had a stroke of luck. He met Samuel de Champlain.

In 1599, when Nicolet was only a year old, Champlain, the son of a French sea captain, was himself the commander of a vessel that sailed to the West Indies, and four years later he voyaged to the St. Lawrence River. A company of merchants in France had decided to launch a colony in New France, and Champlain was sent there to explore and to draw maps. His exploits are familiar to every schoolboy in Canada and the United States. He explored the coast of New England; in 1608 he founded the city of Quebec; the next year he discovered the lake in western New York that still bears his name; and in 1615 he discovered and named Lakes Huron and Ontario. No wonder this pioneer is remembered and honored as the founder of New France!

The French in the first half of the seventeenth century, by discovering and exploring the Great Lakes, opened the door to the Mississippi Valley, and they passed through the door in the second half of the century. Champlain was the leader in the earlier work of discovery and in fact did much of it himself. No one man could explore all New France, however, and he knew it. On his many trips back to France, where he told about his discoveries and showed his maps, he kept his eyes open for promising young men who might help him to carry on his work in the New World. He wanted youths who had courage and had no fear of the hardships that inevitably accompanied a plunge into the wilderness. In Cherbourg, in 1618, he found Jean Nicolet, liked him, and asked him to go out with him to Quebec to study the Indian languages and to be an interpreter.

The Cherbourg boy accepted the invitation. Champlain sent him to live in an Algonquin Indian village, and this was the beginning of a schooling in which Nicolet learned to speak the Indian languages, to trap and hunt, and to live in the wilderness. He learned also the meaning of hunger and hardship. One winter he lived for seven weeks with no food except bark stripped from trees.

Every summer Nicolet left his home among the Algonquins and traveled down the St. Lawrence to Quebec to tell the governor about his life with the Indians and to repeat stories he had heard of tribes and lands and waters far to the west. After fifteen years of trial by wilderness ordeal, Nicolet got a promotion. He was given the job of interpreter and clerk at the fur-trading post of Three Rivers. And the next year, in 1634, Champlain, who thought the route to China might lie through the Great Lakes, chose Nicolet to go west. He was told to make peace among the Indian tribes and to win their friendship for France, but he was also to be prepared in case the "People of the Sea" should prove to be Chinese.

Nicolet's voyage occupies a high place in American history, for it resulted in the discovery of the lake on the shores of which Chicago, Milwaukee, and other great American cities were to be built in the nineteenth century, and it was a further step by the French toward the wealth of mid-America.

Having visited the Winnebago on Green Bay, Nicolet started the return voyage eastward in his canoe. His goal was Quebec, where he intended to make his report to Champlain; but he spent the winter in a Huron village, and it was not until 1635 that he was able to reach the French city on the St. Lawrence. Champlain was now an old man; later in the same year he died;

but before his career ended he had the satisfaction of hearing from the lips of the man he had brought out from Cherbourg the story of a great expedition into the West.

Nicolet went back to the trading village of Three Rivers, and seven years later, in 1642, while on his way to Quebec, he was drowned when his canoe was swamped by waves.

Nicolet did not find a western route to China, but, representing the great Champlain, he discovered the Middle West. Before long other Frenchmen were floating their canoes on western waters. Explorers already knew about the existence of Lake Superior, and in fact Nicolet himself had heard of this vast northern lake and had visited a Chippewa village at the strait where the waters of Superior pour into the lower lakes. Meanwhile, the French were wondering about that great river the Winnebago had told Nicolet about, the river that ran southward to the sea, the highway to the open land of the continent.

Labyrinth of Pleasure

Not long after the middle of the seventeenth century a Frenchman whose daring fully matched that of Jean Nicolet pushed his way into the region beyond Lake Michigan. He found it so beautiful that it set him dreaming about a far future when this country might be a "labyrinth of pleasure" for millions of people.

This imaginative traveler was Pierre Esprit Radisson, fur trader, fighter, woodsman, adventurer. The western region that he saw was "so pleasant, so beautifull and fruitfull" that it made him sad to think the world had not known about it long before and populated it. Here were countless acres of wonderful lands, "plentifull of all things," that might be turned into gardens — while in the Europe of his youth millions of people were poor and miserable and countries went to war for nothing more than a "rock in the sea" or "for a sterill land and horrid country."

Radisson's seventeenth-century dream came true, but not for two centuries and not before geographical puzzles far more complex than those of the fabled Theseus were unraveled by men curious both about channels to the land and about the channeled land.

The chronicle of Radisson, as complicated and intricate as the labyrinth he described, has been told in scholarly detail by a brilliant historian of the Midwest, Dr. Grace Lee Nute, in

her memorable *Caesars of the Wilderness*. It is difficult to reduce it to brief compass without turning it into the dates of
empire and the dry skull of fame, but some of the flesh and
blood of the story may be at least suggested.

Radisson was born in 1636, probably at Avignon in France.
When he was only fourteen or fifteen, his family went out to
New France and settled in the little village of Three Rivers.
The boy Pierre was captured by the Iroquois one day when
he wandered off with some companions to hunt ducks and
geese. The boys who were with him were killed, but his life
was spared. His spirit and courage caused him to be adopted
into the family of an Iroquois chief who gave him the name of
Orimha, which, like the French name *Pierre*, means a "stone."
He had one adventure after another, escaped, was recaptured
and tortured, escaped again, made his way to New Amsterdam
and took ship for the Old World, visited Paris, and then returned to his relatives in the Canadian village of Three Rivers
two years after he had left on his little hunting excursion.

He found that his sister Marguerite had married a fur trader
named Médard Chouart, better known as the Sieur des Groseilliers, a curious name that means "Lord of the Gooseberry
Bushes" and apparently was taken from the name of a farm
near his birthplace in the Marne River Valley in France. The
brothers-in-law soon became fast friends and partners, and in
the period between 1654 and 1660 they journeyed, either
singly or together, into the great Northwest. It was on these
journeys that they visited the world's future "labyrinth of
pleasure."

On the first western trip young Des Groseilliers and a companion made their way, like Nicolet, to Lake Michigan, which
Radisson, who later undertook to write the story of this trip,
called the "delightfullest lake of the world." Des Groseilliers
followed its western shore to Green Bay and then struck off
into the woods of Wisconsin. There is at least a possibility
that he traveled as far as the Mississippi River, for Radisson

writes that he "went into the great river that divides itselfe in 2 . . . because it has 2 branches, the one towards the west, the other towards the South, which we believe runns towards Mexico." Some students even assert that he journeyed up the Mississippi into the Minnesota country as far as Prairie Island, below the site of the present city of Hastings. From the account that Radisson wrote, however, we cannot be wholly certain just where his daring friend did go, and it seems doubtful that he did in fact see the great channel. We do know that he saw the wonderful country west of Lake Michigan, where he lived among the Indians, traded for furs, and had many an adventure before returning to Quebec.

Des Groseilliers reached Quebec with a fleet of fifty canoes manned by red men and loaded with choice furs and was saluted "with the thundring of the guns and batteries of the fort." He was entertained by the governor and cheered and admired by everyone. The truth is that, because of Huron-Iroquois wars, the French fur trade had declined and there was a fur famine in eastern Canada. So it is not difficult to understand why the people of Quebec rejoiced over the success of a daring trading expedition to the distant West. Three ships at Quebec bound for France would have returned to the mother country without furs, Radisson tells us, had it not been for this expedition.

Soon the two adventurers were jointly preparing for an even more daring plunge into the western wilderness. This time they planned to push farther north than Des Groseilliers seems to have gone on the first trip. They understood that if they wanted the choicest of beaver skins they must head for the north country. But the governor, the Marquis d'Argenson, got wind of their plans and refused to authorize them to trade unless they agreed to pay him half the profits of the new venture!

This was twice as much as the usual levy on fur traders, and Radisson and Des Groseilliers refused to make such a pledge. One August night in 1659 they slipped away from

Three Rivers secretly, without official authorization. Up the Ottawa River they went, then by the way of Lake Nipissing and the French River to Lake Huron, and along its northern shores to Sault Ste. Marie. Instead of turning toward Lake Michigan, however, they now entered Lake Superior and paddled along its southern shores.

After crossing Keweenaw Point they stopped to build a little log cabin on Chequamegon Bay, probably the first white man's house in the Upper Midwest. In this cabin they left most of the goods they had brought with them to use in trading for furs with the Indians. Then they set off overland, with some Indians, toward an Ottawa Indian village on a little lake seemingly located in what is now Sawyer County, Wisconsin. Near the center of this county today there is a village called "Radisson."

The Indians living in the seventeenth-century village to which the Frenchmen went had never seen a white man before. Radisson in his own story of the journey suggests how astonished they were when they saw the two Europeans. "There is nothing but cryes," he writes. Cries of wonder, perhaps, at seeing men whose skins were white. Cries of delight, perhaps, at seeing the trade goods that Radisson and Des Groseilliers brought with them. For the white men had gifts for the natives — strange and useful things they had never seen before. These included kettles, hatchets, knives, sword blades, combs, looking glasses — the looking glasses not less wonderful because they were made of bright tin rather than of glass.

The Frenchmen lived in the Indian village during that winter, and the ground was heavy with snow. They had to make rackets, "not to play att ball, but to exercise ourselves in a game harder and more necessary." The two men wore these rackets, or snowshoes, on their feet when following a deer, and were thus prevented from sinking into the soft snow at each step.

Even with snowshoes to help them in trailing game, the hunters could not get enough food, and the Indian camp became the scene of misery — of starvation, suffering, death. To fight hunger the Indians had to kill and eat their dogs, devour roots, and chew the bark of trees. And their white visitors "became the very Image of death." Radisson sometimes found it hard to tell whether a man was living or dead, for some of the starving people seemed to be only skin and bones.

One day, while the natives and their French visitors were suffering from hunger, two Sioux Indians, followed by a dog, appeared in the camp. The dog was lean, but Radisson took an irresistible, hungry interest in it. One night he crept near the hut where the Sioux were sleeping, the dog came out, the Frenchman led it away, then stabbed it with his dagger. Here was a meal for the starving men — they even scraped up the snow that had been stained with the dog's blood to use in seasoning their kettles.

The white men managed to live through the winter, but they as well as the natives suffered intensely. When Radisson later wrote about this experience he exclaimed, "Good God, have mercy on so many poore innocent people!" Mercy came when the crust of snow on a near-by lake got soft enough that deer walking on it broke through; then it was easy for the Indians to catch them.

In the spring Radisson and Des Groseilliers attended a great Indian council, to which came people of eighteen different tribes, including the Sioux — "the nation of the beefe," that is, the buffalo hunters. A great square fort, or inclosure, was built for the occasion.

The Indians presented a most picturesque appearance. The faces of most of the men were daubed with many colors, and their hair was "turned up like a Crowne" and cut evenly. It was trimmed, Radisson tells us, not with scissors, but with fire. "They leave a tuff of haire upon their Crowne of their heads, tye it, and putt att the end of it some pearles or some Turkey stones, to bind their heads." Their ears were pierced in five places. They smeared themselves with thick grease, and every Indian had a crow's skin hanging at his girdle. Their leggings were decorated with pearls and native embroidery.

In the midst of all this finery the Frenchmen, brothers in spirit to the man who carried thunder, did not miss the chance to impress the Indians with the grandeur of the white man. They delivered speeches, but these were not enough. Radisson and Des Groseilliers had twelve guns; they called these their "artillery," and they shot them off in state. They drew their swords and long knives, so that some of the Indians hardly knew whether to run or to stay. But the Frenchmen's most spectacular piece of showmanship was to throw gunpowder into the council fire, making a violent explosion and a cloud of smoke. The next day they gave gifts to the Indians and explained why they were in the red man's country.

When twentieth-century America reads of such exploits, it can perhaps understand why Radisson exclaims, "We weare Cesars, being nobody to contradict us." Caesars indeed — "Caesars of the wilderness."

After these adventures Radisson and his brother-in-law traveled considerably in the north country and even claim to have gone as far as Hudson Bay, though this claim seems to be a spurious one made to enforce their later interest in a Northwest Passage. When they started back for Chequamegon Bay, they were convinced that the North, with its riches of beavers, was a region of tremendous future importance for the fur trade of North America. On reaching the Wisconsin bay where a year earlier they had built their hut, they found that Ottawa Indians had established a village at this place.

Finally, with a great escort of Indians and a fleet of a hundred canoes loaded with furs, Radisson and Des Groseilliers left the upper country to return to Montreal and Quebec. Forty of the canoes turned back when the Indian paddlers learned there was danger of an attack by the fierce Iroquois on the Ottawa River, but the rest went on and safely reached their destination.

The firing of cannon greeted the brothers-in-law when they arrived at Montreal, where everybody was glad "to see so great a number of boats that did almost cover the whole River." But at Quebec the stealthy departure of the two traders for the West had not been forgotten. They were arrested, and the governor made them pay one fine after another, taking away from them most of the profits of their expedition.

Radisson was bitterly angry about this treatment by the Quebec official. "Was not he a Tyrant," he exclaimed, "to deal so with us, after wee had so hazarded our lives?" And Des Groseilliers was so indignant that, after his release from arrest, he made a trip to France to protest to high officials of the French government and to ask for redress, but he had no success. So he journeyed back to Canada and there rejoined his brother-in-law.

Some time after this the two Frenchmen met, at Port Royal in Nova Scotia, a Boston sea captain whom they tried to interest in a fur-trading expedition to Hudson Bay. The captain finally agreed, probably in 1662, to sail his vessel into the north, for they convinced him that he would be amply repaid by the rewards from northern furs. He reached Hudson Strait late in the season, met fierce storms, and to the great disappointment of the Frenchmen decided to return to Boston rather than risk the loss of his vessel by wintering in that inhospitable region. So back they went.

In Boston again, the traders tried to get other vessels for a journey into northern waters, but without success. Fortunately they met at this time some English officials who were much interested in the wonderful tales Radisson and Des Groseilliers had to tell, and one of them, Colonel George Cartwright, advised the Frenchmen to go with him to England, where they might be able to get capital and backing for trading enterprises in the Hudson Bay country.

So in 1665 Radisson and Des Groseilliers crossed the Atlantic. But not without adventure, for the vessel in which they sailed was captured by the Dutch and they were landed in Spain. When they finally reached England, it was the year of the Great Plague, and because of the disease raging in London, King Charles had temporarily moved his court to Oxford. There an audience with the king was arranged for the Frenchmen. They told the king their story of fur-gathering in the wilds of America and asked for assistance in tapping the trade of the Hudson Bay region. He was interested, but it was Prince Rupert, his cousin, and a group of great nobles and merchants who gave the traders their chief support.

By the spring of 1668 an expedition was ready to start. It was provided with two vessels, the *Eaglet* and the *Nonsuch*. Radisson was to go on one, Des Groseilliers on the other. The instructions given to the captains concluded with these words: "Lastly wee desire and require you to use the said Mr. Gooseberry and Mr. Radisson with all manner of civility and courtesy and to take care that all your company doe beare a particular respect unto them they being the persons upon whose credit wee have undertaken this expedition which wee beseech Almighty God to prosper." This document was signed by Prince Rupert and five other men.

So the two vessels started on the long and dangerous journey to Hudson Bay. The *Eaglet*, with Radisson on board, after encountering furious storms, had to return to England. Radisson himself was deeply disappointed, but he used his time in London to prepare for another expedition and to write an account in French of his early travels and adventures in America. An English translation of this account somehow fell into the hands of Samuel Pepys, the English diarist, and ultimately it was placed in the Bodleian Library at Oxford University, where it was filed away. More than two hundred years after Radisson wrote the account, it was found in the Bodleian Library and published, and thus the story of this seventeenth-century trader and explorer became known to the world.

While the *Eaglet* was limping back to an English port, the *Nonsuch* pushed on through stormy seas. Finally, after two months, it reached Hudson Bay, sailed down to the base of James Bay, and there cast anchor. Under "Mr. Gooseberry's" direction a fort was built and named in honor of the English king, and from this center every effort was made to encourage the neighboring Indians to bring in huge supplies of furs to exchange for trinkets and other goods that had been brought out from England. In this trading Des Groseilliers' long experience stood him in very good stead.

The next year the *Nonsuch* returned to England loaded with a wonderful cargo of furs. The men who had supplied the money to equip the expedition were delighted with the rich returns from their investment. Prince Rupert and his associates now proposed that a great company be organized, to which would be given not only the right to exploit the fur trade of the Hudson Bay region but also the ownership of the land and the power to govern it. So was chartered on May 2, 1670, the Hudson's Bay Company — "The Governor and Company of Adventurers of England Trading into Hudson's Bay." The region of which the company was made the proprietor was called Rupert's Land in honor of the prince who had played so large a part in furthering the enterprise.

The founding of this great trading company, which still exists and is powerful more than two and a half centuries after its organization, marks the climax of the careers of the two Caesars of the wilderness. They lived to join in many later adventures, however, and to make one voyage after another to Hudson Bay. In 1682, once more in the service of New France, they led an expedition to the bay. There Radisson outwitted two groups of English traders and gathered up a great harvest of furs to take back to Quebec. When these were seized by the governor because Radisson had attacked the English, with whom France then was at peace, the irrepressible Frenchman deserted the French service once more and returned to England. His brother adventurer, Des Groseilliers, remained in Canada, going back to his much-loved Three Rivers. Radisson was again at Hudson Bay in 1684, this time to capture a French fort commanded by a son of his old friend, Des Groseilliers. Ultimately Radisson settled down in London, where he had married the daughter of Sir John Kirke, on a small pension from the fur-trading company he had served. In London, in 1710, this "Caesar of the wilderness" died.

Black Robe and
Trail Blazer

In the name of the most high and redoubtable sovereign, Louis the Fourteenth, Christian King of France and Navarre, I now take possession of all these lakes, straits, rivers, islands, and regions lying adjacent thereto, whether as yet visited by my subjects or unvisited, in all their length and breadth, stretching to the sea at the north and at the west, or on the opposite side extending to the South Sea. . . . Long live the King!"

Thus Daumont de Saint Lusson, nobleman of France, took possession of the American mid-continent in the name of his king. And black-robed priests with crucifixes in their hands, Indians with feathered headdresses and strings of bear and moose teeth around their necks, fur traders in rough leather jackets, French soldiers flashing their swords or waving their plumed hats in the sunlight, all echoed his shout.

It was a summer's day — June 14, 1671. Indians and white men had come from the surrounding country to Sault Ste. Marie, the "jumping-off place," to attend this high ceremony. The French set up a great cross, and beside it a cedar pole on which they nailed a metal plate engraved with the royal lilies of France. The soldiers fired their guns, the priests made speeches, the Indians — scarcely knowing what all this was about — shouted as loudly as anyone. Toward evening a bonfire was lighted, and around it the priests sang hymns and psalms of praise.

Thus the King of France claimed all America, known or unknown, visited or unvisited, from sea to sea. But his subjects were not content that any part of the land they now held by virtue of official claim should remain unvisited and unknown. Nicolet and Radisson had indeed traveled westward and northward, but no Frenchman yet had sailed southward along the Great River — the "Mechassipi" or "Micissipi."

Among the crowd around the bonfire that June night of 1671 was the son of a wagonmaker, Louis Jolliet, still a youth in his twenties but already known as a daring explorer and a good surveyor.

Talon, the governor of New France, had heard of Jolliet's courage and skill and picked him as a good man to explore the mysterious river of the West, and he made his choice known to his successor in the governorship, the celebrated Count Frontenac. Soon afterward young Jolliet received a letter from Frontenac, telling him that he was to go and "discover the south sea . . . and the great river Mississippi, which is believed to empty in the California sea" — a challenging and majestic mission conveyed in a few simple words.

Jolliet was not to go alone. With him would travel Father Marquette, one of the black-robed priests from the mission of St. Ignace on Michilimackinac Island — a young and vigorous priest skilled in mapping, acquainted with Indian languages, and "resolved to do and suffer everything for so glorious an undertaking."

These two men spent a winter in making plans and preparations for their expedition. They questioned every Indian who could tell them anything about the Great River, and from what they learned they made a rough map to guide them, marking down on it the name of each tribe they expected to meet and each important village they would see. By the spring of 1673 they were ready. With two bark canoes and five men and a supply of Indian corn and smoked meat, they started from the little mission at St. Ignace, undeterred by Indian warnings of frightful monsters to be encountered, of rapids that would destroy their canoes, and of summer heat "that would roast them alive."

Like Nicolet, Jolliet and Marquette went first to Green Bay. From there they followed the Fox River to its end in a little lake. Here they had to carry their canoes and supplies a long way overland, heavy and toilsome work; but presently they got their canoes afloat again, this time on the waters of the Wisconsin River. Seven days they sailed along this stream, which they correctly believed ran into the Mississippi itself. They passed by many vine-covered islands and also countless sand bars which slowed up their progress.

It was the seventeenth of June, a month from the day they left St. Ignace, when at last they reached the junction of the Wisconsin and the Mississippi and launched out on the waters of the Great River that stretched away hundreds of miles to an unknown sea. This was one of the great moments of American history, and something of its greatness is caught in the quiet and undramatic eloquence with which Marquette recorded his feelings. He was filled, he said, "with a joy which I cannot express" as he found himself "on this so renowned River."

As the explorers turned southward, the scene began to change. The hills and forests characteristic of Wisconsin disappeared. The voyagers were coming into the wide, flat prairie country, where moose and deer browsed and buffaloes clumped over the plains or waded noisily into the river. One of these great beasts the travelers shot for food. "Monstrous fish" flopped against their canoe; wild turkeys flew over their heads.

For more than a week they saw only wild beasts and birds — never a sign of man, although they were constantly on the watch for Indians. Each night they landed on the lonely shore, built a fire and ate their evening meal, and then, in order to be safe from attack, put out their fire and paddled their canoes to the middle of the stream again. There, under the stars, they anchored their boats and went to sleep. One man stayed awake all night to keep watch. As soon as day dawned, the voyagers drew up their anchors and started on their way once more along a river that seemed to have no end.

On June 25 the two Crusoes found footprints on the shore. They did not know whether the men who had made the footprints would turn out to be friends or enemies, but they were eager to see a human face again. Leaving their five men in the canoes, Jolliet and the missionary followed the prints. They came to a little beaten path, and the path led them to an Indian village. No one seemed to be about, for it was early in the morning. With a loud "Halloo" the white men proclaimed their coming. Then squaws, children, young men, and old men poured out to stare at the strangers. When Marquette learned that the Indians were of the Illinois tribe, he was glad, for they were supposed to be kinder to strangers than most Indians, and he had longed to see them and teach them.

There began a bustle and stir in the village — a village of huts at the site where the city of Peoria, Illinois, stands today — as the Indians prepared a feast for their white visitors. The old chiefs of the villages round about gathered together, and all were polite to the guests. They fed them on porridge boiled in grease, cooked fish, and buffalo meat. They also offered them dog meat. When they served the fish, the Indians picked out the bones, cooled the food by blowing on it, and then put it, piece by piece, into their visitors' mouths. They ate from wooden dishes, using spoons made from buffalo bones.

The next morning, when the peace pipes had been smoked and one of them given to the travelers, the young men escorted Marquette and Jolliet down to the riverbank again and watched them paddle away. Cheered and encouraged by so much kindness, the explorers went on toward the south. Before very long they passed some rocks on which were paintings of Indian gods — with faces like men, in green, red, and black.

The Illinois had warned the travelers of dangers that lay ahead, and it was not long before these began to show themselves. The waters of the river started to roar and churn, and the little boats were almost overturned by the swift, foaming current or knocked to pieces by the fallen trees that floated about. The voyagers soon understood that this commotion was caused by the swirling, muddy Missouri River rushing in to join the Mississippi. The Missouri suggested to Marquette the "means to discover the Vermillion or California Sea."

The party escaped this danger, but they soon encountered a new difficulty. They were far south now, in the land of sugar cane, and millions of mosquitoes plagued them day and night. Sometimes these pests were so annoying that the travelers could escape them only by wrapping themselves in the heavy cloth used as sails for the canoes.

Most of the Indians they met were friendly. One tribe, however, started to attack them, paying no attention to Marquette's friendly shouts. At last he made them understand that they were not enemies, since they had with them the peace pipe of the Illinois.

Despite dangers, the white men continued their journey until July 17, when they reached the mouth of the Arkansas River. They now knew that the Mississippi must empty its waters into the Gulf of Mexico. If they went farther they were likely to be taken prisoners by the Spaniards, so they turned back northward, beginning a long and weary struggle against the powerful current. When they reached the mouth of the Illinois River, they turned up that stream and made their way to the southern point of Lake Michigan. From there they followed the lake shore to Green Bay, reaching it late in September.

The next winter Marquette, although sick and feeble, returned to the Illinois country, driven on by his zeal to convert the Indians; but in the spring, while on the return trip to his mission station at St. Ignace, he died in the wilderness, near a Michigan stream that is today known by his name. His companions buried him and hastened on to St. Ignace to tell their sad news. A few years later a party of Indians opened the grave, gathered up Marquette's bones, placed them in a birch-bark box, and then, with a procession of thirty canoes, bore them to the mission station where Marquette had lived. There the remains of this missionary and explorer were given final burial.

Meanwhile, Jolliet had started for Quebec to report his discoveries to Count Frontenac, the governor-general of New France. Just before reaching Montreal he had an accident that nearly cost him his life. His canoe overturned in a swirling rapid, and two of his voyageurs and an Indian boy were drowned. Jolliet managed to save his own life, but he lost a chest containing his diary and other papers. He had left a copy of the diary at Sault Ste. Marie, so when he met the governor he told him that in due time he would show him that copy. He had not yet learned that soon after he left the Sault, the mission house, where he had left the copy, had burned. The world was thus deprived of the diary of this explorer and discoverer, though he later drew a number of maps that have been preserved.

Fortunately, we have the record written by Father Marquette, and in it we can read the story of the men who discovered the upper waters of America's mightiest river, the mouth of which had been explored more than a century earlier by the sons of Spain. Men from the East took up the challenge of men from the South in opening the land through which the great river channeled its way.

Cavalier and Friar

Aт Seneffe in Flanders, near Brussels, a bloody battle was fought on an August day in 1674 between the Dutch under the Prince of Orange and the French under the Prince of Condé. A Belgian friar was present on the field giving comfort to the wounded and uttering prayers over the dead. On the same battlefield was a cavalier of France, serving as squire to the Marquis de Lassay. The marquis was wounded three times and had two horses killed under him, but his squire went through the fierce eight-hour fight unwounded.

The friar was Louis Hennepin, and the squire was Daniel Greysolon, Sieur du Lhut. On that day of smoke and blood in Flanders they did not meet, but six years later they met under the summer sun of the midwestern wilderness, in the heart of the Sioux country, surrounded by red-skinned hunters and warriors.

Du Lhut was born of an old French family at St. Germain-en-Laye, near Paris, in 1636. His father was of the lesser nobility, his mother the daughter of a wealthy merchant in Lyons, and in that southern French city he grew up. Like many young men of his class, he was bred to be a soldier, and when he was enrolled in the King's Guard, Louis XIV's own select regiment, a brilliant career was open to him at Versailles, the center of the Grand Monarch's empire.

Upon all this Du Lhut turned his back when he was thirty-six. Not that he did not prize the honor of serving in the king's own regiment — as long as he lived he liked to call himself a "Gentleman of the Royal Guard." But he was attracted by adventure and fortune in the New World. Some of his relatives had gone there already, among them his uncle, Jacques Patron, a rich merchant in Montreal. After being commissioned as a captain in the marine service, Du Lhut in 1672 left Versailles and sailed for Canada. He had been there only about two years when he was recalled to France to join the Prince of Condé's expedition to Flanders, and there he fought with his old comrades of the Guard.

In the same year, not long after the battle of Seneffe, Du Lhut returned to Canada, this time with his young brother, Claude Greysolon, Sieur de la Tourette; and for four years the two lived in Montreal. They were years when the imaginations of many adventure-loving men in Canada were deeply stirred. Count Frontenac, the governor of New France, was determined to have the western country further explored, the fur trade developed, the power of France extended. Louis Jolliet returned from the splendid journey of exploration he had made with Father Marquette to the Father of Waters. In 1676 the governor sent an engineer named Randin out to the Lake Superior region to make friends with the Indians and to win their trade for the French. Jesuit missionaries were braving the perils of the West to establish stations there and to work among the natives. Sometimes Indians fresh from the woods of the West could be seen on the streets of Montreal.

As Du Lhut watched this pageant of events from his home in Montreal, he was fired with the ambition to explore unknown regions for the glory of France and above all to blaze a path to the far Pacific. In 1678 he sold his house in Montreal and with seven companions set out for the West.

This was the beginning of a long career of adventure. Du Lhut was to be one of two great trail blazers under Count

Frontenac. The other was Robert Cavelier, Sieur de la Salle, who about the same time was given a royal commission to explore the Mississippi Valley. La Salle is of course better known in history than Du Lhut, for he explored the Mississippi to its mouth in 1682 and took possession for France of the whole valley under the name of Louisiana. But before La Salle planted the flag of France in the far South, Du Lhut blazed a way into the Upper Midwest. The veteran of Seneffe was to prove himself a bold wilderness fighter, but he also had a force of character and a power of judging men and events that won victories for him more successfully than bullets could have done.

As Du Lhut and his companions started westward, they were thinking of the glory of reaching the shores of the Pacific. But first they had to deal with the problem of wars among the Indians of the Lake Superior country, for Indian fighting had closed the great northern lake to the French fur traders. So Du Lhut's party spent the winter of 1678–79 near Sault Ste. Marie and there won the friendship of the Chippewa. Then in the spring, fearing "not death, only cowardice or dishonor," they started for the western end of Lake Superior to hold a council with the fierce and little-known tribe of Sioux. Not far from the site of the modern city of Duluth they met the Sioux, and from them Du Lhut secured promises of peace with the Chippewa.

After this council Du Lhut made his way far into the Minnesota country to a great Sioux Village at Mille Lacs. Here he held councils with the warlike Sioux on the shores of a beautiful inland lake, made campfire speeches telling of the mighty king half a world away, and won promises of friendship for the sons of France.

What a fascinating story Du Lhut might have written! But he was a man of action, not of words. "On the second of July, 1679," he wrote simply, "I had the honor to set up the arms of his Majesty in the great village of Nadouecioux called Izatys, where no Frenchman had ever been, nor to the Songaskitons

38

and Houetbatons, distant 26 leagues from the first, where also I set up the arms of his Majesty in the same year 1679."

Who were these strangely named people? The Nadouecioux were of course the Sioux, and the Songaskitons probably were the Sisseton tribe and the Houetbatons the Wahpeton. By setting up the king's arms Du Lhut probably means that he nailed to a tree the royal emblem of Louis XIV, signalizing the rule of France over all this wild region. The lake that is today known as Mille Lacs, Du Lhut named Buade, the family name of Count Frontenac.

Before he turned back, Du Lhut sent three of his men to push on into the interior. During their travels they met some Indians who gave them salt that had been brought out of the West. The Frenchmen later reported to Du Lhut that "it was only twenty days' journey from where they were to the discovery of the great lake whose water is not good to drink." Du Lhut had no knowledge of the existence of the Great Salt Lake, and he doubtless thought the salt water was the Pacific Ocean.

Meanwhile, the explorer had returned from Mille Lacs to Lake Superior, and in September he arranged another great Indian council, this time between the Sioux and the Assiniboin, who had been at war for many years. After getting their promises of peace among themselves, he went north to winter at Kaministiquia, at the site of the later Fort William, Ontario.

In June 1680, probably with the thought of solving the mystery of the "lake whose water is not good to drink," Du Lhut started upon a new adventure. Taking two canoes, an interpreter, and four of his young comrades, he followed the Lake Superior shore as far south as the mouth of the Bois Brulé River and then turned up that stream. Canoeing was slow and hard work, for he and his men had to cut down trees and break about a hundred beaver dams in order to get through. From the Brulé the Frenchmen carried their canoes over a portage to the St. Croix and then easily paddled their way down to the Mississippi.

At this point Du Lhut received startling news. He was told by Indians that somewhere below on the Mississippi a great band of Sioux were holding three white men as prisoners. Without hesitation, and taking only one canoe, he hurried downriver with his interpreter and two of his young Frenchmen to rescue the unknown prisoners. He had not forgotten the pledges of friendship that the Sioux had made only the summer before. On July 25 he came upon the roving Sioux and with them he found the three white men. One was none other than Louis Hennepin — and so the gentleman of the Royal Guard and the Belgian friar met in the wilderness six years after that August day when they both stood on the battlefield of Seneffe.

Father Hennepin was born in 1640 in the village of Ath, Belgium. More than three hundred years have passed since that time, but his name has not been forgotten in his native town. Like the great American city of Minneapolis, with its Hennepin Avenue, Ath has a *Rue Hennepin*, and though it has no monumental statue of the explorer like the one that stands in the heart of the Minnesota metropolis, it does boast a curious old town pump on which his name is inscribed.

Hennepin began his religious training early and while yet a young man became a Recollect friar. He loved both travel and adventure. Sometimes he would visit such seaports as Calais, and he himself has told how, in cowl and sandals, he would hide behind the doors of drinking houses to listen to the tales of sailors, even though the smoke of their tobacco made him sick. "I was very attentive," he says, "to the Accounts they gave of their Encounters by Sea, the Perils they had gone through, and all the Accidents which befell them in their long Voyages. This Occupation was so agreeable and engaging, that I have spent whole Days and Nights at it without eating; for hereby I always came to understand some new thing, concerning the Customs and Ways of Living in remote Places; and concerning the Pleasantness, Fertility, and Riches of the

Countries where these Men had been." For a time, after traveling in Holland as a missionary, he served as an army chaplain, and that was how he happened to be with the army of the Prince of Orange at Seneffe.

The next year, in 1675, Hennepin was on his way to the New World. He sailed in the company of the great, for on the same vessel were La Salle, returning from Paris, where he had sought support for his plans of exploration and occupation, and the newly appointed Bishop Laval of Quebec.

After arriving in Canada, Hennepin served as a traveling missionary, gaining experience with dog sledge in winter and with canoe in summer. Fate seemed to link his fortunes with those of La Salle, for after some years he was sent to Fort Frontenac, on the spot where Kingston, Ontario, now stands, and there the commandant was La Salle.

La Salle had made a second journey to France to advance his plans for binding the Mississippi Valley to New France by means of exploration and the building of forts. In September 1678 he was ready to launch an epoch-making expedition, and Hennepin was selected to go with him. The friar was sent on to Fort Frontenac after being dined by Count Frontenac and blessed by Bishop Laval.

Thus Father Hennepin embarked upon the adventure that was to bring him fame. From Fort Frontenac he crossed Lake Ontario to Niagara. There, under the direction of Henri de Tonty, La Salle's chief lieutenant and a cousin of Du Lhut, a vessel of forty-five tons called the *Griffin* was being built for the journey to the upper lakes.

While he waited for the boat to be completed, Father Hennepin saw one of the most famous sights in America, and to him we are indebted for the first description and drawing of Niagara Falls. "The Waters which fall from this vast height," he wrote, "do foam and boil after the most hideous manner imaginable, making an outrageous Noise, more terrible than that of Thunder; for when the Wind blows from off the

South, their dismal roaring may be heard above fifteen Leagues off." He described the falls as "a vast and prodigious Cadence of Water." There was nothing like it, he thought, in the whole world.

On August 7, 1679, the *Griffin* set sail from Niagara, the first sailing vessel to cut through the waters of Lakes Erie, Huron, and Michigan. Three Recollects were in the company that La Salle took with him: Gabriel de la Ribourde, Zenobé Membré, and Louis Hennepin. Despite storms the *Griffin* at last reached Michilimackinac and then sailed down Lake Michigan to the mouth of Green Bay. There La Salle was met by a party of traders who had been sent in advance to collect furs. They had been so successful in their quest that La Salle decided to pack the furs into the *Griffin* and send the vessel back to Niagara, with instructions to return to western waters promptly. The *Griffin* sailed away — and was never heard of again.

Meanwhile, La Salle, with fourteen men and five canoes, was paddling down Lake Michigan. At the mouth of the St. Joseph River he was joined by Tonty, who had come down from Michilimackinac by the east shore of the lake. There they built a fort. Then the party pushed on until on New Year's Day of 1680 they reached Peoria Lake, a widening of the Illinois River, and here La Salle built a palisaded fort that he called Fort Crêvecœur, Fort "Heartbreak."

With the approach of spring La Salle was tormented with fears about the *Griffin*. He had expected the vessel to bring out the equipment for building a boat in which he could descend the Mississippi. When it failed to come, the explorer decided to make the thousand-mile journey back to Fort Frontenac, and on March 1 he set out, leaving Tonty in command of the Illinois fort. How in the face of terrible obstacles La Salle accomplished his purpose and finally achieved the great goal of traversing the Father of Waters to its mouth is one of the epics of American history.

Instead of following this familiar story, however, we turn toward the Northwest, for on the day before La Salle left Fort Crêvecœur for the East he sent out an expedition of three men to explore the northern waters of the Mississippi and to build a fort at the mouth of the Wisconsin. The leader of this group was a voyageur named Michel Accault. The second member was one Antoine Auguelle, who because he came from Picardy was also known as Picard du Gay. And the third was Father Hennepin.

On the last day of February 1680 these men started from Fort "Heartbreak." They paddled their canoe down the Illinois to its junction with the Mississippi, then turned northward. Their way was made difficult both by the current and by ice in the river, but all went well until April 11. On the afternoon of that day they suddenly saw a war party of 133 Sioux, in a brigade of thirty-three canoes, come sweeping down the river toward them. In a moment they were surrounded. Some arrows were fired at them by the howling savages, and at first it seemed certain they would be killed. As they were drawn ashore, however, they made signs that they were friends, and after an anxious night they were offered the pipe of peace.

The Frenchmen's lives were spared because some of the Sioux thought that if these men were killed it would put a stop to the coming of other Frenchmen with tobacco, blankets, knives, and other trade goods. By signs Hennepin made the Indians understand that their enemies, the Miami, against whom their expedition was directed, were far beyond their reach, and finally the war party, with the three white men as prisoners, started northward. The project for building a fort at the mouth of the Wisconsin had to be given up.

The friar soon found himself in trouble. It was his custom to read prayers every day from a book that he carried with him. But when the Indians heard him they became frightened, for they thought this was magic and the book an evil spirit.

Hennepin's companions were also alarmed, but for another reason. Accault told Hennepin that if he did not give up the custom, all three of them would be killed; and Auguelle begged Hennepin to pray only when the natives could neither see nor hear him. So at one point where a stop was made, the friar went into the woods with his little book — but the Indians followed him! He "knew not on what side to turn to pray." Then a new idea came to him: he began to sing the prayers, and at once the Indians were delighted. They now thought the prayer book was a spirit that taught Hennepin to sing for their amusement.

One Indian chief, named Aquipaguetin, made life miserable for Hennepin. Sometimes he would weep on the friar's shoulder, then threaten him with death, and then take away some of his trade goods. The chief was carrying with him some bones of a dead relative, which he kept in a bag of skins trimmed with black and red porcupine quills. Often he would begin to weep over the bones and would keep up the flow of tears until the white men gave him some gifts. Once, to stop his weeping, the prisoners threw on the bones "several fathoms of French tobacco, axes, knives, beads, and some black and white wampum bracelets." Aquipaguetin made them fear that if they did not give him gifts he would kill them. When he had used up his tears, he would call upon one of his sons to weep for him. As the party crossed Lake Pepin there was so much grief of this kind that Hennepin named it the "Lake of Tears."

Somewhere near the site of St. Paul the warriors left their canoes and started with their captives on an overland march to the Sioux village at Mille Lacs. It was a hard march for the friar. When he lagged behind, weary and footsore, the savages hastened his steps by setting fire to the grass behind him. But instead of being killed when Mille Lacs was reached, Hennepin was given "a robe made of ten large dressed beaver skins, trimmed with porcupine quills," and was adopted into the family of Aquipaguetin to take the place of a son who had been killed by the Miami.

The Indians also rubbed wildcat oil on Hennepin's legs, thighs, and the soles of his feet, for they thought the fat of such an agile animal as the wildcat would cure the lameness and soreness induced by the march. He was given steam baths. This was done in a cabin covered with buffalo skins, and to produce steam the natives placed red hot stones in the cabin and then sprinkled them with water. While the friar was being steamed, the Indians rubbed him with their hands, all the time weeping. Just why they wept no one seems to know.

Father Hennepin baptized a sick Indian child at Mille Lacs, and he speaks of it as the "first Christian child among these tribes."

Hennepin had not been long among the Indians before he began to make a dictionary of their words, and in doing this he found that the Indian children could help him. For example, when he wanted to learn their word for "run," he would run back and forth across his cabin until they guessed what it was he was trying to get them to say. Then he would write the word.

When summer came the Sioux set out for the prairies to hunt buffaloes, and they took the three captives with them. Hennepin thought his friends in Illinois would try to send a load of supplies up the Mississippi for himself and his two comrades. So when the hunting party reached the mouth of the Rum River, he and Auguelle got permission to go downstream as far as the Wisconsin River to find out whether or not the supplies had been sent. Accault, who liked hunting and disliked Hennepin, chose to continue with the Sioux.

This canoe trip of Hennepin's led to his discovery of a waterfall that he named in honor of his patron saint, Anthony of Padua. To this day it is known as the Falls of St. Anthony, though its wild beauty and natural state are things of the past, for it has been harnessed to make power for the flour mills of Minneapolis that have been built alongside it.

If Hennepin and Auguelle went down the Mississippi to the mouth of the Wisconsin, they soon returned, for in a short time they were again with Accault and the Sioux hunters. It was now late in July. On the twenty-fifth a swift canoe, paddled from the north, suddenly appeared among the Sioux. In it sat the stern-faced Du Lhut.

Du Lhut was angry about the captivity of Hennepin and his companions, for the Sioux had broken their promise of friendship. He took Hennepin in his own canoe and told the Indians they must return to their village at once. When the party reached Mille Lacs, Du Lhut haughtily refused to smoke the pipe of peace. He scolded the tribesmen fiercely and told them he would turn his back on the Sioux country. He understood that if the Sioux were disrespectful to one Frenchman, they might be so to all. He was determined that no white subject of the French king should suffer at their hands.

By his dignity and fearlessness this one white man cowed the Sioux chiefs. He demanded that they release their captives, and he decided that he himself would lead Hennepin and his comrades out of the wilderness. This was a generous decision, for it meant postponing, perhaps giving up, his plan to push westward in search of the Pacific.

Hennepin, who was very vain, would never admit later that he really had been a captive of the Sioux and had been rescued by Du Lhut, but there is no doubt that this was the case.

Du Lhut, with Hennepin and the other white men, now left the Sioux country. They traveled by way of the Mississippi to the Wisconsin River, went up that stream, carried their canoes across to the Fox River, and then paddled down to Green Bay. After stopping to visit at the mission of St. François Xavier, they went to the mission station of St. Ignace on the Straits of Mackinac, where they spent the winter.

In the spring of 1681 Hennepin left for Fort Frontenac, and not long thereafter he sailed for Europe. There he wrote his *Description of Louisiana*, published at Paris in 1683 — a vivid story of his adventures, though its pages, as someone has said, "abound in exaggeration and self-glorification." The book was popular in Europe and was soon translated into Italian, Dutch, and German. Fourteen years later Hennepin brought out another book, at Utrecht, entitled *A New Discovery of a Very Great Country*, and in this he makes the absurd claim that after leaving La Salle's fort in Illinois he had first traveled down the Mississippi to the Gulf of Mexico and then returned to make his way into the Minnesota country!

He never came to America again, though he tried to interest the English in sending him, and he had his account of New World travels published in England. He was in Rome in 1701, but where or how he died no one knows.

In the same year that Hennepin's book was published in Paris, the tireless Du Lhut, now licensed to trade with the western Indians, was at Mackinac ready for another journey into the Minnesota country. After his return with Hennepin he learned that he had been branded an outlaw and the leader of the *coureurs de bois* by the intendant of New France. It was true that when he first went west in 1678, his journey had not been regularly authorized. But he was not a *coureur de bois*; he was an explorer and peacemaker; and he may even have had secret instructions from Count Frontenac himself.

When he hastened to Quebec to lay his story before the Canadian officials, he was promptly arrested, but Frontenac, who admired him and understood the value of his services to New France, protected him during his arrest by keeping him in his own house. Later Du Lhut journeyed to France in an attempt to secure a royal pardon. This quest was unsuccessful, but when he returned to Canada he was given a license to trade.

From Mackinac in 1683, therefore, he once more set out for the Sioux country. This time he traveled by the Fox-Wisconsin route and up the great river which three years earlier he had descended with Hennepin. When he arrived among the Sioux, they welcomed him with respect and pleasure, and they made a new pact of friendship with the French. Soon he started for the Lake Superior country by way of the St. Croix River, and probably he built a small fort at the portage from that river to the Bois Brulé. In the north country he attempted to win the friendship of the Indian tribes, and he sent his brother Claude, the Sieur de la Tourette, to build a post at Lake Nipigon. Claude carried out his instructions, naming the post Fort La Tourette. Du Lhut, meanwhile, built another fort at Kaministiquia, where he had wintered on his first journey to the West.

He seems now, once more, to have been on the point of starting an expedition to the Far West. Learning, however, that two Frenchmen had been murdered by natives at Keweenaw Bay and that no one had dared to punish the murderers, he set out for Mackinac, arrested the two guilty men, gave them a trial in the midst of several hundred Indians who might at any time have overwhelmed the few white men he had with him, and then supervised the execution of the murderers. By such bold measures he forced the Indians of the West to respect the lives of Frenchmen.

Time after time Du Lhut was prevented by events from going in search of the elusive western sea. Iroquois wars, his appointment to the command of the French post at Detroit, and special military councils kept him from realizing his early dream. In 1688 he traveled once more into the Minnesota region by the Fox-Wisconsin-Mississippi route, then pushed his way into the North, and attempted to challenge the widening influence of the English in the Hudson Bay area. He planned yet again to start west, but was recalled to eastern Canada.

One night in August of 1689 a vast horde of Iroquois fell upon the little French settlement of Lachine, near Montreal, in an orgy of murder, torture, and capture. Du Lhut, still seeking to uphold the safety and dignity of the French, struck a quick blow in return. Taking canoes and some thirty men who were experts with the paddle, he went up the Ottawa to a lake where he suspected some Iroquois would be waiting to strike at French traders who might pass. Du Lhut ordered most of his men to crouch as he neared the point where he expected an attack, so that the Iroquois would suppose the canoes to be lightly manned but heavily loaded with goods.

The ruse was successful. Four canoes full of Iroquois shot out from shore, and the Frenchmen pretended to be retreating in terror. But as the exultant Indians closed in, Du Lhut suddenly ordered his men upright, his canoes flashed round, in an instant the French overturned every Indian canoe, and all but three of the Iroquois were either killed by blows from the French paddles or were drowned. The three captives were taken back to Montreal, where they were burned alive as a reprisal for the horrors of Lachine.

Some years later Du Lhut commanded Fort Frontenac for a time. But he was now growing old and was racked with pain from gout; so he soon returned to Montreal. In that city on a winter day in 1710, in the midst of old friends, the gallant nobleman died.

"Well does the noble city at the head of our greatest lake bear the name of this nobleman of Old and New France," exclaims a well-known historian after summarizing the services of Du Lhut. What had he done? "He had added to New France an empire in the Northwest, had explored the routes from Lake Superior to the Mississippi, had ventured farther west than any of his confreres, and had made French alliances with the greatest and most populous of the northwestern tribesmen." But perhaps the finest tribute to this explorer-statesman of the early Northwest was that paid him soon after his death by the governor of New France. He said of Du Lhut, "He was a very honest man."

Blue Earth and Beaver Skins

Wɪᴛʜ a group of Sioux watching every movement he made, Nicolas Perrot, French explorer and trader, poured some brandy into a cup of water. He was angry and was determined to teach the Indians a lesson they would not soon forget. The place was Fort St. Antoine on the east side of that widening of the Mississippi known as Lake Pepin, and the time was 1688. Perrot had just returned from a trip to Green Bay and had learned that while he was absent Indians had stolen some of his trade goods.

As the Sioux crowded around him, Perrot told them they must return the goods they had stolen. If they did not, he said, he would burn up their lakes and marshes. Suddenly he set fire to the brandy. To the startled Sioux this white man was a magician who could make water burn. They returned the stolen articles.

The Frenchman who used this trick knew of other ways to impress the natives with the white man's power. In 1685 he had established a small trading post at the foot of Mount Trempealeau, at a spot in Wisconsin where today a beautiful state park bears Perrot's name. The next year he went some miles up the Mississippi and built Fort St. Antoine, where two years later he played his little game with brandy and water. On a May day in 1689 he staged at this fort a ceremony not unlike the Sault Ste. Marie pageant of 1671. A number of officers and traders as well as a Jesuit priest were there, and an audience of Indians watched the proceedings. Guns were fired, hymns sung, and Louis XIV of France was proclaimed king over the Upper Mississippi country, while the assembled Frenchmen shouted "Long live the King!"

Among those present when Perrot thus claimed the Middle West for France was a Frenchman named Pierre Charles le Sueur. Four years after the ceremony at Fort St. Antoine, he built a trading house on Madeline Island in Chequamegon Bay on the south shore of Lake Superior. In 1695 he was again in the Upper Mississippi country, where he built a fort on Prairie Island, not far from the present city of Hastings, Minnesota.

Le Sueur wanted to win the friendship of the Sioux for the French, and that same year he took a Sioux chief on the long trip to eastern Canada to make an agreement with the governor, Count Frontenac. He also took with him a Chippewa chieftain and persuaded the two Indian leaders to agree to peace between their two tribes. The French wanted these tribes, eternally at war, to live at peace — their battles interfered seriously with the French trade. Promises of peace were easy to make, but difficult to keep; and in this instance the Sioux chief died before he could return to his own people.

Later Le Sueur went to Paris to apply to the king for the right to control the fur trade of the Upper Mississippi region for ten years, and also to work mines. A high official in New France, when he learned of Le Sueur's strange request, said, "The only mines that he seeks in those regions are mines of beaver skins." Still, Le Sueur got what he wanted. By 1700 he was again in America, and in April of that year, with a little sailing vessel, two canoes, and nineteen men, he started northward from the mouth of the Mississippi on a journey to the upper Northwest.

The party advanced as far north as the Falls of St. Anthony, discovered twenty years earlier by Father Hennepin. Jean Pénicaut, one of Le Sueur's companions, described the falls as "the entire Mississippi falling suddenly from a height of sixty feet, making a noise like that of thunder rolling in the air." The Frenchmen then turned back to the St. Peter's, or Minnesota, and went up that river until they reached the mouth of the "Makato," now known as the Blue Earth River. They made their way a short distance up that stream, until, forced to stop by ice, they decided to build a fort in which they could spend the winter. This was on the last day of September 1700, "when winter, which is very severe in that country," had already begun. The post was named Fort L'Huillier for a French official who had done Le Sueur some kindness.

While the men were working on the fort, seven French traders from Canada, who had been robbed of their goods and their very clothes by the Sioux, took refuge with Le Sueur. They were given clothes and food, and they remained at the fort through the winter. This incident is interesting evidence of the fact that many traders visited the Upper Midwest whose names have not come down to us and whose diaries and letters, if any, have not come to light.

Obviously, we know about Pénicaut and Le Sueur because they recorded their experiences. Pénicaut, for example, tells us many details of the winter passed by the French in this lonely post on a tributary of the great channel. "Half our people went hunting," he writes, "whilst the others worked on the fort. We killed four hundred buffaloes, which were our provisions for the winter, and which we placed upon scaffolds in our fort, after having skinned and cleaned and then quartered them. We also made cabins in the fort, and a magazine to keep our goods. After having drawn up our shallop within the inclosure of the fort, we spent the winter in our cabins." The shallop was the open boat the Frenchmen had brought up from the lower Mississippi.

The buffalo meat dried on the open scaffolds at first made the party sick. There was no salt with which to flavor it, and they got so tired of the unseasoned dried meat that they "hated the very smell" of it. But presently they got used to it and, Pénicaut tells us, would eat six pounds each a day and drink four bowls of meat broth. "As soon as we were accustomed to this kind of living," he records, "it made us very fat, and there was no more sickness amongst us."

Once Le Sueur gathered the Sioux together, made them a speech, and gave them "fifty pounds of powder, as many balls, six guns, ten axes, twelve armfuls of tobacco and a hatchet pipe." "The Sioux are all great smokers," Le Sueur records, "but their manner of smoking differs from that of other Indians. There are some Sioux who swallow all the smoke of the tobacco, and others who, after having kept it some time in their mouth, cause it to issue from the nose." He noted that the Sioux were good shots with bow and arrow and that they sometimes would kill ducks on the wing. Their lodges, he writes, were made "of a number of buffalo skins interlaced and sewed," and they could carry their houses with them wherever they went.

Perhaps the most celebrated event connected with Le Sueur's expedition was the mining of what was supposed to be copper ore. In fact, LeSueur appears to have known from an earlier trip into Minnesota about the peculiar blue or green earth of the region. It was really nothing but clay and had long been used by the Indians as coloring matter. Le Sueur seems to have believed that it was precious ore, however, and when in the spring of 1701 he started downriver on his way to France, he had about two tons of the colored clay loaded into his boat. He had also three canoes loaded with furs, secured in trade with the Sioux. There had been a good deal of trade with the Indians during the winter, and once the savages brought in "more than four hundred beaver robes, each robe being made of nine skins sewed together." Le Sueur reached the mouth of the Mississippi safely, and in 1702 he sailed for France, but we know nothing of what became of the "ore" he took with him.

Twelve Frenchmen remained at Fort L'Huillier when Le Sueur returned to France. They were sadly in need of powder and bullets, and when Le Sueur left he promised to send a load of supplies north from the Illinois country. He kept his promise, but the canoe that carried the supplies was wrecked at some treacherous spot in the Mississippi and its precious cargo went to the bottom.

The next winter Fort L'Huillier was attacked by a war party of Fox Indians who believed their enemies, the Sioux, were getting firearms from the Frenchmen. The attack was a surprise, and three Frenchmen, caught unawares some distance from the fort, were killed. The others managed to hold off the Indians, but after they had gone, the survivors buried the trading goods they still had, abandoned the fort, and started downriver to the sea.

More than two hundred years after the last act in this early forest drama, the site of Fort L'Huillier was located, and today a bronze marker stands near it; but nobody has succeeded in finding the cache of trading goods buried by the Frenchmen in Minnesota in the days of Louis XIV.

War and Falling Stars

Traders on the streams and in the woods of the West had to move warily in the early years of the eighteenth century, for the Fox Indians of Wisconsin were on the warpath and no one knew when the war whoop might ring out and the scalping knives flash. The Foxes were fierce fighters, and wily, like the animals whose name they bore. They sought friendship with the Sioux as insurance, so that if they lost their wars in the south against the Illinois tribes and against the French, they could retreat with safety into the north country.

Notwithstanding the dangers west of Lake Michigan, the French were still dreaming of exploring the vast, unknown lands toward the Pacific. In the lower Mississippi Valley, French posts marked the progress of occupation by men who followed the trail of La Salle, but the Northwest stretching away toward the setting sun from Lakes Michigan and Superior was still very much a mystery.

In 1721 the Jesuit, Charlevoix, was sent into the West to ascertain ways and methods of solving this mystery. When he reached Green Bay he met a band of Sioux Indians, and they told him about trading with other Indians who lived near salt water far to the west. Once again, salt water! The kind of report that had come to Du Lhut's ears some forty years earlier! What did it mean? The Great Salt Lake? Or the sea that washed the shores of Cathay?

Charlevoix made his way as cautiously as he could to the Mississippi and the Illinois country. There he found that the knives and axes of the Fox warriors had struck terror into the hearts of France's Indian allies. Despite dangers and difficulties, he managed to get back to eastern Canada and make his report. There were two ways of exploring the West, he said. One was by going to the head of Lake Superior and following the water route to the interior. The other was by going north from Wisconsin into the Sioux country. To use the second, however, it would be necessary to win the friendship of the Sioux, and a strong fort would have to be built somewhere on the Upper Mississippi — a fort to serve as a wedge between the Sioux and the fighting Foxes.

The French government in 1723 gave permission for an expedition to the Upper Mississippi and the building of a fort there, but partly because of the Fox wars this was delayed for four years. To send an expedition into the West cost money: canoes and equipment were needed; a fort must be built out in the Indian country; and there French soldiers and traders would have to live, perhaps for years. All this meant planning, effort, money. Merchants in Montreal saw in such an expedition a chance to get bargains in furs from the Sioux and were willing to equip it in return for a three-year monopoly of the trade. They promised to have built in the wilderness a fort, a chapel, a house for the commanding officer, and another one for the use of missionaries. The Sioux had told Charlevoix they would welcome the "black robes."

The French governor, Charles de Beauharnois, gladly entered into an agreement with the fur merchants of New France, and a short time later, in June 1727, the expedition started from Montreal with a little fleet of canoes. The leader was an officer named Réné Boucher, who bore the title of Sieur de la Perrière. In his party were two Jesuit missionaries, Michel Guignas and Nicolas de Gonnor.

It took nearly five weeks for the flotilla of canoes to reach Mackinac, the great trading center of the Northwest. There La Perrière and his men spent nine busy days. They bought new and larger canoes that could be used on the rough waters of Lake Michigan, and in these they reloaded their supplies. They also joined in the social life of the post, tasting the joys of civilization for the last time before entering the wilderness. But at length they started on a week of paddling around the north shores of Lake Michigan to Green Bay, where they arrived on August 8.

They were now on the edge of the Indian country. Notwithstanding the fact that the French had made a truce with the red men, La Perrière half expected to be attacked. He and his party were on the alert as they paddled up the Fox River. But there was no ambush. Instead, the Winnebago came down to the river's edge with peace pipes in their hands and invited the white men to a feast of bear's meat. This made the Frenchmen rejoice, for now the road to the Upper Midwest seemed clear.

The fleet of canoes reached the Mississippi and turned northward. To Father Guignas the bluffs along the great river, as he made his way into the Minnesota country, looked like high mountains. Day after day the Frenchmen paddled against the current until on September 17, 1727, they reached Lake Pepin. Here, at sundown, they landed, selecting a spot on a low point on the west side near the upper end of the lake.

The next few days were very busy. "The day after landing," Father Guignas tells us, "axes were applied to the trees and four days later the fort was entirely finished." It consisted of a "plat of ground a hundred feet square surrounded by stakes twelve feet high with two good bastions." Within this inclosure three large log buildings were erected. One was thirty-eight feet long and sixteen wide; the other two, a blacksmith shop and a storehouse for goods, were a little smaller. Before the end of October the houses were finished, and "everyone found himself lodged peacefully in his own home." A little village had sprung up inside the walls of the fort.

The Frenchmen were now eager to go hunting. They had heard tales of great herds of deer they would be sure to find, but actually they had little luck. Before long Sioux Indians came to the fort and put up ninety-five skin tents around the inclosure.

Meanwhile, Guignas and De Gonnor began their work as missionaries. They built a chapel which they called the Mission of St. Michael the Archangel — possibly the first Christian mission established on Minnesota soil. The Jesuit missionaries went to the wilderness not only to preach to the Indians, but also as scientists, to study the geography and natural conditions of the region. Before they left Montreal they asked the governor to provide them with a quadrant, for measuring latitude, a telescope six or seven feet long, and several other instruments. They were thus equipped to be the map makers of the expedition.

La Perrière named the post on Lake Pepin Fort Beauharnois for the governor of New France, and in November he held a celebration in honor of the governor's birthday. Father Guignas tells about this birthday party in a letter he wrote while at the fort. "Some very fine rockets were fired off, and the air was made to resound with a hundred shouts of 'Long live the King,' and 'Long live Charles de Beauharnois.'" The fireworks amused the Frenchmen, but they had a somewhat different effect on the Indians. "When these poor people saw the fireworks in the air and the stars falling from heaven," said Father Guignas, "women and children took to flight, and the most courageous of the men cried for mercy, and urgently asked that the astonishing play of this terrible medicine should be made to cease."

It was intended that Fort Beauharnois should serve as a home base from which an expedition should set out for the Pacific, but such an expedition was never attempted, and neither the fort nor the mission lasted very long. Early in the summer of 1728 La Perrière set out with Father de Gonnor to return to Montreal. He left his nephew, Pierre Boucherville, in charge of the fort.

Meanwhile, the position of the twenty soldiers and traders left at the fort had been made very dangerous by events farther south. The Foxes had broken their truce and massacred many French soldiers in the Illinois country. Beauharnois determined to teach these Indians a lesson they would long remember; in fact, he wanted to exterminate the tribe. In 1728 he sent an army from Montreal to make war on them. It was made up of four hundred Frenchmen and more than twice as many Indian allies. From Mackinac this force advanced into the country west of Lake Michigan hoping to have a pitched battle. But the Foxes got word of its coming, and when the French expedition reached the Fox villages, they were deserted; the Indians had fled to the interior. All the Frenchmen could do was to burn the villages and destroy the fields of corn they found. They could not catch the Indians, and finally the army had to retreat and return to Canada.

With the woods full of hostile Foxes, the garrison at Fort Beauharnois was in great danger. The commander of the retreating French army managed to send a message advising them to give up the post and make their escape, but some of them decided to remain. The new commander, however, with Father Guignas and eight or ten others, tried to slip down the river to the Illinois country.

In three canoes they glided down with the current, and all seemed to be going well until one foggy morning they saw some Indians running along the riverbank, while others paddled out in canoes to stop the white men. They were all taken prisoners, not by Foxes, but by friends of the Foxes. In the hands of these natives they faced torture and death, but luckily one or two of them escaped. This alarmed the Indians, for they feared that a body of French soldiers might be summoned. They held the others as prisoners for a long time but were afraid to put them to death; and the next spring the Indians released the white men, who returned to Montreal in safety.

The feud with the Foxes continued. The French were not able to stamp out the tribe that opposed them so bitterly and bravely. They continued, however, to maintain a post on Lake Pepin off and on until 1737. After that the French had no post on the Upper Mississippi until 1750, when a noted French officer and trader, Paul de la Marque, Sieur de Marin, went into the Middle West and built one not far from the site of old Fort Beauharnois. He was the leader of a group of traders who were associated with the governor of New France in the control of the Upper Mississippi trade. For a half dozen years he and his sons commanded this post. But the period of French control was nearing its end, and Marin's fort was, in fact, the last French post on the Upper Mississippi.

Under Northern Skies

The northern boundary of the United States from Lake Superior westward runs through a tangle of lakes, rivers, and portages. When it reaches the largest of all the lakes separating Minnesota from Canada, it suddenly leaps northwestward. Through the Lake of the Woods it threads its way past numerous islands, leaving some on the American side and others on the Canadian, until it approaches a long narrow inlet, where it veers westward, dividing the inlet in two. At its innermost point the boundary line turns southward, and it runs straight down to the forty-ninth parallel, where it swings west and heads for the Pacific Coast.

The land on the north side of the inlet in the Lake of the Woods is Canadian, while that on the south side is American. The American territory is separated from the rest of the United States by Buffalo Bay, a southwestern projection of the lake. This isolated bit of land, comprising about a hundred and fifty square miles, is known as the Northwest Angle.

That this Angle should be American rather than Canadian provokes endless curiosity among those who scan the map, but the explanation is simple. It goes back to the treaty of 1783, which provided that the boundary from Lake Superior was to follow the line of water communication to the Lake of the Woods, run through that lake to its northwestern point, and then follow a course due west to the Mississippi River. Geography in this instance outwitted diplomacy, for the Mississippi was conspicuously absent from the region west of the Lake of the Woods. After the Louisiana Purchase it was suggested by Americans that the boundary, instead of engaging in a futile pursuit of the Mississippi, should run along the forty-ninth parallel, and this proposal was adopted in the Convention of 1818, with the added provision that a boundary line should be drawn due south from the Northwest Angle point to the forty-ninth parallel.

The Northwest Angle is no mere geographic curiosity. It was on the south side of the inlet separating Canada from the United States, on what is now American soil, that La Vérendrye and his French associates built Fort St. Charles in the seventeenth century. Here was a central point for vast plans, a depot on a pre-pioneer route of trade and travel. With this fort are intertwined the dreams of a great French explorer and fur trader. From this spot were projected a series of far-flung posts; this was the base for ambitious expeditions toward the unknown West. On these northern waters sped canoes of hardy voyageurs; to this fort came wilderness priests; on an island of this lake occurred one of the darkest tragedies of French-Canadian history; and here were enacted the last scenes in the drama of the French regime in the region west of Lake Superior.

La Vérendrye seems to have derived the inspiration for his plunge into the Lake Superior hinterland from tales of western rivers told him by Indians at his Lake Nipigon post — notably by a certain Auchagah, who had journeyed a considerable distance into the West and had picked up rumors of a river that emptied its waters into a great salt sea and of armor-clad men who rode on horses. La Vérendrye believed this tale contained some truth, and he persuaded Auchagah to draw a map on birch bark tracing the route of his travels beyond Lake Superior.

This map La Vérendrye sent to Beauharnois, the governor

of New France, and in 1730 he saw the governor personally and disclosed his ambition to make an expedition to the sea of the West. He asked for money, supplies, and a hundred men. The governor approved the plan and forwarded to Versailles a request for its authorization.

Pierre Gaultier de Varennes, Sieur de la Vérendrye, was then forty-five years old and had already had a varied career. He was born in New France in 1685, at Three Rivers, where his father was governor and his mother's father, Pierre Boucher, had been governor. When he was only twelve years old he entered the army. In his twenties he went to France, and there in 1709 he fought and was wounded at Malplaquet, the decisive battle of the War of the Spanish Succession. A few years later he returned to Canada and became an officer of a colonial regiment. He married Marie-Anne Dandonneau du Sablé in 1712 and had four sons — Jean Baptiste, Pierre, François, and Louis Joseph — all of whom ultimately were at Fort St. Charles.

The king's reply proved disappointing, for, although Louis XV authorized a western expedition, he was unwilling to make a grant for its expenses. He did promise La Vérendrye a monopoly of the fur trade beyond Lake Superior. The governor had already given him a similar assurance, and this enabled him to get financial support from a number of Montreal merchants interested less in exploration than in beaver skins.

So in June 1731 the veteran of Malplaquet started from Montreal for the West with his three eldest sons, his nephew La Jemeraye, and a party of about fifty soldiers and voyageurs. At Michilimackinac the expedition was joined by a Jesuit priest, Father Mesaiger, and on August 26 the canoes carrying the Frenchmen landed at Grand Portage on the north Superior shore. La Vérendrye, facing a mutiny among his men, who were reluctant to push into the unknown hinterland of the Great Lakes, took most of them north to spend the winter at the mouth of the Kaministiquia River, while La Jemeraye, with one of La Vérendrye's sons, one voyageur, and a guide, crossed the portage to the Pigeon River and made his way as far as the western end of Rainy Lake, where he built Fort St. Pierre, naming it in honor of La Vérendrye.

The next summer, in 1732, the commander joined the men at Rainy Lake and then, with his followers and an escort of fifty Indian canoes, struck out for the Lake of the Woods, where he established Fort St. Charles. This was the second in a chain of French forts that was ultimately to include Fort Maurepas, at the mouth of the Red River; Fort Rouge, at the junction of the Red and Assiniboine rivers, where much later the metropolis of the Canadian Northwest was to be built; Fort La Reine, some distance up the Assiniboine; and Forts Dauphin and Bourbon, erected by La Vérendrye's sons in the Saskatchewan country.

Fort St. Charles was named in honor of the Canadian governor, Charles de la Boische, Marquis de Beauharnois, for whom, as we have seen, Fort Beauharnois on Lake Pepin also was named. The fort on the Lake of the Woods was surrounded by palisades—a double row of spruce, aspen, and oak stakes from twelve to fifteen feet high. The east and west sides of the inclosure measured a hundred feet long; the other two sides, sixty. There were two gates, one on the north side, which faced the lake, the other on the south, giving access to the neighboring forest; and there was also a watchtower. Inside the inclosure were houses for the commandant and the missionary, a chapel, four main buildings, a powder magazine, and a storehouse. The establishment as a whole was somewhat smaller than Fort Beauharnois—one of the Frenchmen stationed there described it as "but an enclosure," inside which were "a few huts of square logs, calked with earth and covered with bark."

The records leave no doubt that the fort was frequently the scene of much bustle and activity. In the spring of 1733 La Jemeraye got ready to journey back to Quebec to report on the progress that had been made and to obtain fresh supplies. Three canoes, filled with furs collected during the winter, were sent to Lake Superior, and they returned in August laden with merchandise. As many as a hundred and fifty canoes arrived at the fort in one day, each carrying two or three Indians and a load of meat, buffalo fat, bear oil, wild rice, and other things to trade. One day some three hundred warriors on their way to attack the Chippewa of Madeline Island stopped at the fort, and the next day five hundred more came on an expedition against the prairie Sioux. After forts were established to the west and north, men were dispatched from Fort St. Charles with supplies and merchandise for these newer posts, or returned with furs to be packed for the journey eastward to Montreal.

Old records enable us to look in on a trading council held at Fort St. Charles with a party of Cree and Assiniboin Indians in the winter of 1733–34. When the Indians arrived they saluted the French flag that was flying over the fort with three volleys, to which La Vérendrye and the twenty Frenchmen who were with him replied. Then the chiefs were allowed to enter the fort, where compliments were exchanged and they were given tobacco and provisions. The next day the Indians presented the Frenchmen with gifts of beaver skins and about a hundred pounds of buffalo meat, and they in turn were given a sack of corn and a large supply of tobacco. "My children," the white leader said to them, "I will tell you tomorrow what are our Father's orders to me regarding you, and shall let you know his will."

On the next day, New Year's Day 1734, the Indians thronged into the fort at ten o'clock in the morning. The Frenchmen had placed at the center of the grounds thirty pounds of tobacco, forty pounds of bullets, two hundred gunflints, twenty axes, sixty knives, sixty ramrods, sixty awls, and supplies of glass beads, needles, and vermilion. Before distributing these gifts, however, La Vérendrye made a speech. The great chief of the Frenchmen, he said, would be glad to learn of the Indians' visit. The French were numerous, there was no land unknown to them, they had only one chief, and La Vérendrye was his mouthpiece. If the Indians obeyed this chief, he would send many Frenchmen each year to satisfy their needs; but they in turn must bring in plenty of skins in exchange.

The next day La Vérendrye again entertained the chiefs, giving them cloaks, shirts, breeches, leggings, powder and shot, axes, daggers, knives, hatchets, beads, and flags. Incidentally, he asked them if they had any knowledge of iron and was interested when one of them said he knew of several places where iron could be found.

This scene discloses La Vérendrye in the role of a negotiator and trader. But he was also a farmer. The fort had been established with an eye not only to trade, but also to fishing and hunting, the availability of wild rice, and good land. The Frenchmen cleared the land the first year by burning. Abundant wild rice enabled them to save their corn for seeding. They planted corn and peas, and of the latter La Vérendrye reported a harvest of ten bushels for one of seed. He also made some effort to teach the Indians to sow corn.

But with all his care, life at the fort was precarious. Heavy rains in 1733 damaged the wild rice crop, and that autumn La Vérendrye sent ten men to the other side of the lake with tools to build a shelter at the mouth of a river and with nets for fishing. The fishing was excellent. That fall the men caught more than four thousand whitefish, not to speak of trout, sturgeon, and other varieties of fish. They returned to Fort St. Charles on May 2, 1734, after the ice had melted, having lived during a northern winter on the food furnished them by lake and country.

The problem of food was not the only serious one that faced white men in the primitive West. Sometimes there must have been grave danger from forest fires. Jean-Pierre Aulneau, a young Jesuit missionary who went out to Fort St. Charles in

1735 to take the place of Father Mesaiger, thus described his trip from Lake Superior to the Lake of the Woods: "I journeyed nearly all the way through fire and a thick stifling smoke, which prevented us from even once catching a glimpse of the sun."

In 1734 La Vérendrye, worried over his debts and the demands of his creditors, journeyed the long way to Montreal and Quebec to reenlist their support and to report to the governor. He returned to Fort St. Charles with his youngest son, Louis Joseph, the following year. Early in 1736 he suffered a great loss in the death from exposure of his nephew La Jemeraye, and then, before the year was over, an even heavier blow fell upon him.

Provisions, goods, and powder ordered by La Vérendrye in Montreal the previous year had not yet arrived at the fort. Since they were badly needed, the commander decided to send three well-manned canoes to meet the brigade that was on its way west. The plan was for this party to secure some of the supplies and hurry back to the fort with them. Jean, the explorer's eldest son, was selected to lead this relief expedition, and he took with him Father Aulneau and nineteen voyageurs.

Not long after leaving the fort Jean and his party beached their canoes on an island in the Lake of the Woods. And here they were surprised by a large Sioux war party, looking for revenge upon the French for maintaining friendly relations with their own bitter enemies, the Cree and Assiniboin. All the white men were killed and beheaded.

The course of this terrible tragedy we can only imagine — perhaps a seemingly friendly arrival of the enemy, masking treachery, or possibly a stealthy approach that caught the Frenchmen unawares, then the sudden attack, the blood-curdling yells, a spirited defense, finally stillness.

Eventually La Vérendrye learned what had happened, and his heart was heavy with grief. "I have lost my son, the Reverend Father, and my Frenchmen, misfortunes which I shall lament all my life," he said. Later he had the bodies of his son and the priest and the skulls of the voyageurs buried beneath the chapel of Fort St. Charles. He had the fort itself rebuilt and "put in such a condition that four men could defend it against a hundred." There was no thought of giving it up, but the next spring the garrison of Fort Beauharnois on Lake Pepin was withdrawn by its commander, St. Pierre, because of the increasing hostility of the Sioux, who were gloating over their trophies from the North. The tragic affair on the island in the Lake of the Woods thus compelled the abandonment of the French post on the Upper Mississippi.

We usually think of the voyageurs who served La Vérendrye as nameless, but it is interesting to know that in Montreal are preserved copies of the engagements they made with him and his business associates before they departed for the post of "Winnipegon" in the North—that is, for Fort St. Charles. The Minnesota Historical Society has transcripts of no fewer than twenty-one of these documents dating from 1731. They give us such names as Jacques La Vallée, Paul Chevalier, François Provanche, Joseph De Laurier, Pierre Le Boeuf, Roc Touin, Antoine Millet, and Jean Baptiste Renaud, as well as the terms and conditions of their employment. A typical agreement called for a year's service at a compensation of five hundred livres payable in beaver skins after the return of the engagé, who promised to help in "going up and coming back," to paddle canoes, to transport merchandise and furs, to be obedient and faithful, and not to leave without the consent of his employers.

Let us give an honored place in the story of Fort St. Charles to the French-Canadian voyageurs—gay of heart, bright of dress, superbly skilled in the art of handling the *canot d'ecorce*, singers of "*A la clair fontaine*" and other ballads, pioneers of western waters. They have earned it, for they manned the canoes that carried explorers and fur traders into the heart of the inland empire, they built the fort itself, and nineteen of them died alongside the commandant's son and the Jesuit father in that bloody hour on Massacre Island.

When in 1737 La Vérendrye revisited Montreal — a journey of two months and eighteen days — he was pressed by the governor to forward his exploration of the farther West. The governor in turn was urged on by the impatient colonial minister in France, Count Maurepas, who evidently believed that La Vérendrye had succumbed to the lure of beaver skins.

The truth seems to be that La Vérendrye had never forgotten his ambition to find the western sea, but he clearly regarded the expansion of the power of New France as fundamental, a first essential. He would set up new trading posts, win the loyalty of the Indians, increase French trade at the expense of the English in the North, and thus establish a firm base for an advance to the mountains and sea of the Far West. It must not be forgotten that from the first he had in effect been left by the government to shift for himself in his western enterprise, to make his way without government funds. He was obliged by every circumstance to take a realistic view of the problems that confronted him in the wilderness.

Upon his return to the West in 1738 La Vérendrye made his famous journey to the land of the Mandan Indians in the Missouri River country, taking with him two of his sons and a large party of voyageurs and traders. His reports give an interesting picture of the Mandan. He found them to be industrious, living in spacious dwellings, making excellent wickerwork, using earthen vessels, and "great eaters . . . eager for feasts." Every day, he said, they brought him "more than twenty dishes" of corn, nuts, and pumpkins, "always cooked." He was especially impressed by their cellars, "where they store all they have in the way of grains, meat, fat, dressed skins and bearskins."

Before he returned to Fort La Reine, which was now the French base in the West, La Vérendrye instructed two of his men to remain behind with the Mandan, and when they re-joined him the next autumn they brought him circumstantial reports, gathered from Indians who had visited the Mandan, of white people living far to the west in towns "near the great Lake the water of which rises and falls and is not good to drink."

Clearly, if the mystery of the sea whose water was not good to drink was to be solved, a more ambitious exploration was called for. Such a venture was undertaken in 1742. Since La Vérendrye himself was unable to join in it, two of his sons were put in charge of it. "On January 1st 1743," wrote one of them, "we were in sight of the mountains." And a few days later they reached the foothills of the mountains.

This was farthest west for the Vérendryes. Most scholars today believe they reached, not the Rockies, but the Black Hills. When the explorers returned to the Missouri, they buried an inscribed lead plaque as a record of their journey. A hundred and seventy years later that plaque was picked up by a South Dakota school child who was playing on a hill above Fort Pierre — a message from the eighteenth to the twentieth century.

La Vérendrye was alive to the possibility of using the Sas-katchewan River approach to the farther West, but ill, under a fire of criticism, and burdened with a debt of more than forty thousand livres, he was obliged to return again to Que-bec. There he found that he still retained the confidence of the governor, but that Maurepas' skepticism had increased. He was therefore denied a merited promotion in military rank and relieved of his position as commandant of the western posts. His achievements spoke for themselves, however, and in 1746 he was promoted to a captaincy. Three years later he won an even higher honor: the coveted Cross of St. Louis. Two of his sons received promotions in the military service, and he him-self was reinstated as commandant in the West.

It was too late, however. He intended to go back to the

wilderness in 1750 "to continue the establishment of posts and the exploration of the West," but the intention was never realized, for on December 5, 1749, at Montreal, he died. He had not discovered the western sea, but, as Beauharnois once said of him, he had given himself "wholly to the task and devoted to it the whole proceeds of the new posts which he established with so much trouble and care and with extreme risk."

Fort St. Charles had been at first the western capital of the empire that La Vérendrye was carving out in the interior Northwest. After some years it seems to have yielded priority of importance to the newer posts established in more strategic centers of the Canadian Northwest, but it continued to be a scene of activity until the eve of the British conquest, when it fades from the records. It was undoubtedly the longest occupied French post on Minnesota soil. For how many years the palisades and chapel and other buildings of the fort escaped the ravages of fire we do not know, but we do know that ultimately they were destroyed. As long ages passed, the very site was forgotten.

In more modern times, however, the story of Fort St. Charles and other posts of the West began to arouse interest. La Vérendrye himself has been accorded a high place in the history of Canada and the American Northwest; monuments in honor of his achievements have been erected in Quebec, Three Rivers, Winnipeg, and other Canadian cities, as well as in the North Dakota village that bears his name. And scholars have studied his journals and letters with great care. In these vivid records the old fort comes to life again, the voyageurs ride western waters, and La Vérendrye himself lives and breathes.

Back in 1889 an old man named Alneau told a Jesuit at La Vendée, in France, that his family possessed a package of letters written by a relative, a Jesuit priest, who had been massacred by Indians in North America a hundred and fifty years earlier. Thus was brought to light another important contemporary source of information, the letters of the martyred Jean-Pierre Aulneau. And in 1890 the Jesuits of St. Boniface College, Manitoba, stirred by interest in Aulneau's life, tried to identify the island on which he was killed. They went to the Lake of the Woods, and on an island associated by tradition with the massacre they placed a memorial cross. Later, in 1905, the Archbishop of St. Boniface had excavations made on this island, which is on the Canadian side of the boundary line, in a futile search for relics, and he had a small memorial chapel built.

In 1902 a search had been made for the site of Fort St. Charles. A party from St. Boniface landed on the north shore of the Northwest Angle inlet, and there, at a spot pointed out to them by an Indian chief, they unearthed an old fireplace. This spot they believed to be the site of La Vérendrye's fort. It was investigated further in 1907, but in 1908 a new expedition under the auspices of the Historical Society of St. Boniface, which had been organized immediately after the discoveries made in 1902, rejected the earlier identification and found the exact spot where the fort had stood. It was on the south, or American, side of the inlet, not on the north.

The ruins of a large fireplace were the first discovery. Then on subsequent days, though the buildings and palisades had long since crumbled away, the fort took shape in the minds of the searchers. Here had stood the chapel, there the priest's house, over there the quarters of the commandant. Remains of the posts which enclosed the fort were found, and buried in the soil were discovered a pair of steel scissors, a carpenter's chisel, a shoe buckle, two iron handles, several knife blades (one with the name "Alice D." on it), a staple for a lock, nails of several kinds, iron rings, and beads.

But the most dramatic find was made at the site of the chapel. There the skeletons of Jean Baptiste de la Vérendrye and Father Aulneau and the skulls of the massacred voyageurs were found. In all, nineteen skulls and five skeletons were uncovered, two of the latter clearly those of Jean Baptiste and the Jesuit father, for the two had been placed together in a wooden box and bore evidence of wounds. And with them was found confirmatory evidence: two keys, another bunch of five keys, a piece of gilt glass, beads such as belong to a rosary, the hook for a priest's cassock, a shoe buckle, a hunting knife, an awl, and a few other objects.

It is sad to be obliged to add that all the material found by the excavators at Fort St. Charles was stored in the old St. Boniface College and was lost or destroyed when that building was swept by a devastating fire in the early 1920s. A few bones were found after the fire, but even these could not certainly be identified as the relics from Fort St. Charles, since nine students and one Jesuit father were burned to death in the fire. Fortunately, however, the finds were recorded in pictures before this disaster occurred, and these pictures, together with a sketch plan of the fort drawn by the Reverend Father Blain, S.J., are reproduced in a bulletin issued by the Historical Society of St. Boniface.

Fort St. Charles constitutes a significant and dramatic chapter in the history of the American and Canadian Northwest, and the post commander is a major figure in the epic of the continent. To the central interest of the French fort is added that of the international boundary and of the water channel to the West, as well as the attraction of what is in fact a natural wilderness park.

Fort St. Charles stood by the waters of a majestic international lake, studded with picturesque islands, its waters teeming with pike, whitefish, and the royal muskellunge, its irregular shores entrancing in their wild beauty. And the primeval northern charm of the Lake of the Woods makes its appeal today to Americans and Canadians as, long years ago, it stirred the sons of New France, whose chansons floated across its waves.

Prophet of
Mighty Kingdoms

THE first explorer to reach the Upper Midwest after the triumph of the English in their great struggle with the French was certain that thousands of people would sometime live in this region and that they would build wonderful cities. His name was Jonathan Carver. He came into the Minnesota region in 1766, three years after the treaty had been signed by which New France became a British possession. He did not precisely anticipate Whittier's phrase, "The land lies open," but he wrote, "There is no doubt that at some future period, mighty kingdoms will emerge from these wildernesses, and stately and solemn temples, with gilded spires reaching the skies, supplant the Indian huts, whose only decorations are the barbarous trophies of their vanquished enemies."

Carver did more than visit the West. He wrote a book about his travels that became very popular in its day and was read by great numbers of people in the Old World, and his book illustrates one of the greatest achievements of the early trail blazers. Their letters, maps, reports, and books lifted the curtain of mystery that had veiled western America from the eyes of the world, and once the curtain was raised, people began to think about the natural wealth and beauty of the land that lay open.

In May 1766 Jonathan Carver set out from Boston for the western post of Mackinac. He had already had a taste of adventure, for he had served as a captain in the French and Indian Wars. The commander of the Mackinac garrison was Major Robert Rogers, who also had fought in the war and had performed many daring exploits. When Carver wrote his book he did not tell about his connection with Rogers, but we know now that the plan for his journeys was all worked out by Rogers.

Perhaps Rogers was not himself a trail blazer, but his imagination and his planning made it possible for others to win fame in exploring. He devised a system of government for the whole region that centered at Mackinac. He tried to win the friendship of the western Indians. And he conceived the idea of sending an expedition to the Pacific Coast. The British government long before had offered a prize of a hundred thousand dollars to the man who should find the Northwest Passage, a waterway from Hudson Bay to the Pacific Ocean. Rogers believed that if he sent an expedition overland to the west coast, it could find, far north on that coast, the water passage that would lead back to Hudson Bay.

In going into the Northwest, Carver was merely carrying out Rogers' orders. He was to go into the Sioux country around the Falls of St. Anthony and there try to win the friendship of the Indians. He was to get the promise of the red men to send representatives to a peace council to be held at Mackinac. And he was to join a great expedition to the Pacific Ocean.

So Carver started westward from Mackinac. He followed the route the French traders had so often taken, going first to Green Bay, then up the Fox River, over a portage to the Wisconsin, and down the Wisconsin to the Mississippi. Then he turned up the great river and went to Prairie du Chien. This village, containing about forty buildings and some two hundred Indian warriors, was a place to which many traders went. Carver called it "one of the most Delightsom Settlements" he saw during his travels.

From this village he again set out with a Frenchman and an Indian, and on November 14, 1766, he came to a great cave in the banks of the Mississippi. This was not far from where the city of St. Paul now stands, and it has ever since been known as Carver's Cave. Entering the cave through a small opening, Carver found a room about thirty feet wide. Sixty feet back from the entrance he came to a lake. "I Cast a Stone which I Could hear fall at a distance and with a strange hollow sound," he writes in his diary. "I tasted of this water and found it to be very good."

The Indians told him that some of them had tried to explore the lake, using a canoe and torches, but they saw strange lights at a distance and heard queer sounds. So they gave up and called the cave *Wawkon Teebee*, which means the "House of Spirits." Carver, however, thought the ghostly lights were reflections and the sounds echoes. When he came out he noticed a stone at the entrance, with a number of curious Indian marks cut in it and to these marks he added the insignia of the king of England.

On the same day, November 14, Carver got as far as the mouth of the Minnesota River, called by the natives the *Wadapawmenesotor*. And the next day he reached the falls discovered nearly a century earlier by Hennepin. Around the falls he saw a wide plain with some oak and hickory trees growing on it. "A more pleasing and picturesque view cannot, I believe, be found throughout the universe," he wrote.

In his book Carver says he traveled up the Mississippi for some sixty miles above the Falls of St. Anthony, but his manuscript diary shows that he did not really make this trip. Many travelers in the history of the world have enjoyed telling wonderful stories about what they have seen and heard, and Carver is not unique in describing trips he made only in imagination. What he really did in this instance was to go back to the Minnesota River. He found a place to camp some distance up that stream and remained there until the next spring.

On April 26, 1767, Carver left his Minnesota stopping place, and on May 1 he was present at a solemn Indian council held near the great cave that he had visited on his northward journey. Here he told the tribesmen about the grand council to be held at Mackinac, and he promised for those who should be sent to attend it a straight road, smooth waters, and a clear, blue sky. He told them that beaver blankets would be ready for them, spread out under a great "Tree of Peace," and that the pipe of peace would be lighted. Carver was adopted as a chief by the natives. Their leader then answered him, promising peace and friendship. He hoped the Great Father would send more traders, bringing guns and powder, tobacco, beads, paints, and different kinds of cloth. Such things, he said, made glad the hearts of the young men, wives, and children.

After this meeting Carver and some of the Sioux chiefs who were going to Mackinac started down the river, and on May 6 they reached Prairie du Chien. There Carver joined Captain James Tute, whom Rogers had appointed leader of the exploring expedition to the Pacific. Second in command was one James Stanley Goddard, and Carver was third, having been made the surveyor of the party. Now they were to begin their search for the river *Ourigan*, or Oregon, which they thought emptied into the South Sea, and for the Northwest Passage.

On May 21 Tute, Goddard, and Carver, with two interpreters, eight workers, and a Chippewa chief as guide, started up the Mississippi. At first they planned to go northward, cross from the Mississippi to the Red River, and then go to Lake Winnipeg and westward, securing at the far-distant Fort La Prairie some supplies that Major Rogers had promised to send by way of Grand Portage on the north shore of Lake Superior. Captain Tute changed his plans, however, because the Chippewa guide was afraid of attacks from the Sioux and because the party did not have enough presents with them for the Indians through whose country they would pass. The explorers therefore turned up the Chippewa River, first placing on a tree at the mouth of that stream a drawing showing their two canoes, so that passing Indians would know who they were and where they had gone. From the Chippewa they went by lakes and streams and portages to Lake Superior. Paddling their two canoes along the shores of this lake, they arrived on July 12 at Fond du Lac, a little Chippewa village at the mouth of the St. Louis River. Carver thought it the dirtiest and most beggarly village he had ever seen.

From Fond du Lac the expedition moved on along the north Superior shore until they came to the village of Grand Portage, and here they suffered a bitter disappointment. Word came from Major Rogers that he was not able to send them any supplies. Despite this, he asked them to go on with their western explorations, but after talking matters over, the party decided to give up its great plan.

Carver's diary ends with the date August 29, 1767. By that time he was back at Mackinac. "Here ends this attempt to find out a Northwest Passage," he wrote.

Rogers had been unable to get the approval of his superior officer for the purchase of supplies for the expedition, and as a result of some trumped-up charges he was put in prison. He was tried and acquitted, and later went to England, where he again attempted, without success, to get financial aid for the discovery of the Northwest Passage. Meanwhile, in 1769, Carver had also gone to England, and in London, eleven years later, he died of want. If he did not win fortune, he did win fame — through the publication of his book, given to the world under the title, *Travels of Jonathan Carver through the Interior Parts of North America in the Years 1766, 1767, and 1768.*

Yankee Trader

A KITCHEN helper in a Connecticut house where the former governor of the state lived was starting a fire with some old sheets of paper. The fire flamed up, and the pages grew black and crumpled away. Just then a visitor noticed that the paper was covered with old, faded writing.

"What is that?" she asked. "It looks interesting."

"You can have it," said the kitchen helper. "It's not worth anything."

The visitor took up the remaining sheets and began to read them. Very soon she realized that what she held in her hands contained the life story of Peter Pond, uncle of the Connecticut governor in whose house the old yellow pages, thrown away as waste paper, were almost lost forever.

It was Mrs. Nathan Gillet Pond who rescued the old trader's story from the flames, and she found it to be a most amusing piece of work. Peter Pond had his own ideas about spelling. He would write *extrodnerey* for extraordinary, *eairley* for early, and *comfortbel* for comfortable. But his handwriting was fairly easy to read, and the story he told very interesting indeed. Only the early part of it was saved, for it was the last pages that were used to start the kitchen fire. But from those that were left we know the story of Pond's visits to the West and his explorations in the Upper Mississippi Valley in the years just before the Revolutionary War began.

Peter Pond was born in Connecticut in 1740. When he was sixteen he enlisted as a soldier to fight for the English against the French and their Indian allies. His parents told him he was too young to go to war, but Peter had heard a military band, and nothing would stop him in his determination to be a soldier. "One Eavening in April," he wrote in his diary, "the Drums an Instaments of Musick ware all Imployed to that Degrea that thay Charmed me."

The life of a soldier gave Peter more than a taste of adventure, and when the war was over, he did not go back to his home in Connecticut, but became a fur trader in the West at Detroit. Once he took part in a duel. He does not tell us the exact reason for the fight, but he says that he was "Exposed to all Sorts of Companey" and that one person abused him in a "Shameful manner." There was a quarrel, followed by a challenge. Pond's comment on the duel is laconic: "We met the Next Morning Eairley & Discharged Pistels in which the Pore fellowe was unfortenat."

In 1733 Pond decided to go to the Upper Mississippi country as a fur trader. He entered into partnership with a man named Felix Graham, who furnished the necessary capital while Pond supplied the experience in organizing and actually carrying on the trade. At Mackinac he got together the trading goods he intended to use in buying furs from the Indians. Some of these goods had been sent out from Albany, New York, and some had been brought to Mackinac from Montreal by Pond himself. He divided his stock of material into twelve parts and loaded it into twelve large canoes. "Each cannew was made of Birch Bark and white Seader," he explains, and "thay would carry seven Thousand wate."

Many of the things Pond took with him are listed in the accounts he kept during his years as a trader. In these business papers he spelled as strangely as in his diary. Among the articles he was prepared to give the Indians in exchange for furs were some "silk Bandanos," "21 paire Trowsars," "44 Rufeld Shirts," "2 nests Tin Kettels," "2 doz Sizars," and eight dozen scalping knives.

Pond employed nine men to work for him as traders, and with his fleet of canoes, he set off for Green Bay and thence by the Fox-Wisconsin route to the Mississippi. On the Wisconsin he and his men saw and killed many rattlesnakes that were swimming across the river. At its mouth they tried their luck as fishermen and made a big haul of catfish. "Thay Came Heavey," Pond records. "At length we hald one ashore that wade a Hundered and four Pounds — a Seacond that was One Hundred Wate — a third of Seventy five Pounds."

At Prairie du Chien Pond made final arrangements with his assistants, who were to spend the winter each on a different stream flowing into the Mississippi and then to bring back to the village in the spring the furs they had collected. Since Pond sent out nine agents to work for him, he must have been an important fur merchant. He understood that if the trade paid well, he could greatly increase the profits of himself and his partner by employing a number of traders.

Not all was business at Prairie du Chien, however. It was a lively village when Pond visited it. There the French liked to play billiards when they came in from their trading stations, and the Indians took part in exciting games of lacrosse. Such amusements were carried on for three or four weeks each spring, and many of those who took part in the festivities had come long distances. In some cases, boats loaded with trade goods were brought to Prairie du Chien from as far away as New Orleans. They were "navagated by thirty-six men who row as maney oars."

After making the proper arrangements, Pond, with two other traders, started up the river. This was in October 1773. Already the rumble of the coming American Revolution was being heard in the English colonies, but Pond probably was not thinking of war or politics as he paddled northward against the current of the Mississippi. Now and then a shot would ring out, however, as he and his friends spied wild game. They had plenty to eat — geese, ducks, and deer and bear meat.

They "Lived as Well as hart Could Wish on Such food," and they even found crab apples along the banks of the river. Canoeing in such circumstances, at a time when trees and shrubs were bright with autumn's reds and browns, must have been pleasant.

Pond had decided to go as far as the mouth of the St. Peter's, or Minnesota, River. When he reached it, he continued up stream until he found a good place for his winter camp. He chose a high bank on which to build his little cabin, and there he made himself as comfortable as he could.

In January 1774 the Indians began coming to Pond's cabin to trade with him, bringing with them the skins and furs of beavers, otters, deer, wolves, foxes, raccoons, and other animals. "Thay ware Welcom," wrote the trader, "and we Did our bisnes to advantage." But he soon found that a near-by Frenchman got more trade than he did. At first he thought this was because the Frenchman was better known to the Indians than he was, but the other trader told him this was not the reason. The Frenchman had learned that the Indians, especially the Indian women, liked to steal little things from him, and so he would leave some small trinkets, knives, needles, or bells on his counter. "For the sake of Stealing these trifels," Pond learned, "thay Com to Sea him and what thay Had for trade he Got." The idea seemed to the Yankee to be worth trying, so he put out on his counter some of his own smaller articles for the Indians to steal, and soon he was getting just as much trade as the Frenchman.

Thus the long months of snow and ice passed. Pond did not find trading a very exciting business, for he remarks, "Well thare was not Eney thing Extrodnerey Hapened Dureing the Winter."

In the spring Pond returned to Prairie du Chien. All his agents had done well, and he and Graham made excellent profits from their trading. Prairie du Chien was crowded with people. Indians in their paint and finery were there; fur traders like Pond, fresh from their winter posts, thronged the village; at the waterfront lay a fleet of a hundred and thirty canoes from Mackinac, and some also from New Orleans. All this shows that before the Revolution the fur trade was a thriving business in the Upper Midwest.

Deciding to spend a second winter in the wilderness, Pond returned to the Minnesota country, and the next winter he really had an "extrodnerey" experience. He learned that a band of Yankton Sioux camped about two hundred miles up the Minnesota River from his place wanted to trade. So he loaded a canoe with trading goods and started on a nine-day trip up the river. When he was only three miles from the Yankton camp he had an unlucky accident. He was caught in a snow storm, and he pulled his canoe up on land and turned it over so he could use it for shelter. But the next morning a sharp gust of wind lifted the canoe up in the air, and when it dropped back onto the frozen ground it broke in pieces. Soon, however, a number of Indians came to his aid. They helped him to get his goods to the camp, the pipe of peace was smoked, and then Pond began a brisk trade with them.

When the trading was finished the Indians all left. Pond remained with his furs, but he had no canoe in which to take them down to his trading post. He had only an Indian boy to help him. Finally he decided to leave the boy to look after the furs while he made a quick trip back to his post to get another canoe. He was delayed by bad weather, and it was fifteen days before he returned to the camp. He found the boy almost dead with hunger. It was too late then to take away the furs by canoe, for the river was frozen, so he put them on some high scaffolds and left them there until the next spring. After the winter had passed he went upriver again, found the pelts still there, and took them down to the trading post. In all, the furs he gathered in 1774–75 were worth nearly twenty thousand dollars.

"The Spring is now advancing fast. The Chefes Cuming

with a Number of the Natives to Go with me to Mackenac to Sea and Hear what thare farther Had to Say . . ." Here Pond's diary ends. The rest of his own story was burned in the Connecticut kitchen stove, but we know something of what he did after he left the Minnesota Valley in 1775. He made a journey to Grand Portage later in the year, and then went far into the Northwest, to Lake Winnipeg and the Saskatchewan River. For the next few years he traded with Indians in that region, and in 1778 his travels took him even farther north, to the Athabasca country. And two years later he reached the Great Slave Lake, far to the northwest of Hudson Bay.

Pond was among those who formed the Northwest Company, one of the most famous of the fur-trading companies, and he also won fame as a map maker. During his years of travel he had gained personal knowledge of a vast section of the American and Canadian Northwest. It was this knowledge that led him to prepare some remarkable maps of the West, one of which is said to have been in the hands of Benjamin Franklin when that great statesman was negotiating with the British on the boundary question at the end of the Revolutionary War.

Pond lived until 1807, thirty-four years after he made his first trip to the Upper Mississippi. These years had been packed with great events, but the Upper Midwest region that Pond had visited by way of the great channel was still a wilderness.

The True Source

THE mystery and power of America's mightiest river captivated the imaginations of men through more than three hundred years of discovery and exploration—and no wonder. Little more than a trickle at its source, a tiny stream that one can step across, it winds its way down through the heart of a continent from North Star State to the Gulf, broadening and deepening as it runs "unvexed" to the sea, flowing not only through the open land of America but also through the epic of America's history.

Where did it take its rise? West of Lake of the Woods, as diplomats guessed in the eighteenth century? Below the forty-ninth parallel? In some unknown lake of the Upper Midwest?

Late in the eighteenth century a British surveyor and trader for the Northwest Company, David Thompson, found what he believed to be the Mississippi's source while returning from a trading visit to the Mandan villages on the Dakota plains. "Turtle Lake," he called it, and it was not far from the actual source.

Long after the Revolutionary War the British continued their control of the beaver and muskrat empire of the Northwest, but Americans had not forgotten the claim of the United States to this great region—a claim based solidly on the treaty of 1783. Under Jefferson this claim blossomed into action, and in 1805, seven years after Thompson's journey, a dashing young American soldier-explorer, Lieutenant Zebulon Pike, followed the Mississippi northward to what he believed to be its headwaters. He left St. Louis on August 9 in a keelboat, with twenty men and provisions for four months on the Upper Mississippi, and he was under instructions, among other things, to "ascend the main branch of the Mississippi to its source."

In the middle of October winter overtook Pike near the site of Little Falls, Minnesota, and there he built a fort to use as a winter base. Early in December he started northward again with sleds over a frozen river. On one occasion a sled, heavily loaded, crashed through the ice, and during a part of the journey the weather turned so cold that Pike's men had to build fires every three miles to keep from freezing. It was this expedition, undaunted by the cruel Minnesota winter, that pushed on to Sandy Lake, to Leech Lake, which Pike considered to be the "main source of the Mississippi," and to Upper Red Cedar Lake, now known as Cass Lake, which he described as the "upper source of the Mississippi."

Upper Red Cedar Lake was again pronounced the source of the Mississippi in 1820, when Governor Lewis Cass of Michigan Territory led an exploring party to its shores. This expedition is of special interest, for among its members was a mineralogist, Henry R. Schoolcraft, then twenty-seven years old, a native of New York whose education had been received at Middlebury and Union colleges.

Cass and his party left Detroit on May 24 in three huge birch-bark canoes; on July 5 they entered the mouth of the St. Louis River, passed the present site of Duluth, and landed at the American Fur Company's post of Fond du Lac. By way of a well-known route broken by numerous difficult portages — up the St. Louis and East Savanna rivers and down the West Savanna — Cass reached Sandy Lake. He then proceeded up the Mississippi to Upper Red Cedar Lake, which was named Cassina, and this the governor supposed to be the "true source of the Mississippi." Schoolcraft did not quite agree, however, and he took note of the fact that Cass Lake had two inlets. Inlets from where?

Before Schoolcraft had an opportunity to solve the mystery of those inlets, another explorer was destined to pass through the north country in quest of the headwaters of the Mississippi. This was the romantic Italian, Giacomo C. Beltrami. He arrived at Fort Snelling in the spring of 1823 on the *Virginia*, the first steamboat to ascend the Upper Mississippi from St. Louis. With Major Stephen H. Long, Beltrami left for the Red River country in July. At Pembina, on the Canadian border, they separated, and the Italian, with an interpreter and two Chippewa guides, struck into the wilderness to the southeast, where he thought the source of the Mississippi to be.

Although Beltrami's guides deserted him and he was left to search alone, he succeeded in reaching Red Lake. There he obtained the services of a half-breed guide, who led him by stream, lake, and portage to a heart-shaped lake situated about halfway between Red and Cass lakes. This he named Lake Julia. Although it had no visible outlet, Beltrami believed its waters to "filtrate through its banks both northward and southward, and he pronounced" it to be the "most southern source of the Red River and the most northern source of the Mississippi."

Unfortunately, Beltrami did not bother to search out a lake called *Omushkos*, of whose existence the Indians told him, although he did describe it as the western source of the Mississippi and showed it on his map. He came very close indeed to winning the honor of being the discoverer of the Mississippi's beginning.

The early 1830s found Schoolcraft in the Indian service, while Cass had now become secretary of war. In this capacity, Cass in the spring of 1832 authorized his former mineralogist to lead an expedition into the country west of the Great Lakes. Schoolcraft was directed to visit the Chippewa of the Upper Midwest, to try to bring about a lasting peace between them and the Sioux, to gather as much information about them as he could, and to see to it that as many as possible were vaccinated. For purposes of "evangelical observation" a missionary, William T. Boutwell, was attached to the party, Dr. Douglas Houghton went to vaccinate the Indians, and a military escort consisting of ten soldiers commanded by Lieutenant James Allen was provided.

This large and well-equipped party left Sault Ste. Marie on June 7, 1832, and went by way of Fond du Lac and the Savanna portage to Sandy and Cass lakes. Schoolcraft engaged Ozawindib, "the Yellow Head," a Chippewa Indian whose home was at Cass Lake, to guide his party. This native led the explorers to Star Island in Cass Lake, where his village was located. From this place Schoolcraft planned to push on into the wilderness, through one of the inlets he had observed in 1820 to the source of the Mississippi. He drew maps, collected five small canoes in which to travel, and engaged additional guides. Early on the morning of July 11 he led a select party of sixteen persons out of Cass Lake by way of a stream he said was the Mississippi.

The travelers ascended this stream to Lake Bemidji and then turned south, following the east fork of the Mississippi, now known as the Yellow Head or Schoolcraft River, to its beginnings in a swamp. Then early on the morning of July 13, they began the trek along a hardly noticeable portage path leading toward the southwest. The Yellow Head, carrying a canoe, led the way and the others followed, some loaded with baggage, others bearing canoes. Through woods and underbrush they picked their way in Indian file.

"Every step we made . . . seemed to increase the ardor with which we were carried forward," writes Schoolcraft. "The desire of reaching the actual source of a stream so celebrated as the Mississippi — a stream which La Salle had reached the mouth of, a century and a half (lacking a year) before, was perhaps predominant; and we followed our guide down the sides of the last elevation, with the expectation of momentarily reaching the goal of our journey. What had been long sought, at last appeared suddenly. On turning out of a thicket, into a small weedy opening, the cheering sight of a transparent body of water burst upon our view. It was Itasca Lake — the source of the Mississippi."

The Indians called the lake *Omushkos*, the Chippewa name for elk, and fur traders who knew of the lake used the name Lac la Biche, or Elk Lake. But Schoolcraft was not content with names taken over from others. He felt that the occasion of its discovery called for a new and fitting name, and while coasting along the south shore of Superior with Boutwell, on his way to the interior, he gave thought to originating a splendid name for the lake he felt sure he would discover. He asked the missionary for some classical words that would convey the meaning of true source, or head, of a river.

Boutwell seems to have been a trifle rusty in his Latin, but he jotted down the words *veritas* and *caput*. Schoolcraft, after studying them, amputated the first syllable of *veritas*, slashed off the last syllable of *caput*, joined what was left, and had *Itasca* for the name of the true source of the Mississippi.

Many years later Schoolcraft himself implied that the origin of the beautiful name *Itasca* was in fact a very different one, saying he had adopted it after learning about some of the "mythological and necromantic notions of the origin and mutations of the country" entertained by the Indians. This somewhat cryptic language seems to be an allusion to the legend of an Indian maiden who was wooed by Chebiabo, the ruler of the lower regions. He bore her away to his dominions below the earth, and her tears, as she eternally weeps for the upper world, form the springs that well up into Lake Itasca. This charming legend, reminiscent of an ancient Roman myth, was told as early as 1853 by Mrs. Mary H. Eastman, a writer who knew the Minnesota country, and she names the weeping maiden *Itasca*.

Alas for the legend, in 1832, after the discovery of Lake Itasca, Schoolcraft visited Fort Snelling and there wrote a letter to a Galena newspaper in which, referring to the lake that he described as the "true source of this celebrated stream," he says that he named it "La Biche or Itasca lake (from a derivation of the expression veritas caput)."

Schoolcraft and his party remained at Lake Itasca only a few hours. Up the long southeast arm they paddled to the island that has since been known as Schoolcraft Island. Here they put up a pole and raised the American flag. The Yellow Head told the explorers that a tiny creek, much too small to be called a river, was all that flowed into Lake Itasca from the south, and both Schoolcraft and Allen accepted the Indian's statement. Leaving to later explorers the task of making a detailed examination of the shores of the lake, they took their departure through its northward-flowing outlet, which they were surprised to find about ten feet wide with an average depth of more than a foot. This was the main stream of the Mississippi, and they followed it to Cass Lake. There, on Star Island, called by the explorer Colcaspi or Grand Island, Schoolcraft gave the Yellow Head a "flag and the president's medal, thus investing him with chieftainship." On July 16, three days after the discovery of Itasca, Schoolcraft and his men were making their way southward to Fort Snelling.

While Schoolcraft was solving the problem of the source of the Mississippi, he did not neglect the instructions he had received from Cass when he left the Sault. On every suitable occasion he cautioned the Chippewa to keep peace with the Sioux; he made a count of the number of Chippewa in the bands around Lake Superior; and he gathered a wealth of information about the fur trade.

Meanwhile, Dr. Houghton was busy vaccinating more than two thousand Chippewa in the Upper Midwest. By questioning Indians and traders he learned that during a period of some eighty-five years the Chippewa country had been swept by five fearful epidemics of smallpox — a gift of the white man to the red — and he found the Indians only too ready to submit to vaccination when they were told it would prevent this dread disease.

Though the existence of Elk Lake undoubtedly was known to fur traders long before Schoolcraft's visit to it on July 13, 1832, historians have not hesitated to honor Schoolcraft as its discoverer. One trader, William Morrison, long years after Schoolcraft's trip, put forward the claim that he was the real discoverer of the lake because he had passed it on trading journeys in 1804 and 1811. Dr. William Watts Folwell asserts that this "claim may well be just, but the failure to make any report or record, and a silence of forty years or more, debars Morrison from credit as an exploring discoverer." This is as much as to say that there is a difference between finding and discovering.

So, three hundred and seven years after De Soto set out from Tampa Bay, an American explorer discovered the "true source" of the Father of Waters, and the Mississippi lay open, from mouth to source, known and mapped, for the sons of the Old and New worlds.

Part II. People on the Land

Pioneer of Culture

On board a schooner that sailed down Lake Michigan from Mackinac to Green Bay in the fall of 1834 was a lithe and muscular young man named Henry Hastings Sibley. He had studied law in his native city of Detroit, but he had given up "irksome" law books to find a more active and adventurous life. Now twenty-three, he was on his way to the Indian frontier to be a trader for the American Fur Company.

Despite his youth, he was not unprepared for a career in the wilderness, for he had already served as a clerk in the American Fur Company. In 1829 he had visited Chicago when it was only a stockade and a half dozen dwelling houses. And he had known danger on the treacherous waters of Lake Michigan. When the bark canoe in which he and nine voyageurs were crossing Saginaw Bay struck a submerged rock a mile from shore, he thrust his overcoat into the jagged hole made by the rock, ordered his men to paddle for shore, and managed to beach his canoe safely.

The Sibley family in itself represents the westward movement of the American frontier. Henry's mother, Sarah Sibley, a lady of gentle culture, was the daughter of one of George Washington's colonels who sought his fortune on the Ohio frontier after the Revolution. His father, Solomon Sibley, going west from Massachusetts, went first to Marietta, then to Cincinnati, and finally to Detroit just after the British gave it up under Jay's Treaty. There the elder Sibley rose to be mayor and eventually chief justice of the territorial supreme court. And Henry himself, with two years of training in Greek and Latin, some study of law, and a practical schooling in fur trading, represents in his migration from Michigan to Minnesota another step in the identification of the Sibley family with the American westward movement.

When the schooner reached Green Bay in October, Henry Sibley at once started up the Fox River by canoe. After portaging to the Wisconsin River, he boarded a little stern-wheel steamer that was just leaving for Prairie du Chien. From that village he traveled northward on the Mississippi and arrived, late in October, at the junction of the Mississippi and Minnesota rivers. He climbed the high hill overlooking what was to be his home region for more than fifty years and was struck with the beauty of the surrounding country, one landmark of which was the stone walls and blockhouses of picturesque Fort Snelling. But when he went down to the village of Mendota, where he was to live for nearly a quarter of a century, he was disappointed to find there only a few crude log huts.

Nonetheless, the vast fur empire of which Sibley was to be the lord was centered at Mendota. There the furs gathered at many stations scattered across the Minnesota country were assembled, sorted, packed, and prepared for shipment to Mackinac, New York, and the Old World. A faded old Sibley manuscript tells us what furs and pelts were collected in 1835 — and incidentally stirs the imagination with its hint of the wild life of the old Middle West. Of chief importance were 389,000 muskrats, worth about $44,000, but the "Sioux Outfit," as Sibley's agency was called, also handled more than a thousand otters, an equal number of buffalo robes, three thousand deerskins, three thousand minks, two thousand raccoons, and a large assortment of beavers, martens, bears, wolves, foxes, badgers, wild cats, and rabbits.

Occasionally Sibley made long trips to inspect the far-flung trading posts of his empire; and he liked to join the Sioux

Indians in their great winter hunts, sometimes leaving in October and not returning until March. The French Canadians, from whom were drawn the bulk of the traders, clerks, and voyageurs — the veins and arteries of the fur trade — won Sibley's respect and admiration. He describes them as a hardy, cheerful, courageous, honorable, and chivalrous race. In an enterprise based upon good faith between employers and employees, goods "amounting to hundreds of thousands of dollars, nay millions, were annually entrusted to men, and taken to posts in the Indian Country, more or less remote, with no guarantee of any return except the honor of the individual, and it is creditable to human nature," Sibley testifies, "that these important trusts were seldom, if ever, abused."

In later years Sibley liked to say that he had been successively a citizen of Michigan, Wisconsin, Iowa, and Minnesota territories without moving from his residence at Mendota. The statement was true, and its explanation lies in the successive changes in political boundaries that marked the advance of settlement. By 1848 the fur trade had declined; lumbering and farming had begun; and the time had come to create Minnesota Territory. Sibley promptly emerged as a political leader.

When Wisconsin was made a state in 1848, a large portion of the former Wisconsin Territory, which had extended westward to the Mississippi, was left a "no-man's land without law or government." The people of that excluded area at once began to agitate for the organization of Minnesota Territory. Meanwhile, however, some ingenious and audacious frontiersmen suggested that the part of old Wisconsin Territory that had been left out of Wisconsin state was still the Territory of Wisconsin. An election was held, and Sibley was named delegate to Congress from Wisconsin Territory.

He went to Washington for the opening of Congress, appeared before the House Committee on Elections, and argued his cause skillfully and with dignity, declaring that it was unthinkable that Congress should deny to frontier American

97

settlers the blessings of government and legal status. To his own surprise, his argument carried the day and he was seated as a delegate. Thus it came about that both the state and the Territory of Wisconsin were represented in the same Congress at the same time. As delegate, Sibley used all his force and diplomacy to bring about the creation of Minnesota Territory, and in the spring of 1849 his efforts were crowned with success.

Then came Minnesota's first great boom. The frontier community, numbering less than five thousand people in 1849, grew by leaps and bounds and by 1860 had become a commonwealth of 172,000 inhabitants. Throughout this vigorous decade, Sibley played a prominent part in Minnesota's politics. He was the territory's delegate at Washington from 1849 to 1853. In 1857 he served as president of the Democratic branch of the convention that framed the state constitution. And later in that year he was elected the first governor of the state, which was admitted to the Union May 11, 1858.

As governor, Sibley dealt intelligently and honestly with the problems of the young state. One of his policies deserves special mention: his insistence, in respect to the common schools and the University of Minnesota, that the funds accruing from the lands Congress had granted for these institutions should be preserved "forever inviolate and undiminished."

As early as 1850 Sibley had urged upon the government the need for an intelligent and friendly Indian policy. "You must approach the Indians with terms of conciliation and real friendship," he declared, "or you must suffer the consequences of a bloody and remorseless Indian war." Unless the system was changed, he predicted, a new Philip or Tecumseh would band the Indians together in a last desperate stand against the whites. His warning went unheeded, and in August 1862 the Sioux went on the warpath, with Little Crow as the new Philip.

Governor Ramsey at once asked Sibley, his old rival and

steadfast friend, to lead a military force against the war-in-flamed Indians; and Sibley, who knew the Sioux and their language and also understood the underlying causes of the revolt, accepted the trust. He commanded the volunteer forces that suppressed the outbreak, and in 1863 he led a campaign on the plains of Dakota against the Sioux, who, he found, were good fighters, skilled in attack and retreat, very nearly a match for their white foes.

Sibley retired to private life in 1865, but he continued for many years to be a dynamic force in the state. He was one of the founders of the University of Minnesota, and for many years he continued to act as a member and as president of its board of regents. He also served the Minnesota Historical Society faithfully in many ways and was its president for a dozen years. He lived until 1891.

In his private as well as in his public life, Sibley gave expression to genuine cultural interests. One of his early letters to New York, written in the fur-trade period, includes an order for such books as Prescott's *Ferdinand and Isabella* and *Conquest of Mexico*, Hallam's *Middle Ages*, Thiers' *French Revolution*, and Froissart's *Chronicles*. He was himself the author of a series of portraits — graphic character sketches — of some of the unusual figures of the early Northwest, and in an extensive work he detailed the life and adventures of Jack Frazer, a notable Scotch-Sioux hunter and warrior of the Northwest. He also told a part of his own story in his *Unfinished Autobiography* and various papers of reminiscences. Through all Sibley's writings runs a strain of affection for Minnesota and of faith in the state and its people. It was a "land where Nature had lavished her choicest gifts." The "sun shines not upon a fairer region."

Sibley was a subscriber to the *Spirit of the Times*, a leading sports magazine in nineteenth-century America, and in the columns of that magazine were printed from time to time articles from his own pen on hunting and on Indian customs and warfare. In signing these contributions to the literature of the frontier West, Sibley used the pseudonym, "Hal — a Dacotah." What the editor of the *Spirit of the Times*, William T. Porter, thought of Sibley's contributions may be judged from the following comment, which appears on the editorial page of the issue for April 11, 1846:

We heartily commend to each of our readers an original article . . . in to-day's paper. For twelve years past the writer has been residing on the west side of the Mississippi, during which period he has spent a great portion of his time hunting Buffalo and other game on the boundless prairies between that river and the Rocky Mountains. He is a most accomplished gentleman, a ready writer, and enthusiastically devoted to field sports. Our friend dates his last letter from St. Peters, near the Falls of St. Anthony; it will be read with thrilling interest. Referring to a promise made us when we last had the pleasure of seeing him, he writes: "You know I only promised to sound my trumpet when the music of the finer instruments should have ceased." We have no idea of his getting off under this plea; we don't recollect anything about this reservation to which he alludes; moreover, what does he mean by "finer instruments?" We insist upon it that no one has written upon the subject of Buffalo Hunting and Prairie Sporting generally, better than himself, and he might as well make up his mind at once that *the readers* of this paper have a claim upon him which *we* intend to look after. We shall do it, too, by hook or by crook, if we have to chase him with a sharp stick among a roving band of Sioux.

Whether or not Porter found it necessary to carry out his threat we do not know, but for a number of years following 1846 readers of the *Spirit of the Times* continued to enjoy thrilling reports of frontier adventure by "Hal — a Dacotah." The account that called forth the editorial comment quoted above is reprinted in the pages that follow.

A BUFFALO AND ELK HUNT IN 1842
By Hal — A Dacotah

Dear "Spirit." — It is a fact much to be regretted that the game on the Western Prairies is rapidly diminishing in number. A residence of twelve years on the West side of the Mississippi, during which time I have made very many hunting excursions, has satisfied me that the larger animals are fast disappearing, and will soon be exterminated. Upon the plains which were the scene of my sports in former years, where the Elk and Buffalo were to be found by hundreds and by thousands, the hunter may now roam for days together, without encountering a single herd.

Nor is this surprising, when we reflect that of the Indians west of the Mississippi, at least a hundred thousand subsist entirely by the chase, and the improvidence of these people is so great, that often ten times as many cattle are killed as can be consumed by a camp, either by being driven over precipices, or by other methods. What will become of these starving thousands when buffalo shall have failed altogether, is a question which I am unable to solve. Present appearances indicate with much certainty, that ere twenty years have elapsed, but few buffalo will be found, and those only on the immense plains of New Mexico, or on the distant prairies which skirt the base of the Rocky Mountains.

In the month of October, 1842, I took with me eight horses and carts, in charge of five Canadians and one American, and with my old hunting companions, ALEX. F[ARIBAULT] and JACK FRAZER, wended my way towards the buffalo region. We expected to find these animals at or about the *Minday Mecoche Wakkon*, or Lake of the Spirit Land, a distance of a hundred and fifty miles. The first few days we amused ourselves with shooting grouse, ducks, and geese, of which there were a great abundance. One of the party knocked over twenty ducks at a single shot, nineteen of which were secured. Of course we did not lack for provant. As we advanced farther inland, where we hoped to find elk, a veto was put on all discharges of fire arms at small game, as the report of a gun will set the keen-eared animals in motion at the distance of miles. On the seventh day out, Jack Frazer reported that he had seen some game, but whether buffalo or elk he could not tell, as they were too far off. Our glass being put in requisition, we soon found them to be a small herd of the latter, lying down at the base of a hill about six miles off.

Notwithstanding the excitement which warmed us at the prospect of a chase, the beauty of the scene which broke upon our vision from the height whereon we stood, attracted the attention of the most thoughtless of the party. A large lake, which might have been taken for the "Glimmer Glass" of COOPER, stretched itself out at right angles with our course, about a mile beyond where the elk lay. The prairie, clothed in its variegated autumn garb, appeared to rise and fall like the undulations of the ocean, and in all directions might be perceived points of woodland giving forth all the different tints and hues peculiar to an American forest. A thin belt of lofty trees encircled the lake, showing through their intervals the bright sheet of water, which lay, unruffled by a breeze, in all its glorious beauty. It seemed almost a sacrilege against Nature thus to invade her solitudes, only to carry with us dismay and death. But other, and certainly not more holy thoughts, soon dissipated in us all sense of the magnificence of the scene. Our measures were taken to circumvent the elk.

Alex., Jack Frazer, and myself, as the only experienced hunters, were to approach and fire, while the others of the party mounted their horses, and were stationed under the cover of the hill, except one man, who remained in charge of the carts and baggage. With this man I left my hunting horse, ready saddled, with instructions to mount as soon as he heard our guns, and come with all speed to my stand. These precautions taken, and having stripped ourselves of all superfluous clothing, we commenced the delicate operation of approach. A few yards brought us in full view of the herd, which, unsuspicious of danger, were lolling lazily in the sunshine. Throwing ourselves flat upon the ground, we wormed ourselves along with Indian stealthiness, under cover of the short grass.

We had proceeded thus about half a mile, when we came to a marsh, which it was found we must necessarily pass. The water here was two feet deep, and the exertion of crawling through the knotted grass, and of securing, at the same time, our guns from moisture, while we kept ourselves concealed, was excessively severe. By dint of unremitting efforts we passed silently through this serious obstacle, and emerged upon dry ground within sixty yards of the game. We here examined our arms, renewed our primings, and sprang upon our feet, not wishing to fire until the elk rose. As these magnificent creatures bounded off in great confusion, our double barrels were discharged, and three elk fell dead. Jack F., who sported a single barrel, made a clean miss, as usual. In fact, he was a miserable shot. With an eye like an eagle, firm nerves, and active withal as a wild cat, it was not one of Jack's "gifts" to shoot well. Unfortunately, Alex. F. and myself had aimed our second barrels at the same large animal, which came to the ground riddled with balls and buckshot, otherwise we might have secured a fourth without doubt. As the remaining fifteen or twenty fled at full speed, we could hear the shouts of the horsemen as they discharged their pieces. They failed, however, to hit a single elk.

My horse was presently at my side, and as soon as I was mounted, the noble animal entering into the spirit of the chase, set off at racing speed. The elk were now a mile ahead, and I passed successively each of the Canadians on their jaded horses, vainly struggling to keep with the chase. Wright, the American, who was well mounted, was thrown headlong from the saddle, and when I overtook the herd after a run of six miles, I perceived his horse running side by side with the elk. I had left my double barrel behind, trusting to a revolving pistol to do execution. But my hands were so benumbed by long immersion in the cold water, that I could not pull the trigger. Shifting the revolver to my left hand, I managed to discharge it at a large female elk, at a distance of not more than ten feet.

The ball took effect *a posteriori,* and the animal was so much wounded that she plunged headlong into a wide boggy stream, through which, after incredible efforts, she succeeded in passing, leaving me no other alternative than to abandon the chase, the nature of the ground rendering it impossible to cross.

I succeeded in securing the runaway horse, with which I returned to my companions, who had already made preparations to encamp on the border of the lake. Here we spent one day in preserving the meat of the slain elk, which was accomplished by cutting it into thin slices, when it was spread out upon a scaffold, and a fire kindled under, which soon dried it thoroughly.

The next morning there were myriads of ducks and geese in and about the lake, and the discipline of the camp was so far relaxed as to allow a few shots to be fired among them, which afforded us an ample supply.

Continuing our course southwestwardly, we reached Lac Blanc, a fine sheet of water, which bore upon its surface swan, geese, and ducks in great numbers, which we did not disturb, as there were fresh "sign" of elk and traces of buffalo. From this point we followed a small stream which ran through very swampy ground, and which was literally covered with wildfowl. These poor creatures were not at all shy, giving evidence of their utter ignorance of the arts of the great destroyer, man. In fact, geese, mallard, and other wild ducks, were innumerable, and I doubt not that either good shot of the party might have destroyed a thousand in a day. But we were in search of nobler game, and not a single discharge of a gun was permitted.

The day after we struck the stream, and while we were still following it, Jack Frazer was going along in the high grass at a little distance from the party, when he threw himself suddenly from his horse, and appeared to seize hold of some object at his feet, at the same time calling for assistance. There was a general roar of laughter when we reached him. He had seized two large raccoons which were sleeping quietly in the grass, each one by the tail. Startled at this unexpected assault upon their nether extremities, the coons made a joint effort to nab our friend Jack, who, with tail hold fairly fixed, endeavored to evade their bite by jumping about in all directions. He was so expert with his sudden pulls and twitches, that he escaped without injury for a little time, until, encumbered with the weight of his victims, he ceased hopping, and at that moment one of them got Jack by the leg, when he incontinently gave up the battle. With a desire to see fair play, none of us would interfere while this farce was being enacted, but seeing our *compagnon* so badly treated, we revenged him by knocking the coons on the head.

The accidental discharge of a gun by one of the men caused me to lose a shot at three buffalo. They had been quietly feeding on the low grounds along the stream, when, hearing the discharge, they dashed away over the open prairie. After holding a *conseil de guerre*, we concluded not to follow them until the next morning, as the day was already far spent. Selecting a favorable spot, we encamped, and the arms of the party were put in order for the expected sport. A large buck came out of the woods at the opposite side of the stream, without perceiving us. We could not allow him to be fired at. The next morning Jack Frazer was despatched with the most active of the Canadians to reconnoitre. In a short time they returned, and reported that three buffalo were lying down in one of the low places in the prairie. Two men were then placed in charge of the carts, with directions to proceed slowly along at an angle slightly deviating from the line to the buffalo, while the rest of us, seven in number, mounted our horses and prepared for the chase.

Approaching the bulls within three hundred yards, we charged down the hill upon them at full speed. The first flight of the buffalo is comparatively slow, but when pressed by the huntsman, the rapidity with which these apparently unwieldly animals get over the ground, is amazing. Alex. F. and myself having the fleetest horses, each of us singled out a victim, leaving the third to be dealt with by the remainder. We were shortly alongside, and our double barrels told with deadly effect, the huge beasts rolling on the ground in death, within a hundred yards of each other. The other horsemen followed the remaining buffalo, discharging numberless shots at him, but notwithstanding each man swore that he had hit him, the bull got clean off, and his pursuers were brought to a sudden halt by the sight of a large herd of cattle, which they were unwilling to disturb until we joined them.

Meanwhile the prairie had been set on fire by some Indian to windward of us, and as the wind blew violently, the flames came down upon us with such rapidity that we had not even time to secure the meat of the two buffalo killed. It was decided to attempt a passage through the flaming barrier, leaving the men with the carts to get to some shelter ere the fire reached them. Five times did we approach the raging element, and as many times were we repulsed, scorched and almost suffocated, until, by a desperate use of whip and spur, we leaped our horses across the line of fire, looking, as we emerged from the cloud of smoke, more like individuals from the lower regions, than inhabitants of this earth.

It took some time to recover from the exhaustion attendant upon our enterprise when, being fully prepared at all points, we went off in search of the buffalo. We shortly discovered them on the top of a hill, which was bare of grass, and to which the fire had driven them. Alex. F. and myself made a large circle to gain the rear of the herd, and the rest placing themselves out of view, waited for our charge. When about half a mile distant, the huge mass set itself in motion, and the herd, composed of several hundreds, took to flight. We were soon among them, and the discharge of fire-arms from all the horsemen were incessant and well-sustained. Alex. F. and myself had each shot two cows, and others of the party had succeeded in bringing down an animal or two, when we all bore down en masse close to the heels of the affrighted buffalo. Jack Frazer's horse stumbled over a calf, fell, and threw his rider headlong from the saddle. Merely casting a glance to ascertain that Jack's neck was not broken, away we sped, until horse after horse gave out, and in a short time I found myself alone with the herd, the nearest of my companions being a quarter of a mile in the rear.

There was a very fine fat cow in the centre of the band, which I made several attempts to separate from the others, but without effect. She kept herself close to an old bull, who, by his enormous size, appeared to be the patriarch of the tribe. Being resolved to get rid of this encumbrance, I shot the old fellow behind the shoulder. The wound was mortal, and the bull left the herd, and went off at a slow gallop in a different direction. As soon as I had fired I slackened the speed of my horse to enable me to reload, determining to pursue the retiring mass, trusting to find the wounded animal on my return.

Unfortunately I changed my mind, and rode after the bull to give him the *coup de grace*. I rode carelessly along with but one barrel of my gun loaded, when, upon getting near the buffalo, he turned as quick as lightning to charge. At this critical instant I had risen in my stirrups, and released my hold on the bridle rein. At the moment the buffalo turned, my horse, frightened out of his propriety, gave a tremendous bound side-wise, and, alas! that I shall tell it, threw HAL clear out of the saddle, and within ten feet of the enraged monster!

Here was a predicament! Imagine your humble servant face to face with the brute, whose eyes glared through the long hair which garnished his frontlet like coals of fire — the blood streaming from his nostrils. In this desperate situation I made up my mind, that my only chance for escape was to look my enemy in the eye: as any attempt to run would only invite attack. Holding my gun ready cocked to fire if he attempted a rush, I stood firmly, although I must confess I was awfully frightened, and thought my last hour had come! How long he stood there pawing and roaring, I have now not the least idea, but certainly thought he was a long time making his decision what he should do. At last he turned slowly away, and I gave him a parting salute, which let out the little blood left in his body. He went a short distance and fell dead.

I did not fail to render due homage to that Almighty Being who had so wonderfully preserved my life. The frequenter of Nature's vast solitudes may be a wild and reckless, but he cannot be essentially an irreligious man. The solemn silence of forest and prairie — the unseen dangers which are incident to this mode of life, and the consciousness that Providence alone can avert them; all these have the effect to lead even the thoughtless man, occasionally, to reflection.

The only one of the party within view now came up. I was so near the buffalo when dismounted, that he thought I had struck him with the barrels of my gun. I despatched him in search of my horse, which, as is usual in such cases, had followed the herd of buffalo at full speed. I now felt much pain in one of my feet, which had received a serious blow when I fell. I had to use my hunting knife to free me from sock and moccasin, and in ten minutes I was unable to walk, or even stand without support.

Knowing the man who had gone after my horse to be a mere tyro in woodcraft, I feared he would not be able to find his way back to me, and being ten miles from camp, with no fuel to light a fire, and clad in scanty Indian costume, the prospect of spending a cold October night where I was, was any thing but agreeable. I had no other alternative than to load my gun heavily with powder, and discharge it in quick succession, hoping that some of my comrades would hear the reports and come to my aid. After a short time spent in this pleasant exercise, I perceived Jack Frazer, who, having recovered his horse, was looking for the rest of the party, when my gun attracted his attention. I despatched him after the missing man, and he soon returned with him and my horse. When I mounted it was with difficulty I could support myself in the saddle.

On our way to camp, we discovered a single buffalo cow feeding. Jack started off in pursuit, and I had the pleasure of witnessing a most beautiful chase, albeit unable to take part in it. The cow made for the height of land opposite, and as she reached the summit Jack overtook her, when she turned and charged him furiously. I thought it was all over with him, for the animal was within three feet when he discharged his gun. I saw her fall before the report of his gun reached my ears: the ball had broken her neck. Had it taken effect in any other part, Jack must have been seriously injured, if not killed.

When we got to the camping ground, all the party were assembled. The injury I had received was of too serious a nature to allow of rest. I passed a sleepless night, and being satisfied that it was necessary to have surgical assistance as soon as possible, I determined to return home — offering to leave four men with Alex. and Jack, if they were disposed to continue the sport. The disappointment was a serious one, but my hunting companions refused to leave me, and it was arranged that the next day should be employed in securing the meat of the buffalo killed, and the day following we should leave for home.

In the morning, while the men went in search of the meat, we rode over to get a view of "Minday Mecoche Wakkon," or "Lake of the Spirit Land," already mentioned. This beautiful sheet of water has an island in it, which the Sioux Indians never venture upon — as they believe it to be the residence of demons. Their traditions say, that in days of yore, several of that tribe landed upon the island from a canoe, when they were instantly seized and devoured. Hence the name. We saw several others disporting themselves in the Lake, apparently not much afraid of us, or of the spirits of the island.

When all was ready for our departure homewards, I told my companions that as our progress would be necessarily slow with the loaded carts, they would have time to scan the country on either side of us, and perhaps find buffalo, and they could easily rejoin us at night. This plan suited them well, and they were off bright and early, while we retraced our trail — myself on horseback, leading the procession. About noon I perceived, directly in our line of march, a large herd of elk, and I made a signal to the men to halt. I then despatched them to give the elk a volley, bidding them to be very careful in approaching, while I, with my game leg, rode to windward to endeavor to get a shot as they passed.

Having ensconced myself snugly in ambush, I presently heard a rustling in the bushes, and a huge buck came bounding out close to me. I could have keeled him over with a load of No. 6, but I forbore to pull trigger on him, lest I should spoil the sport of my party, and he got safely off. In two minutes after the whole herd of elk went dashing past, but at too great a distance for me to shoot. The men, as I feared, made a bungling attempt to get near the elk, and had been discovered. There must have been a hundred or more in this band, and we watched their movements with lively pleasure as they bounded over the prairie. Alex F. and Jack Frazer joined us in the evening, having three buffalo tails pendant at their belts — trophies of the number slain — they had fallen in with several large droves of buffalo, and might have killed many more, but, as the meat could not be taken, they very properly abstained from useless slaughter.

We hastened homewards as fast as our trammelled condition would allow, only now and then shooting a few ducks or other wild fowl, wherewith to make a *bouillon* in the evening. On the 22d day after our departure from home, we reached our domicils, having in the interval killed 16 buffalo, 3 elk, 8 raccoons, 12 wolves, 7 geese, 244 ducks, and 80 grouse, besides sundry other small snaps not worth recording.

When I next go on a buffalo hunt,
"May you be there to see."

The Land Takers

"THERE was something impressive in these vast stretches of level fertile land, which seemed to offer such unusual opportunities," wrote the son of an immigrant of the North Star State, telling the saga of his father and mother. "There was sunshine and song of birds, a luxuriant growth of grass and wild flowers. It was America, or their part of it, as they first learned to know of it."

The immigrants, whether hailing from the East or from across the Atlantic, were land takers — and the land did not lie truly open until they had in fact taken it, broken its age-old sod, and metamorphosed the wilderness into farms.

Explorers, guided by star and compass and the channels of rivers, made their way to that land, tasted its sunshine, heard its song, saw its luxuriant growth. Traders supplied with blankets and trinkets and whisky cajoled the red men into gathering up annual fur harvests from woods and streams and lakes. And red-sashed shanty boys cut down the primeval white pine to build up the Middle West, singing to the accompaniment of ax and saw ballads to the "noble Big Pine Tree" and to their own carefree way of life:

> Blow high or low, no fear we know,
>   To the woods we're bound to go,
> Our axes swing, the woods do ring
>   With shanty men, heigho!

But neither the explorers nor yet the fur traders and lumberjacks opened the land in the final sense of breaking sod and building farms. That was the job of the land takers, the pioneer farmers. Traders and soldiers, it is true, scratched the land and planted, on their few cultivated acres, such vegetables as potatoes, peas, beans, lettuce, cucumbers, and radishes, but as late as the census of 1850, a year after Minnesota became a territory, there were recorded only 157 farms in its whole widestretching area.

In the 1850s and 1860s many states and territories of the Middle West competed fiercely for settlers from the East and Europe. Each one needed muscle and brawn to exploit its resources. Each one insisted that it had superior advantages. Each pointed to serious drawbacks in competing areas. Disquieting questions were asked. Could Minnesota, with its "Hyperborean" climate, actually produce wheat? Could the summers of the north country support a profitable agriculture?

Minnesotans set out to answer such questions affirmatively and to get the needed manpower for a new frontier community. In 1853 the territorial legislature sent a Minnesota exhibit to the Crystal Palace world's fair of that year in New York. William G. Le Duc, a remarkable pioneer in more fields than one, was placed in charge of it and after fantastic adventures managed to transport to the eastern metropolis not only specimens of cultivated grain actually raised in Minnesota, but also furs, wild rice, an Indian canoe, and, incredible as it may seem, a live buffalo bull.

Le Duc had been informed that the distinguished editor of the *New York Tribune*, Horace Greeley, had spoken of Minnesota — most mistakenly — as a "barren land"; so he invited the great editor to see the exhibit, and particularly his samples of grain. Greeley came and saw, and the result was another editorial that praised the fertility of Minnesota's soil and spoke favorably of the adaptability of its climate.

Two years later the territory stationed a "Commissioner of Emigration" in New York to invite immigrants to settle in Minnesota. The governor of the territory, in asking for such a commissioner, made a bitter complaint. He had been besieged, he said, with letters asking him if the Minnesota winters were not so cold that stock froze to death and "man hardly dare venture out of his domicile"!

Meanwhile, visitors, after the fashion of Horace Greeley, came and saw — and wrote their impressions. For example, Fredrika Bremer, the Swedish novelist, turned ecstatic prophet when she saw the Minnesota country. "What a glorious new Scandinavia might not Minnesota become," she exclaimed. "Here would the Swede find his clear romantic lakes, the plains of Skåne, rich in corn, and the valleys of Norrland — the climate, the situation, the character of the scenery agrees with our people better than any other of the American states, and none of them appear to me to have a greater or more beautiful future before them than Minnesota."

Miss Bremer's countrymen agreed with her appraisal, and her lyrical praise was soon reenforced by letters from settlers themselves, who described the region as a veritable Land of Canaan. And it was also reenforced by the organized propaganda of land companies, by the negotiation of treaties with the Sioux and Chippewa legalizing white land claims, and in due time by the advertising of railroads and towns, all joining in the exuberant chorus of the American West:

> We have room for all creation, and our banner is unfurled,
> With a general invitation to the people of the world.

> Then come along, come along, make no delay,
> Come from every nation, come from every way;
> Our lands they are broad enough, don't feel alarm,
> For Uncle Sam is rich enough to give us all a farm.

Settlers from the older states and from Europe, looking for good land and for happiness, "came along" to Minnesota in the 1850s and 1860s.

A hard journey, that from Vermont or western New York out to the Mississippi and then upriver by steamboat or by rough roads overland in covered or uncovered wagons — but a much harder one for the European immigrants! As someone has said, "If crosses and tomb stones could be erected on the water as on the western deserts, where they indicate the resting-places of white men killed by savages or by the elements, the routes of the emigrant vessels from Europe to America would long since have assumed the appearance of crowded cemeteries."

But thousands of settlers, native and immigrant, got out to the frontier, whatever the ordeal of travel, and at once they found that their real job was just beginning. An Englishman who pioneered in Minnesota in the 1860s wrote that in America a man "buys a farm very much in the sense that a sculptor buys a statue when he purchases a block of marble — the raw material is there, the manufactured article will appear only after much toil, trouble, expense, and anxiety."

That was the problem: the manufacture of a farm. Once land had been bought at auction or claimed by squatter's rights or entered under the Homestead Act, the first concern of the settler was of course to build a house. Often, as in *Giants in the Earth*, it looked more like a "bulwark against some enemy than anything intended to be a human habitation." Sawmills were likely to be far away, but even if they were near at hand, there was the nice problem of money to pay for lumber — and few pioneers had any money. Usually in the Minnesota country the prospective farmer built a log cabin or, if he found himself on the treeless prairie, a sod hut.

When William Boutwell, the missionary, moved into his "log mud-walled cottage" in northern Minnesota in the 1830s, he wrote, "This is a palace to me though I have neither chair, stove, table, or bedstead. Our windows, which are deerskins, admit a very imperfect light."

Prairie folk built huts of pieces of sod made secure by a

mortar of clay and buffalo grass. Hugo Nisbeth, a Swedish traveler of the 1870s, found some of his countrymen literally burrowed into a hillock, with a room that "measured about twelve feet in width by twelve to fourteen in length and was something over eight feet high. Just within the door to the left stood a cast-iron stove, an object that is never wanting in America, farther over to the left was a child's bed, in the middle of the floor stood a table and chest, and to the right was a large bed and a sort of cupboard, where several household utensils were kept. The furnishings were completed with two or three chairs. Above the table hung the portrait of Charles XV. From the stove a chimney went up to the center of the hut, where a hole had been broken in the dirt roof. Daylight came in through the door!"

Pioneer beginnings could be pitifully crude, but the house was sanctuary — sanctuary from storm and rain and icy cold or glaring sun. Something to start with — and the day would come when a better house could be built.

Meanwhile there was the urgent problem of breaking sod and starting the farm. That meant oxen. That meant hard work. In 1840 two farmers not far from the future St. Paul and Minneapolis turned three acres of sod in six days, using four yoke of oxen. If the sod happened to be unusually tough, more oxen were needed, and there is actually a record of the use of as many as ten yoke to a single plow. A natural garden, many thought Minnesota, but the garden could be stubborn before yielding its fruit. Land broken one spring might have to lie fallow until the next before it could be planted. A slow process, but each year the frontier farmer added to his broken and opened domain until ultimately most, if not all, his land was under cultivation.

Preparing the land with the plow was not enough. It also had to be fenced before crops could be safely planted, for in frontier days livestock was permitted to run at large. Laying the rail fences — if one could get rails; sod, if not — was work for the winter, with many a cold evening spent in "grinding up" the axes.

Notwithstanding the cynical dictum of Dr. Samuel Johnson, a man must live — and eat. In early days, while laboriously hewing a farm out of the wilderness, the frontiersman ate fish, game, wild rice, such provisions as he might have brought with him in his western trek, perhaps vegetables planted as quickly as possible after reaching the land. But the long winters might reduce food supplies to virtually nothing. A family in southern Minnesota in 1859 lived on potatoes and limited supplies of bread for seven weeks in a stretch (the last four without salt). Another family lived for a winter almost wholly on potatoes and maple syrup. "The want of salt bothered the pioneers more than anything else," wrote a woman recalling childhood in the Minnesota River valley in the 1850s. Coffee was a luxury, but substitutes made from ground corn-meal crusts or parched rye did not seem too unacceptable.

Abundance did not necessarily follow hard on the heels of breaking and fencing, though the farmer and his family awaited crops with a huge optimism after planting grain or potatoes or corn. The immemorial hazards of farming were not absent, even from the beginning. An Indian agent wrote in 1842 that "cold weather in May, the ravages of the blackbirds, worms, and ground squirrels, the several frosts between the 10th and 20th June, and the subsequent dry weather" had almost completely destroyed his crops. In the 1850s a noted pioneer farmer, Mitchell Young Jackson by name, recorded his worries in a diary. His "corn and oats must fail," he wrote, "unless we have rain soon." They had been "badly cut by the worm and squirrel" and not more than half his field was standing. In October he found his corn "much injured by frost," and he added plaintively, "I am not well suited with Minnesota weather this season." But, well suited or not, one usually did somehow survive.

When the winds came howling down from the north and

winter snows mantled the lonely farms of the frontier, field
work came to a standstill, but the ambitious land taker was not
idle. If one dips into another farmer's diary, that of William R.
Brown for the winter of 1845–46, one finds such items as
these: "chopped and hauled 5 loads of firewood" — "hauled a
load of hay" — "butchered a hog" — "commenced putting up
the fence" — "mended the sled" — "done some little jobs about
the house." The pioneer farmer did not merely twiddle his
thumbs from fall to spring. His callouses did not wear off.

No less strenuous than man's work, however, was that of
the wilderness Marthas. Travel, for example, was somewhat
different from that on the smooth paved roads of a century
later. Boutwell, recording a portage in the 1830s, casually remarks, "My dear Hester, like a true heart, followed me through
mud and water half-leg deep," carrying "a few small cooking
utensils."

Such travel was but prelude to long and busy days of cooking, washing, ironing, tending children. Often the frontier
woman pitched in on the field work of the emerging farm, but
more often she filled out her hours with the tasks of spinning
yarn, knitting socks, churning butter, molding candles, making soap, taking care of the cellar or spring house. On three
successive days, William Brown noted in 1845, his Martha
was preoccupied with "hard soap." She made five pots, one
that her husband judged "excellent," and one, alas, that
"would not thicken."

Happiness there was in many a frontier cabin amid the busy
self-sufficiency of pioneer living, and often merriment. Friend-
ships there were, too, the assuaging bonds of common origin or
of speech or of church, though the visits of ministers might
be rare enough. Sometimes voluntary association eased the
strenuous jobs of building or harvesting. But loneliness and
insecurity, and the ordeal of childbirth far from the comfort-
ing security of competent medical care often left minds darkly
overcast, like that of the forlorn Beret in Rölvaag's powerful

novel of pioneering — Beret who could not find even a tree to hide behind.

As if all this were not enough, Indian menace added to the feeling of insecurity, especially when the Sioux were on the warpath. "God be thanked, I kept my life and sanity," exclaimed one Minnesota woman after the unspeakable ordeal of an Indian raid in which her husband and one son were killed, another son wounded, and her two daughters carried off as captives.

There came a time when the frontier amenities eased the ordeal, though accidents could sometimes interfere with such amenities, as when poor Martha Brown failed to attend a wedding because the horses had run away. The church, once it was established, was a community center, and on Sundays when services were held the entire family made a pilgrimage to worship. As villages and towns sprang up, the American lyceum movement spread to the frontier, and sometimes the ladies attended with their husbands. Jackson records a lyceum meeting in the 1850s, with "Gents & Ladies" present, at which the affirmative carried in a discussion of the proposition that the liquor dealer is the "biggest scoundrel in the world."

The chance of seeing a play was remote for most farmers and their wives, but Allen Dawley, another country diarist of frontier Minnesota, on one occasion made this record: "Attended a Dramatic Entertainment in the Evening given by a Kellogg company for a free Reading Room." This farmer's dramatic criticism was succinct: "Performance poor." Less rarely the frontier people had the fun of hearing strolling singers like the Hutchinsons, with such songs as "The Cot Where We Were Born," "My Mother's Bible," "Pauper's Funeral," and "There's a Good Time Coming." Occasionally there might be a ballad that caught the very spirit of the pioneers themselves:

> We'll cross the prairies as of old
> The Pilgrims crossed the sea,

And make the West, as they the East,
The homestead of the Free!

Books were few but not unknown in the frontier country
homes, including almanac and Bible, both pored over with unending zeal and interest — the one still touched by the wit and
wisdom of Poor Richard, the other a buttress of faith amid
frontier trials, "a threat held over the head and a rainbow before the eye," as Della Lutes has said.

Probably one could easily exaggerate the place of diversion
and entertainment in the lives of the wilderness Marthas, but
it is not easy to overstate their faith in the future. In soil and
hard work they saw the glowing promise of better days. "It
was less for our sakes that we set out," said an immigrant
woman, "than in order to provide our children with a decent
living."

Initially the most practicable — and profitable — form of
frontier farming was vegetable gardening, for the farm homes
and for such local markets as could be reached, but experiments in grain growing were made relatively early in the
Minnesota country. In 1841, for example, one James Norris
harvested forty acres of spring wheat in Washington County,
and the next year ninety. He gave a definite answer to one
of the questions of the time: wheat did well in Minnesota. It
seemed to be easy to raise, and there was promise of an expand-
ing market for it. So as the tide of settlers swept in, as the
virgin soil came under cultivation, many turned to wheat raising. The earlier subsistence diversification began to give way
to a one-crop system. King Wheat was ascending his golden
throne.

But it was not easy to transport the harvested wheat to market. The railroad did not reach Minnesota until the 1860s, and
one had to depend on horse or oxen to get the crops to river
towns for transportation to St. Louis and other centers. If
steamboats were few, wheat supplies might pile up in the ship-
ping ports. "Every boat got all the wheat it could carry,"

wrote an old steamboatman, recalling pioneer days, "and the shippers begged, almost on bended knees, for a chance to ship five hundred sacks or a hundred, or fifty — any amount would be considered a great favor." A visitor in 1859 to Hastings, a bustling Minnesota town on the Mississippi, described the scene he saw: "wheat everywhere; wheat on the levee; wagon loads of wheat pouring down to the levee; wheat in the streets; wheat in the sidewalks." And wheat in the fields too, its colors like "liquid gold," a "marvel of yellow and green," running "before the wind's feet," as in Hamlin Garland's songs of the Middle Border.

Many factors play into the story of the ascendancy of wheat: the swarming of people onto the western lands in the 1860s, the coming of the McCormick reaper and other farm machinery, the Civil War with its demand for increased production, and the gradual westward extension of railroads, which closed up the gaps between farm and market. More and more the open land was wheat land, and by the mid-seventies wheat made up two thirds of all the agricultural production of Minnesota. In the flush of wheat excitement, some men even created fabulous bonanza farms, making a gigantic business from the combination of land, machines, and wheat. Minneapolis grew into the Mill City of the world as business magnates like the Washburns and Pillsburys turned the mountains of wheat into flour.

But the wheat utopia that some people dreamed of did not quite materialize. For one thing, farming marched westward to the rich prairies of the Dakotas; for another, there were servants of King Wheat in other parts of the world — Argentina, Australia, Russia — who added fat acres to the royal domain. As production increased, not only in the West but throughout the world, prices dropped. And unhappily, yields began to decline as the soil gave up its virginity. Smaller yields, lower prices, worldwide competition, and the exactions of middlemen and railroads — these and yet other forces set the king to tottering on his throne.

They also gave rise, on the one hand, to an agrarian crusade and on the other, to a revolution that modernized farming.

It was not easy to fight competition from far-off countries, but the railroads and elevator men and millers were close at hand, and in the 1860s and the decades that followed the farmers organized and fought their battles through such institutions as the Grange and the Farmers' Alliance and through radical third parties, with gifted leaders like Oliver H. Kelley and Ignatius Donnelly. The farmers used the instruments of political democracy in an attempt to restore what they regarded as the economic democracy of the earlier frontier.

The story of the farmers' crusade, from the Granges to Populism, has been told and retold as a chapter in the saga of the midwestern farmer. It is an interesting, even a great, story, with a record of substantial gains alongside defeats and frustration. In the light of history, however, it is clear that the answers to the farmers' problems were not to be found wholly in regulatory laws aimed at the railroads and elevators, significant as these were in the long run. For there was a fundamental difficulty. No legislative act, solemnly signed by a governor, could restore the fertility of soil worn out by continued one-cropping. The farmer could indeed pack up and move off to another frontier and start the cycle anew. And many did, in caravans of covered wagons like ocean fleets that headed for the Red River Valley and the sea of far-stretching acres in the Dakotas. But many others stayed on, and they had to face their problems at home. As the American frontier itself closed in, it became less easy than in earlier days to run away from one's troubles.

Soon the farmers faced a crisis that by no stretch of the imagination could be ascribed to the machinations of monopoly. Instead, many thought it was brought on by God Himself. In 1873 swarms of countless millions of Rocky Mountain locusts, or grasshoppers, flew out of the West and descended upon the wheat fields of southern Minnesota, destroying everything in their voracious greed, like the calamity that Moses brought down upon the land of the Pharaohs. The next summer the winged devourers attacked again, and every summer after that until 1877, when, no one knows why (though some believed the motivating force was a day of prayer set apart by the governor of Minnesota), they rose up in clouds and flew away, no one knows where.

Grasshoppers gone, the prospects for a bumper crop seemed excellent, but in midsummer stem rust attacked the wheat fields of the Middle West, and when autumn came, there was the same dismal story: virtually no wheat to harvest. So a dilemma was upon the farmers, either to give up wheat or to give up their very farms. Some answer had to be found. While political captains tried to win elections and to distil in laws the solutions for agricultural problems, another kind of reform was coming from the soil, from everyday people, from the observation and experience of farmers. Most of them doubtless would have taken alarm if anyone had called them, at the outset of their work, pioneers of agricultural diversification or prophets of modernized farming. They did the day's job, but in every instance something marked them out as leaders. An idea, perhaps; a piece of imagination; a streak of stubbornness; possibly a cherished tradition they were unwilling to give up; perhaps only a curiosity that asked questions and looked for answers.

The roll of names could be a long one, for there is strength and imagination and stubbornness at the grass roots of the national life. What are the sources of the probing researches of scientists? Are they entwined with the life of the land takers and land users? Certainly the frontier experimenters had no conscious purpose of making scientific advances, but in the absence of official experiment stations, they had the open land and they had freedom to experiment.

Look, for example, at a Vermonter named Oren C. Gregg who arrived in Minnesota in 1865. He was a man of varied interests who, among other things, tried his hand at raising wheat in a state that seemed to be going wheat crazy. One day, when hauling wheat to town, he observed another farmer, bigger and stronger than himself, driving a load behind him. "What is the use of your trying to compete with this fellow in raising the same kind of things?" he asked himself, and he pondered the question after selling his wheat. Before long he saw a possible answer. "My grandfather," he said, "used the cow to turn the grass of the old Green Mountains into butter. Why could not I use the cow to turn the grass of the western prairie to butter?"

Gregg turned dairyman and at once put his finger on a custom that to him seemed ridiculous. It was the practice of farmers who owned cattle to have their cows freshen in the spring and go dry in the long winters. Dairy products were at a premium during the non-producing season, but "when the winter broke and the spring grasses started, in May, the old cow was expected to 'come across,' deliver a calf and start her flow of milk, which she did, and another season of corn meal mush and milk opened up."

Gregg had the shrewdness of the born Yankee. If winter was the period of high prices, winter, he reasoned, was the time to have butter and milk for sale. Two and two make four, and sometimes more. So Gregg arranged to have his cows freshen in the autumn — and milked them all winter. He went on to become an apostle of winter dairying, talking his ideas to anybody who would listen to them. One of his listeners said, "You get more for the same amount of butter or cream, and you have the satisfaction of putting it on the market when dealers want it." And he added, "After you get fairly launched in winter dairying, the wheat fields are apt to disappear."

Gregg was a self-made dairy scientist. By selection and improvement through breeding, he sought the ideal dairy cow. To farmers puzzled whether to breed for beef or for dairy, he said bluntly, "Choose ye this day whom ye will serve. If beef then serve him, and if dairy, then serve her."

The man's middle initial was C, and when the University of Minnesota, founding a Farmers' Institute, chose Gregg to be its superintendent and he traveled up and down the state, speaking everywhere about dairying, it was suggested that the C must stand for "Cow." Thus a Minnesota farmer became a pioneer of diversified farming, and — if the story were told in full detail — of cooperation as well, for in cooperatives he saw salvation for his dairymen. His accolade today is "Father of winter dairying in Minnesota."

Peter M. Gideon, who came to Minnesota from Ohio in 1853, was no less a pioneer than Gregg. His passion was apples, not cows. Most Minnesotans, when Gideon appeared on the frontier scene, believed that Minnesota was too far north to grow good apples. Gideon was not convinced. Moreover, he liked his apple pie filled with apples, not with potatoes soaked in vinegar.

Since his boyhood Gideon had been interested in fruit growing. When he migrated to the Minnesota frontier, he took with him thirty varieties of apple seedlings, some small pear, plum, and cherry trees, a bushel of apple seeds, and a peck of peach seeds. Horticulture and Gideon arrived on the same boat. He pioneered on the south shore of Lake Minnetonka — that peerless lake famed nationally in a later day as a popular summer resort — and he promptly planted all his stock of fruit.

After ten years of experimenting, Gideon found all his trees killed by the punishing cold of the winters save one crab. He took stock of his possessions. He had a large family, a cow, a few chickens — and eight dollars. What was worse, winter was coming on and he had no warm clothes. The eight dollars would indeed buy a coat — but what about apples?

Gideon preferred a coatless to an appleless state of being, so he sent his money off to Bangor, Maine, for apple seeds and met the clothing crisis by sewing together two cast-off vests, with sleeves made from the amputated legs of an old pair of pants. "More odd than ornamental," somebody remarked. But the Bangor seeds arrived, and from them Gideon developed the Wealthy apple, a hardy variety that did not winterkill in Minnesota.

The Wealthy (so named for Gideon's wife) was first noticed publicly in an announcement in the *Western Farmer* in 1869, and for the next thirty years — Gideon died in 1899 — the man distributed Wealthy seedlings throughout Minnesota and the surrounding states. One Minnesotan declared that the Wealthy apple was the best apple produced since Adam and Eve left the Garden of Eden. Others referred to Gideon himself as Johnny Appleseed.

This land taker and apple planter has not been forgotten. Every year at Excelsior, on the shores of Minnetonka, Apple Day is celebrated, an Apple Queen rules for a day, and the praises of Peter Gideon are sung.

Another people's pioneer of diversification was an immigrant who came to Minnesota in 1857 from Kulsheim in the Tauber Valley of the Duchy of Baden. A distinguished American historian has written about "culture in immigrant chests" — this German immigrant brought agriculture in a bag. Wendelin Grimm was his name, and his bag held twenty pounds of alfalfa seed.

He planted the seeds on his farm in the spring of 1858 and continued stubbornly to plant again every spring, though there were some winters when most of his alfalfa was killed. He gathered up the surviving seed with care and kept on planting, with the result that his alfalfa won the battle against Minnesota's cold. Most observers and students accept the view that Grimm himself did not realize the "practical or the scientific importance of his experiment in acclimatization." This may be true, but he knew well that the "everlasting clover" he grew did things to his cattle.

He fed the alfalfa to beef cattle. In a particularly bad corn year — 1863 — his cattle were sleek and fat, and a neighbor asked him where he got corn for feed. "Kein Körnschen," he replied, "nur ewiger Klee" (Not one kernel, only everlasting clover).

Inevitably Grimm's neighbors took an interest in this wonder clover, and he was quite willing to sell seed to one and all. By the late 1880s his county (named for the explorer Jonathan Carver) produced about half the alfalfa grown in Minnesota.

But it took more than the stubborn and patient alfalfa growing of Wendelin Grimm to spread his everlasting clover to the whole Middle West and to Canada. Another Minnesota farmer, A. B. Lyman, became greatly interested in the alfalfa, tried it out on his father's farm near Excelsior, and in 1900 reported the outcome to Professor Willet M. Hays, the head of the Agricultural Experiment Station at the University of Minnesota. Four years later the discovery came to the attention of an agent of the United States Department of Agriculture, who said, "We have been searching the world for a variety of alfalfa that would do just what this variety does. We sent a man to Turkestan this summer at great expense to get something of that kind, but here we know we have what we sought."

Scientific experiments soon confirmed this judgment. One was conducted at Dickinson, North Dakota, after the winter of 1908–9, when the temperature went down to thirty-one degrees below zero. The percentage of alfalfa winterkilled was 83.3 for a common variety, 7 for Minnesota Grimm, and 2.8 for a Grimm variety developed at Fargo.

Scholars found that Grimm's alfalfa had a Eurasian strain that doubtless contributed to its hardiness, but they also found that Grimm's long-continued work in acclimatizing the plant was a major contribution. For the northern tier of states, and for Canada, the fruits of the bag of seeds from Baden seemed an answer to prayer. In Minnesota alone, alfalfa acreage jumped from 658 in 1900 to 1,184,062 forty years later. The everlasting clover grows today on thousands of fields in the northern stretches of the New World.

In 1924 the Grimm Alfalfa Growers Association erected a bronze marker on Grimm's old farm to honor the alfalfa pioneer. A noted agricultural editor, George W. Kelley, commenting on this celebration, said, "Sometimes it is given to a few to recognize and pay tribute to a patient man or woman who in obscurity and perhaps in poverty has worked out great benefits to humanity." The honor paid to Grimm seemed to be an illustration of this generalization. "Civilization advances," wrote Kelley. "Perhaps someday our historians will tell more of the work of such men and glorify less the authors of death and devastation."

The past, in Shakespeare's phrase, is prelude. The people who opened the land have passed from the scene, but the land they opened remains open. The contributions of farming men of ideas, widened and deepened through the resources and ingenuity of science and education along a hundred fronts, form part of the ongoing industry of a new age. Something from the frontier folk has been carried forward in the unbroken sequence of time as a heritage not to be forgotten by the beneficiaries of their hopes and strivings, of their courage and hardihood, of their ideas and work and stubborn will. As one reviews the farm story one is reminded of winged phrases in a speech by Woodrow Wilson. "Did you ever hear of a nation that was renewed from the top?" he cried. "Did you ever hear of a tree that drew its sap from its flowers? Does it not draw it from the dark and silent places of the soil? Does not a nation draw its power of renewal and enterprise, and all its future, from the ranks of the great body of unnamed men?"

The Booming of Gopher Prairie

Wʜᴇɴ folk in covered wagons thronged the trails to the Upper Midwest and land-hungry settlers crowded into steamboats churning north on the Mississippi, the builder and promoter of towns and cities was as typical a figure as the farmer. Town lots were as eagerly sought as quarter sections.

Everywhere men tried to read the future. What was going to happen tomorrow and next year? Would the commerce of the great river turn St. Paul into the metropolis of the West? Would water power build an imperial Minneapolis around the Falls of St. Anthony? Would lumber make Stillwater, in the valley of the St. Croix, a great city? Would Gopher Prairie be the trading mart of its hinterland?

People gambled in futures, bought town lots, sold and bought again. Everywhere towns and villages were boomed with confidence. There was a mania for laying out towns. The town builders of the 1850s, in fact, provided lots for more than eight times the entire population of 1860 in the North Star State. The mania went so far that in 1857 a witty member of the legislature offered a resolution to reserve a third of the future state for the farmers!

In the frenzy of townsite speculation, some people created towns only on paper, some sold lots in the middle of lakes, and more than one easterner, arriving in Minnesota with a beautiful engraved plat of a city, showing schools, parks, and

128

churches, found the town inhabited only by hoot owl and gopher. One Minnesota plat showed a mythical railroad station located on a mythical railroad in a nonexistent town.

But many of the boom towns were real settlements, promoted by the optimism and energy of men who believed in their future. Nininger, on the Mississippi River near Hastings, Minnesota, was expected to blossom out as the New York of the West. A townsite of 674 acres was subdivided into 3800 lots. The town proprietors, advertising Nininger throughout the country, promised a mammoth hotel, a steam ferryboat, and a library. The prices of lots shot skyward, and before long the town had five hundred inhabitants. Its boom unhappily collided with the Panic of 1857, the prices of lots collapsed, disappointed owners moved away, and today Nininger is one of the many ghost towns left in the wake of the westward movement.

Some boom towns did last, however. One of these was founded by a versatile pioneer named Joseph R. Brown. He foresaw a metropolis on the Minnesota River and in 1855 laid out the town of Henderson. In the newspaper he founded there one can catch something of the spirit of the pioneer town builders. In the spring of 1856 he wrote, "In April last the town was surveyed, and the work of clearing out the streets was commenced. At that time there was one tavern and one store erected, and some half-dozen log houses inhabited. During the last summer and fall over sixty buildings were erected. We have no doubt that one year hence the business of Henderson will aggregate business of all the other points on the river." Today Henderson is still on the map; it is still an inhabited village; but the glory that its founder dreamed of never came. What Brown did not foresee was the decline of Minnesota River steamboating and the changes in land travel and transportation that another decade was to bring about.

Some of the midwestern towns were planned by colonization companies. Like individual founders, these companies were fired with faith in the future and did all they could to make their prophecies come true. Zumbrota, Minnesota, was founded in 1856 by a company of New Englanders who wanted to set up a Puritan community without vices in the wilderness, and Worthington was settled during the early 1870s by the National Colony, a company of Ohioans who quickly converted a straggling village into a thriving railroad town.

Fairmont, in southern Minnesota, was promoted by a colonization concern in England. The community was to be the great bean-growing center of western America, and Englishmen, many of them younger sons who knew more about fox hunting and racing than they did about farming, flocked to the community. But another kind of immigrant flocked to the community at the same time — the voracious Rocky Mountain locusts, in swarms of untold millions that darkened the sky. They ate up the bean plants as fast as they emerged from the ground, season after season, and the Englishmen's dreams of an idyllic country life in the West faded away. Yet the settlers left a colorful legacy of character and of culture that has persisted to this day, as all know who have read the charming novel by Maud Hart Lovelace called *Gentlemen from England*.

Inevitably there was fierce rivalry among the frontier towns. Everybody considered his town the superior of all others, particularly of neighboring towns. Local citizens tried to promote town growth in every way. They worked for improved navigation on rivers. They subscribed to the building of roads and railroads. In order to entice new industries into their community they gave business sites, bought stock, and promised tax abatement. And they quarreled lustily with the people of near-by towns.

A classic illustration of municipal rivalry is the long-continued fight between Minneapolis and St. Paul. There are rumors that the rivalry has not altogether disappeared even today, but in any event it was active, even virulent, in pioneer days. St. Paul got the earlier start. It was the capital. It had the fur trade. It was the head of Mississippi steamboat navigation. It was a commercial center of great promise. But, ten miles away, St. Anthony and Minneapolis had the promise of the mighty power of the Mississippi tumbling over the rocky ledge at the Falls of St. Anthony, power for turning the wheels of industry in a great manufacturing city. In 1860 St. Paul, with more than ten thousand people, was the metropolis. Minneapolis and St. Anthony together had less than six thousand. Twenty years later, however, the picture had changed, for Minneapolis, which by that time had absorbed old St. Anthony, had 46,000 people to St. Paul's 41,000.

The rivalry of the two cities continued for many years and led almost to a municipal war when the United States census of 1890 was taken. The returns gave Minneapolis 182,967 and St. Paul 142,581. But there was something queer about the census. It turned out that in Minneapolis, families had been greatly increased by children and boarders who seemed later to have disappeared. Hundreds of houses were reported that nobody could find, and real houses had been filled with imaginary people. Another curious thing turned up: employees had been counted both at the shops where they worked and in their homes. Officially they led double lives.

St. Paul was virtuously indignant as these disclosures were made. It promptly proposed, as a nickname for its genial twin, the pleasant designation of "Pad City." Unhappily, investigations soon revealed that queer things had happened in St. Paul, too. It appeared, for example, that 275 persons resided in the St. Paul Union Depot. A family of appalling size lived in a downtown dime museum. Ninety-one lodgers resided in the building of an eminent St. Paul newspaper, and sixty-eight lived in a near-by bindery.

Minneapolis was now equally indignant, and its newspapers pointed the finger of shame at the city across the river. So the federal government had to act. The census was taken all over again in both cities, and the sad fact came out that in the first count there had been an exaggeration of 18,000 in the Minneapolis report and of 9,000 in the St. Paul report. One man was actually brought to trial on the charge of having overstated the number of people who lived in the St. Paul Union Depot. But he was tried before a jury of St. Paul citizens. After due deliberation they found him not guilty.

Not only in the Twin Cities did local ambition and pride flare into intercity rivalry. In the 1850s, for example, the Stillwater *Union* made numerous charges against St. Paul. For one thing, that city, it was alleged, deliberately delayed all mail destined for Stillwater. For another, its growth was too rapid to be honest. St. Paul was almost entirely dependent upon Stillwater for lumber, however. "So it seems something good can come out of Nazareth," said the *Union*. "But the St. Paul papers won't acknowledge it. They would infinitely prefer to have their eye teeth pulled."

A slightly less genial note was sounded in a newspaper of Osceola Mills, Wisconsin, when it paid its respects to the neighboring village of Sunrise, Minnesota. It urged that the name be changed to Sunset, and added the following comment: "The village is about ten years old, is not of rapid growth, nor fortunate in its settlers. When one neighbor gets mad at another, the custom has been to set his house on fire, kill his hogs and chickens, poison his dogs and cats or pull down his fence and let another neighbor's cattle destroy his crops."

More charitable, if condescending, was the citizen of Stillwater who conceded that he had "on the whole formed a very favorable opinion" of Hudson, Wisconsin. "It appears to contain," he said, "a very intelligent, industrious, and enterprising population, whose principal aim appears to be, to make Hudson, *the* town of the St. Croix Valley; and with the exception of Stillwater, they will doubtless succeed."

There have been many county-seat wars in American history. Sometimes not two but four or five towns were involved in a sharp struggle for the advantage of being designated the county seat. For example, five towns in Freeborn County, Minnesota, in 1857 waged a war of circulars, mass meetings, and votes to decide which one was to have the honor. "Fellow citizens," ran one circular, "Will you be bought and sold? Will you suffer yourselves to be hoodwinked and led into the support of a foreign monopoly?" There was a barrage of charges, but when the votes were counted, the city of Albert Lea had an undisputed claim and the other contestants had to retire. So by democratic processes civil war was held in check.

In Wabasha County, Minnesota, during the late 1860s, an attempt was made to change the county seat from Wabasha to Lake City. Lake City issued bonds up to $20,000 to pay for a courthouse and a jail. Wabasha replied that the county already had a good courthouse, but it promised to build a "good and suitable jail of Brick and Stone." The air was filled with charges, claims, and counterclaims. "Assert your heaven-born rights, and at the ballot box, bury this hellish scheme," begged one Wabasha citizen. And so the election was held. A big vote turned out. In fact, in a county that had a total population of 13,500, some 9480 votes were cast. A newspaper, commenting on the situation, pointed out that whereas in Wabasha there were thirteen votes to each legal voter, in Lake City there were only four. A long legal squabble followed, and eventually the supreme court of the state, reversing a district court ruling, gave the county seat to Wabasha.

The rivalries between frontier towns were many and hot, but we should not forget that there were occasions when towns could and did work together for the common welfare. In the 1850s, for example, the people of Red Wing turned out in a body to help the citizens of Zumbrota build a road connecting the two towns. And no one can read the story of the Sioux Uprising of 1862 without being made aware of the ready sympathy and material aid that Minnesota towns gave to the stricken city of New Ulm and to many other communities that suffered from Indian raids. Sometimes towns cooperated to bring about the construction of badly needed railroads. But usually such cooperation centered about a single specific object; the frontier was a trifle too individualistic for much cooperation along general lines.

On the positive side, town rivalries meant growth and expansion. Throughout the Upper Midwest towns and cities, after periods of self-conscious insecurity, were becoming firmly established. In 1860 only three cities in Minnesota had populations larger than 2500. By 1890 a third of the people of that state lived in cities of this size and larger, and in our own day the number has shot up to more than 50 percent.

City growth inevitably brought with it new problems of regulation, control, welfare, and human relationships. A significant part of the pioneering saga of towns and cities has to do with how people tackled the problem of abuse of government, how they sought to regulate public utilities, grappled with the problems of public health and public recreation, provided libraries, improved schools, modernized police and fire protection, and took other progressive steps. Not the frontier alone, but all America sought answers to the problems projected by the urbanization of our civilization. Today, looking backward, we see that genuine progress was made over a long pioneering way. The communities and officials that blazed trails to modern municipal government are as true pioneers as the people who felled the trees of the Big Woods or broke the virgin sod of the prairies or founded towns in the days of the infancy of the Midwest.

There came a time when the reform and progress of American municipal government demanded wide cooperation, counsel, and planning. In the spring of 1903, in response to a call issued by the Cannon Falls Commercial Club, delegates from thirty-five municipalities and commercial bodies in Minnesota met in St. Paul to form the Municipal and Commercial League of Minnesota. Called to consider railroad rate discriminations against the smaller cities, the league soon widened its field of action to include municipal problems in general. It set up standing committees on municipal charters, public service corporations and municipal ownership, railroad rates and transportation, streets, alleys, and boulevards, health and sanitation, parks and playgrounds, and taxes and insurance; and it set in motion a bureau of information.

That early league was not long active. Difficulties over finance and certain controversial measures contributed to its decline. But however short-lived, it charted a pathway for later organization; it pointed toward a new day in municipal cooperation, and many of its active members took up the cause when in 1913 the League of Minnesota Municipalities was launched.

The League of Minnesota Municipalities demonstrates the capacity of local governments to cooperate in common efforts for the public welfare. It has made a notable record in planning legislative and administrative changes. Through its educational program it has lighted the way to broader understanding, not only for community officials but also for citizens in general, and its centralized Reference Bureau has been a successful laboratory in municipal problems. The League has provided means for the exchange of ideas, the exploration of problems and possibilities, and effective leadership in municipal cooperation.

The League symbolizes the progressive development of American institutions in line with our best traditions. We need to train men and women in the arts of democratic government and administration. We need both leaders and a citizenship that can better understand the direction in which we are moving. We need the vision to understand that local institutions must be adapted to serve the needs of a democracy under changing conditions. We need intelligent planning — for locality, state, and nation alike. And for all these things there is no better foundation than the democratic principles rooted in our common past. If cooperation, education, and organization are the implementing agencies, the clue to progress is the pioneering impulse.

Yankees on the Land

Names on the land of the New World have not yet attracted the kind of serious study that scholars long have devoted to place names in the Old World, and yet what a source of never-ending fascination they provide!

The ingredients and very flavor of life in the Middle West are caught up in the names of the region. In Minnesota, for example, Winona and Waseca testify to the presence, in by-gone days, of the Stone Age folk who once reigned over the land — the Sioux. Kanabec and Koochiching tell of their mortal enemies, the Chippewa. Hennepin, Duluth, Mille Lacs, and St. Louis remind us of the sons of France who sang their way to the region in the time of Louis XIV. Carver, Nicollet, Beltrami, and Albert Lea recall the captains of exploration under the British and American flags. Traders in furs and pelts are fixed on the land in such names as Brown, Rice, Sibley, and Kittson. Ramsey and Swift and Marshall, their terms as governor long since over, are part of the Minnesota nomenclature. German immigrants have left imprints of their Old World memories in New Ulm and Cologne, and the Scandinavians in Bergen, Stockholm, and Denmark, while the utopian dreams of Bohemians are recorded in New Prague.

Where, in this panorama of names, are the Yankees — the salty, enterprising folk out of New England and regions settled by New England, whose imprints on the life of this midwestern region are everywhere: on business and the professions, on school and church, on press and politics, on the fabric of social and cultural life?

Look at the Minnesota map and New England jumps out at you. There is Maine in such names as Stillwater, Bangor, Brunswick, and Argyle. There is New Hampshire in Franconia, Claremont, and Woodbury. And Vermont in Burlington, Orwell, and Bennington. Massachusetts—"there she stands"—in Lexington, Springfield, and Lynn. Connecticut is present in Hampton, New Hartford, and Highwood; and Rhode Island is there in Providence.

It would be easy enough to prepare a map showing the distribution of New England place names in Minnesota, but it is difficult to appraise the New England influence in the history and life of that state.

There is, first of all, the nice problem of estimating the extent of the Yankee element in the population. In 1860, of a total Minnesota population of 172,000, only about 19,000 were New England-born, but there were more than 21,000 New Yorkers, and it is clear that a very considerable proportion of these "York Staters" were Yankees a step or two removed from their original New England states. Similarly, many who hailed from northern Pennsylvania and Ohio and from Indiana and Illinois were New Englanders by family and tradition. By 1870 there were some 28,000 New England-born and nearly 40,000 New Yorkers in a total state population of about 440,000.

Such statistics offer some clues, but they fail to take into account the children and grandchildren of New Englanders, born in Minnesota or elsewhere at some intermediate stage of the westward migration of Yankee families. And when one tries to appraise Yankee influence, it must also be remembered that New England had left deep marks upon American life long before Minnesota appeared in the sisterhood of states. How shall one distinguish between the general influences of

New England, woven into the very fabric of the national life, and those derived by direct or indirect lines of migration from Vermont, Massachusetts, Connecticut, and other New England states?

There is yet another difficulty. The Yankee influence, like the Norwegian or Swedish influence, has been modified by American frontier life itself, and it is no easy matter to disentangle one factor from the many that have gone into the molding of a people in school, church, lodge, convention, and legislative hall. The truth is that many streams of influence, originating in as many different sources, met and became one in the fashioning of the Midwest. Often, therefore, historians take refuge in descriptions, not of the contributing streams, but of the turbulent, swirling whole that we characterize as American.

But how have America and Americans come to be what they are as a whole? That question the historian cannot evade and should not try to evade. The only way to meet it seems to be by specific analysis, however tentative or incomplete its results may be.

New England was early on the Minnesota pioneer scene. The Yankees were descendants of pioneering colonists. They were not afraid to pull up stakes and move. They were colonizers long after the colonial era. They were daring, shrewd, tough-fibered, hard-working, with an alert eye for opportunity. Fresh farms of fertile, virgin land looked good to them. They had an instinct for speculation and investment in the towns and lands of the booming West — and some of them had money to invest. They had the necessary ability and enterprise for taking full advantage of the business and professional opportunities of that West.

An American historian has described the spread of Yankee influence under the title *The Expansion of New England*. That expansion was national, continental. New England brains and energy, New England blood and ambition played a major

part in the entire American westward movement, and when
Minnesota was caught in the sweep of that movement, Yankees were promptly on the spot. They turned sod and created
farms, built towns, set up business, practiced the professions,
started newspapers, organized churches, opened schools, and
contributed leadership and ability to virtually every line of
activity. They played a creative, vigorous part in laying the
foundations of all the states of the Middle West.

These Yankee folk might on occasion be sparing of words,
in a tradition exemplified in a later time by Calvin Coolidge,
but they had an alert consciousness of their Yankee character
and individuality and their own power of leadership. And
they were quick to think of the Upper Midwest as another
New England.

"We regard this Territory as destined to become the New
England of the West," wrote James Madison Goodhue, the
first newspaper editor of Minnesota. No false modesty prevented him from claiming that in the past New England
had "supplied the old States with their education, their laws,
and their religion." But as empire marched westward, he
argued, New England found itself farther and farther from
the national center, with the result that the "demanded supply
of these moral wants" would have to be sought elsewhere
than in New England. The perfect answer to this quest, he
believed, was Minnesota — its climate, soil, and opportunities.
The New England character, he alleged, "dies out upon the
savannahs of the South," so unlike New England's "gravelly
hills." But Minnesota was the ideal spot to nourish New England virtues, and as the western New England, the new New
England, it could and would supply the "moral wants" of the
"teeming millions of the West."

This complacent readiness to look after the moral needs of
the entire West offers more than a hint of a certain Puritanism
and paternalism not wholly absent from the New England
temperament. A New Englander who visited Minnesota in

1856 echoed the same sentiments as he looked about him at the frontier scene. He reflected that the New Englanders had brought with them "all their associations and attainments, their love of order, their correct moral principles, their regard for religious institutions, their industry and sound sense." They were bound to succeed, he thought, particularly since, with these qualities as a firm base, they responded so quickly to the "energy of Western enterprise."

Evidence of the attitude of the pioneer Yankees is afforded by the New England Society of the Northwest, which was organized in 1856 and celebrated its first anniversary by holding a great festival at the Cataract Hotel in Minneapolis on December 22, 1857. "Extensive arrangements had been made for the occasion," said a contemporary newspaper, "and so much interest was manifested, that, at an early hour, the streets of our city were noisy with the din of carriages." The newspaper was proud of the whole affair, for, it said, "an audience had assembled to commemorate the Landing of the Pilgrims, which would honor any city in the Union. They were mostly from the middle class, and our Eastern friends . . . would undoubtedly have expressed profound astonishment at the intelligence and respectability, the cultivation of the mind and the accomplishment of manners that characterized the occasion."

The series of toasts after the dinner included one for each of the New England states. One grandiloquent speaker voiced the wish that Minnesota might "imitate the heroic virtues of her foster mother, till New England industry, New England enterprise, and New England thrift shall build here a glorious superstructure of education and Gospel truth, till Sabbath bells shall echo from hill-top to hill-top, and forests now untrodden shall be filled with the murmur of the common school, ensuring the intelligence and integrity of our people, and making the land we live in like the land we left."

One of the toasts at this banquet was to the "Sons of New

England — As they have done tonight, may they ever exclude from their festive board all intoxicating drinks." If liquor did not grace the banquet, it must be added that the Puritanism of the "festive board" did not impose a curfew on toasts. They went on until three o'clock in the morning!

The characteristic and self-acknowledged New England industry and enterprise found a congenial outlet in the Minnesota lumber industry, which was developed chiefly by lumbermen from New England, particularly from Maine. The historian of the industry writes, "The names of many Maineites who came into the upper Mississippi territory are well known in Minnesota today — De Laittre, Bovey, Eastman, Stanchfield, Morrison, and Washburn," and she adds to the list "Tozer, Hersey, Staples, McKusick," all men from Maine whose names were familiar in the St. Croix lumber region. John McKusick was one of a group of lumbermen who in 1843 built the first sawmill on Lake St. Croix; another in the group was Elam Greeley of New Hampshire. Isaac Staples went to Stillwater in 1853 to represent the eastern lumber firm of Hersey, Staples, and Hall.

Much eastern capital was invested in the Minnesota industry. For example, Cushing, Rantoul, and Company, a Massachusetts concern, invested ten thousand dollars in Franklin Steele's sawmill at the Falls of St. Anthony in 1847. That year, also, Daniel Stanchfield took a crew into the woods to report on the lumber of the Upper Mississippi. He built the first logging camp on the Rum River. Lumbering on the St. Croix had begun nearly a decade earlier at Marine, where such men as George and Lewis Judd of Connecticut and Orange Walker of Vermont were prominent.

Not only men but also techniques migrated from New England west to the pine forests. "The Maine men," writes Professor Agnes Larson, "brought to the Minnesota forests the go-devil and the ax and that instrument so necessary in the drive, the peavey"; and an old lumberman tells us that the early logging camp of pioneer Minnesota was the kind that used to be built in Maine.

Not many Minnesota industries were so sharply marked by New England as lumbering, but it is not far wrong to say of Minnesota, as Dr. Schafer has said of Wisconsin, "There is hardly a general business of any kind which, in the early days of our territory and state, was not largely in the hands of 'York Staters' or other Yankees."

New England zeal for schools and learning was unquenchable. The Yankees who came west were one in spirit with the framers of the Massachusetts school law of 1647, whose purpose was that "learning might not be buried in the grave of our fathers." Of the first five superintendents of public instruction in Minnesota, three were New Englanders. John Marsh, who taught the children of officers stationed at Fort Snelling in 1823, was a Harvard man. Two women from Mount Holyoke Seminary taught in the Belle Prairie Seminary established by Frederick Ayer in 1849. Harriet E. Bishop, who came from Vermont in 1847 to open a school in the infant city of St. Paul, was sent out by the National Popular Education Society, a New England organization that devoted itself to supplying competent women teachers for frontier western settlements. Women sent out by that society established schools also in Stillwater and St. Anthony in 1848 and 1849. It was a Canadian, Martin McLeod, who framed the state's basic public school act, but John D. Ford, a native of New Hampshire and a graduate of Dartmouth, was influential in bringing about the establishment of the first Minnesota normal school at Winona in 1860.

New Englanders also played a significant part in the early years of the state university. John S. Pillsbury, known as the Father of the University, was a native of New Hampshire. He is one of eight men officially designated as "Founders of the University." Two others in the group — Henry M. Rice and Dr. Alfred Ames — came from Vermont. Of five persons recently honored as "Builders of the Name" of the university, all save one was born in New England. They were Cyrus Northrop and Maria Sanford, natives of Connecticut; William S. Pattee, first dean of the Law School, a native of Maine; and Henry T. Eddy, first dean of the Graduate School, a native of Massachusetts. Dr. Northrop and Dr. Eddy were both sons of Yale.

Distinctly a New England product on Minnesota soil was Carleton College, which started with a preparatory department opened in 1867 by Horace Goodhue, a Dartmouth graduate. College work began in 1870, with James Woodward Strong, a native of Vermont, as president, and the next year William Carleton, a Bostonian, gave the college an endowment of fifty thousand dollars. That New England ideals of education marked the institution goes without saying.

Zeal for education was closely allied to that for religion, and in this field, too, New England played an important role in the Upper Midwest. The story of Indian missions in Minnesota would be very different if one subtracted from it the achievements and personalities of Gideon and Samuel Pond and Alfred Brunson of Connecticut, William T. Boutwell and Joseph W. Hancock of New Hampshire, Frederick Ayer and Edmund F. Ely of Massachusetts, and Sherman Hall of Vermont, not to mention many missionaries of New England backgrounds who came from New York and Ohio.

American talent for organization, for working out plans on the basis of well-formulated rules, with a president, secretary, and treasurer, probably is derived to a considerable extent from New England. In the religious field the counterparts of the National Education Society are the American Board of Commissioners for Foreign Missions at Boston and the American Home Missionary Society. The American Board sent missionaries to all parts of Minnesota, and the Home Mission Society dotted the pioneer commonwealth with churches and societies. The first Congregational church in Minnesota Territory was founded at St. Anthony in 1851. Five years later the New Englanders of Minnesota were ready to set up their own general church organization, and the Minnesota Conference of the Congregational Church was established with Sherman Hall as moderator. Only six churches were represented in that action, but by 1874 there were 86 and by 1885 there were 141 Congregational churches in the state. Among the Methodists, the Presbyterians, the Baptists, and other church groups as well, New England backgrounds and influences are unfailingly evident.

The pioneer Congregational conference of 1856 "proceeded with intensity of spirit," according to one record, "to adopt resolutions against slavery and intemperance." An offshoot of the Congregational conference, the Evangelical Sabbath School Society of Minnesota, was formed the next year, and among its chief purposes was the distribution of literature against slavery and intemperance.

This emphasis upon intemperance invites one to consider whether that much-debated manifestation of Yankeeland called Puritanism was influential in pioneer Minnesota. A few items that bear upon this question are these: The territorial legislature passed a law banning work on Sundays and such diversions "to the disturbance of the community" on the Sabbath as hunting, shooting, and sport. More serious, and punishable by a heavier fine, was desecration of the Sabbath by profane conduct. There was an early law against gambling; and in due time Minnesotans were prohibited from attending dances and public shows on Sundays. The Sons of Temperance were organized in the state in 1849, and in 1852 the Minnesota legislature passed a Maine Law, forbidding the manufacture or sale of intoxicating liquors save for medicinal and "mechanical" uses.

Yes, Puritan influences were definitely at work in the Minnesota frontier community; and when one learns that of the 27 members comprising the Minnesota legislature of 1851, nine, or one third, were born in New England and seven others hailed from New York, one has a partial answer to the question of the origin of those influences.

Puritanism was not all grim, as modern research is revealing in its studies of the brighter side of colonial New England. An early commentator, to prove his point that a small Minnesota village "had the distinct stamp of New England upon it," cited a temperance organization and an active lyceum. The lyceum was typical of a cultural interest that had many manifestations. And alongside these were numerous social activities derived from the soil of New England, for New Englanders transferred to Minnesota their holiday celebrations. It would be a mistake not to include in this appraisal some mention of these activities, for they touch the common life.

It was at the suggestion of a group of New England clergymen that Governor Ramsey set aside December 26, 1850, as the first Thanksgiving Day in Minnesota. In his proclamation he enumerated such blessings as abundant crops; freedom from the ravages of blast, hurricane, drought, and epidemic disease; and friendly relations between the pioneer and the red man. He therefore invited solemn thanksgiving: "Let us in the public temple of religion, by the fireside and family altar, on the prairie and in the forest, join in the expression of our gratitude, of our devotion to the God who brought our fathers safely through the perils of an early revolution, and who continues his favors to the remotest of his sons."

So the Thanksgiving Day was duly celebrated. In St. Paul bells were rung at sunrise and sunset. In a morning service Dr. Edward D. Neill compared the "infancy of our favored Territory with that of the Puritan colonies." In the evening a magnificent ball was held at a hall suitably equipped with "transparencies, paintings, pictures, and chandeliers in a style of superb elegance."

In its social life, pioneer Minnesota was much influenced by New England traditions. Look, for example, at a sleighing party for children held in Minneapolis in the 1860s. The ride was followed by a "New England supper," for which the "table was piled with the substantial and the fine," including broiled chicken, "hearty vegetables," jellies, cakes, pies, and puddings. A jolly evening was concluded with the "usual kissing games" and "sedate marching about the big room and near attempts at dancing." Someone, recalling this party many years later, wrote, "The Christmas affair pleased me for it was New England again."

Oyster soup, roast turkey, and plum pudding were main dishes in a Christmas dinner served by a New England woman in Minnesota in 1860. A Christmas celebration at Faribault had a carol service. "The carols were old and familiar Christmas songs," wrote one member of the congregation, "many of which were learned by most of us as Sunday school children in the far off parishes of Eastern cities and villages." In Chanhassen a family from Massachusetts in 1855 found that the community social life centered in the schoolhouse, where old-fashioned spelling bees and lyceums were held.

New Year's calls, it is said, can be traced to an old Dutch custom, but the New Englanders of pioneer Minnesota certainly followed the fashion with vigor. "We had forty calls," wrote one of the members of the Fuller family of Connecticut after the 1853 New Year's, "not as many as I believe we had last year." Another custom from the Atlantic seaboard was that of issuing New Year's greetings to be sold by newspaper carriers.

New England's contribution to Minnesota law and politics was notable. The repeal of the Missouri Compromise in 1854 led to the formation of new party lines, and New Englanders, animated by a crusading spirit directed against both slavery and liquor, threw themselves into the organization of a Republican party in Minnesota. When the constitutional convention was held in 1857, New Englanders constituted 44.4 percent of the Republican wing, but only 20 percent of the

Democratic wing, which was dominated by men of the Old Northwest. It would be a mistake, however, to draw lines of differentiation too sharply. Sibley, the first state governor, was a Democrat and a native of old Detroit, but he was of New England ancestry and traditions. Ramsey, the second state governor, was a Republican and a native of Pennsylvania, with Scotch and German ancestry.

Of eleven Minnesota state governors from 1858 to 1890, only two, Austin and Pillsbury, were born in New England, but five others, Sibley, Swift, Davis, Hubbard, and Merriam, were of New England ancestry. A tabulation of governors, lieutenant governors, secretaries of state, treasurers, auditors, and attorneys general for the period from 1849 up to 1890 lists 64 officials, and of these twenty, or nearly one third, were New Englanders by birth. Probably many of the others, including nine born in Ohio, eight in New York, and eight in Pennsylvania, were of New England derivation.

It may be of comparative interest to note that of sixteen state governors since 1893, no fewer than twelve have been of Scandinavian stock.

A striking evidence of the New England factor in Minnesota law is the composition of the territorial and supreme courts up to 1890, for of 23 chief and associate justices, nine, or nearly 40 percent, were of New England birth, and of the remaining fourteen, seven were from New York. In 1904 a book was published on the bench and bar in Minnesota which included biographies of 220 prominent lawyers. Of these 53, or approximately one fourth, were born in New England. Vermont contributed more than twice as many as any other New England state.

The launching of the press in Minnesota by a New Englander, James M. Goodhue, has already been described. Many other men from the New England states played parts in the newspaper history of the state. The New England element was attracted by journalism, as indeed it was by the professions in general; it is probable that the greatest contributions of New Englanders to Minnesota were made in the professions. In the field of journalism, however, the elements from New England encountered competition, for a survey of leading Minnesota journalists of the pioneer period reveals a diversity of origins.

New England and Minnesota have maintained close relationships with each other from pioneer times to the present. There have been, as one writer phrases it, "bridges facing east," or, as it might be put from another point of view, "bridges facing west," or, perhaps more accurately, intersectional bridges, facing both ways. Such bridges were the National Education Society, the American Home Missionary Society, and the American Board. Such bridges were the letters sent by Minnesotans to relatives and friends in New England; the many newspaper articles and items that appeared about Minnesota and the West in New England political and agricultural papers; the visiting back and forth of relatives; the lecture trips in the West of leaders of thought, including Emerson himself, who spoke in the Twin Cities in 1867; the lecture trips in the East of notable representatives of the Middle West like Bishop Whipple; the education of Minnesotans at Harvard, Yale, and other colleges and universities of the East; and in more recent times the education of many young New Englanders at Minnesota and other universities in the Upper Mississippi Valley.

We need to survey and appraise also the roles played by people from the Middle States, the South, and other sections of America, as well as by Swedes, Danes, Norwegians, Irish, Canadians, Germans, Czechs, Poles, and others who have helped to build the Middle West. We need to understand the intermingling of the many elements that have gone into the making of the composite whole. Goodhue's prophecy that Minnesota would become the New England of the West was made before diverse immigrant streams flowed into the region.

Minnesota became, not a western New England, but a middle-western commonwealth of cosmopolitan origins.

There can be no doubt, however, that New England men and women made notable and permanent contributions to the life and institutions of the region — contributions of a wide sweep both in time and in nature. And the history of the Middle West is crowded with Yankee personalities as salty as they were eminent, men and women of the breed of Samuel Pond, James M. Goodhue, John Pillsbury, and Cyrus Northrop. Without these and many others of their stamp, the drama of the region would have lacked much of its savor.

Some of that savor is caught by Oscar Firkins in a poem honoring a great university teacher, Maria Sanford — a Connecticut Yankee — which closes with these lines:

> Praise her not with smug obeisance,
> Sleek and millinered complaisance!
> Save your peppermint and raisins
>   For the dupe of sugared lies!
> Praise her, travel-soiled and dusty,
> Praise her, vehement and gusty,
> Praise her, kinked and knurled and crusty,
> Leonine and hale and lusty,
> Praise her, oaken-ribbed and trusty,
>   Shout "Maria" to the skies.

A State University Is Born

Many people of our own time, looking at the history of the University of Minnesota, express surprise that it should have been chartered as early as 1851.

The Territory of Minnesota, then only two years old, was impressive on the map, with counties stretching westward as far as the Missouri River, but it was for the most part undeveloped wilderness not yet ceded by the native Sioux and Chippewa — virgin woods, prairies of ranging bison, lonely lakes and rivers. Connections with the outer world were still uncertain and sporadic, and when winter closed the river highway, people had to depend upon horses and sleds and their own sturdy legs.

The pioneer Minnesotans sometimes spoke of the East as "back in the United States." When steamboats docked at the St. Paul wharf, crowds were on hand to learn the latest news from faraway — the reports of the California gold rush, the emergence of the "sprawling tent city" called San Francisco, the policies of the Whig president from Louisiana, General Zachary Taylor, who himself had been the commandant of Fort Snelling as a young officer in the late 1820s; the Compromise of 1850; the publication of a book in 1851 by Harriet Beecher Stowe . . .

To many easterners *Minnesota* was an almost wholly unfamiliar name, and they had no idea where the territory really was. Alexander Ramsey's neighbors in Pennsylvania, after President Taylor appointed him governor of Minnesota Territory in 1849, wondered whether he would go out to Minnesota by way of the Isthmus or the Horn.

Minnesota in 1851, then, was the Wild West, the edge of civilization, the frontier rim of mid-America. Why speak of a university in this almost primitive wilderness? And yet the really surprising thing is that a university was not chartered two years earlier by the first territorial legislature.

Not a few of the pioneers of Minnesota had moved north from Wisconsin and knew that as early as 1838 the Territory of Wisconsin had passed an act to establish a university "at or near Madison, the seat of government"; and that Wisconsin had launched a university in 1848 and opened a preparatory school. Through the 1840s Michigan had a functioning university, and there can be no doubt that Minnesotans knew of its existence. As early as 1817 the Territory of Michigan had projected a pretentious and impracticable "catholepistemiad, or university, of Michigania," but the real University of Michigan was not organized until twenty years later, in 1837. By 1849 it had been in actual operation for eight years and was just then organizing its school of medicine. And the University of Iowa, though its classes did not begin until 1855, had been officially chartered in 1847.[1]

Moreover, the cultural, professional, and political leaders of Minnesota were deeply and genuinely interested in education and saw it as one of the main highways to a great future. Not a few of them, in fact, were themselves college graduates or former college students. In recent times the University of Minnesota has officially recognized eight "founders" and has engraved their names in a permanent roster of founders in the foyer of Northrop Auditorium. Of these eight, four had college backgrounds. Governor Ramsey had studied at Lafayette College in Pennsylvania.[2] John W. North was a graduate of Wesleyan, Edward D. Neill of Amherst, and Alfred E. Ames of Rush Medical College. Henry Hastings Sibley was educated in an academy at Detroit and had been tutored privately in Latin and Greek. The three other founders had common school educations in Vermont (Henry M. Rice), Illinois (William R. Marshall), and New Hampshire (John S. Pillsbury). Isaac Atwater, not given the accolade of founder but nevertheless a prominent figure in the early development of the university, was a graduate of Yale College.[3]

The university question does not seem to have come to the Minnesota surface in 1849, but it did emerge in 1850, and early in 1851 Governor Ramsey recommended to the second territorial legislature that it should memorialize Congress for a grant of 100,000 acres of public land for the endowment of a university.[4] This recommendation set in motion two actions. One was a memorial to Congress requesting the land grant, as suggested by the governor, and the other was an act to establish the University of Minnesota.

The memorial to Congress, approved by the governor on February 19, 1851, referred to the earlier territorial act establishing common schools and declared that a great number had already sprung up in Minnesota.[5] "Many of the youth who are now receiving the rudiments of knowledge in the common schools," it said, "will soon be prepared for the more arduous ascent which leads to the acquirement of a liberal education; and all feel the great disadvantages, and in many instances disability of sending their children abroad for that purpose."

It is curious circumstance that a congressional bill became law on February 19, 1851, assuring a land grant for a university in Minnesota. This federal act reserved "a quantity of land not exceeding two townships, for the use and support of a University" in the territory, "and for no other use and purpose whatsoever," to be taken from public lands "to which the Indian title has been or may be extinguished."[6]

The fact that this congressional act bears the date February 19, 1851 — the very day on which Ramsey signed the Minnesota legislative memorial asking for a land grant — clearly indicates that the movement for a university land grant antedated the events in the Minnesota territorial legislature.

The pivot of this earlier movement was Henry Hastings Sibley. As congressional delegate from Minnesota, he was in a strategic position to work for a university grant, but it is now known that another Minnesota pioneer whose name has not heretofore appeared in the early annals of the university played a significant role in initiating the land grant. This was William G. Le Duc, a pioneer lawyer and bookseller in St. Paul who later won wide fame as a Civil War general, an agricultural leader, and a businessman.

As early as December 9, 1850, Le Duc wrote to Sibley from St. Paul urging him to secure a land grant of 100,000 acres for a university in Minnesota.[7] "There is no more enduring and nobler monument of wise legislation," he said, "than a well endowed [and] well sustained University." He even suggested that the person "through whose exertions it may be established" would receive, and merit, "the approbation of thousands who may throng its halls long years after his physical 'form and semblance' shall be forgotten."

It was Le Duc's hope that the university would be established at Fort Snelling, converting "the school for the soldier into a school for the civilian." This hope was not realized, but there can be no doubt that Le Duc's proposal was reflected in Sibley's action. Le Duc did more than write a letter; he printed and circulated a hundred petitions in support of the move, and he secured promises from "prominent and influential men" to request their friends in Washington to aid a university grant for Minnesota.[8]

Sibley made rapid progress. On February 9, 1851 — ten days before the Minnesota legislative memorial — he wrote Ramsey that a bill granting two townships for a university in Minnesota had passed the House in Washington.[9] It was this measure that became law on February 19, giving Minnesota, not the

100,000 acres that both Le Duc and Ramsey had hoped for, but nevertheless a substantial amount — 46,080 acres, to be selected in subdivisions of not less than one section each. Le Duc's letter of December 9, 1850, is the earliest known advocacy of the establishment of the University of Minnesota.[10]

One could hardly ask Congress for a university land grant, as the territorial legislature of 1851 was doing, without taking action to bring a university into existence, and this matter the territorial house committee on schools promptly took in hand.

The report of that committee, dated February 3, 1851, is one of the first of the basic University of Minnesota documents and deserves to be better known than it is.[11] Dr. Edward D. Neill, the versatile pioneer preacher and historian who later became chancellor of the university and president of Macalester College, is said to have drafted the report, but the committee was headed by John W. North of St. Anthony, with two other members: J. C. Ramsey, a brother of the governor, and B. H. Randall.

North, a college graduate, has been described as "a Yankee with an astonishing flair for cultural, legal, and economic pioneering." He arrived in Minnesota in 1849, helped to found the Republican party in the territory, was a leading figure in the Republican wing of the state constitutional convention, was a milling pioneer in the Cannon River valley, and helped to found the city of Northfield, named for him. Later he moved west, presided over the constitutional convention of Nevada, became a judge on its supreme court, and ended his career in California, where he also served in a high judicial position. He may well have been aided by Dr. Neill in drafting the report of 1851, but there is no reason for supposing that he did not have the competence and vision to write it himself.

The committee said that "the cause of education in the Territory demands the early establishment of an institution of learning, which shall afford to the youth of the Territory an opportunity of obtaining a liberal, scientific and classical education." "Men do not 'gather grapes of thorns, or figs of thistles;' neither does society grow virtuous citizens from the haunts of vice, or exalted minds from the abodes of ignorance and stupidity." The committee believed that "to govern and restrain the ignorant is far more difficult than to educate and fit men to govern themselves." "The children of the present, are the citizens and rulers of the future; and upon their education, depends the character and destiny of our infant commonwealth."

North's committee did not think it was too early to establish a university in Minnesota: "The foundations of some of the New England Universities were laid almost at the commencement of their colonies. As soon as the forests were cleared from their streets, and they had constructed dwellings for themselves, they immediately began to erect institutions of learning for their children. Harvard University, the first in the United States, was founded in 1638, eight years after the first settlement of Massachusetts Bay, and only eighteen years after the landing of the Pilgrims at Plymouth Rock. *There were at that time, only about half as many inhabitants in all New England, as are now residing in the Territory of Minnesota.*"

The report spoke also of Yale and pointed out that both Yale and Harvard, small in infancy, had "kept pace with the growth of our country." In fact, they "have done more than any other [institution] to give an impress of virtue, intelligence and refinement to our national character."

Minnesota Territory was far away from the eastern centers. As the "New England of the West," it needed institutions of learning of its own. So the committee recommended passage of an act to incorporate the University of Minnesota. That the prospective land grant was much in the thought of the committee members is evident from the following statement: "Though such an institution should not come to maturity in many years, it may now receive an endowment in lands, that will increase in value with the growth of the country, and when wanted, will be amply sufficient to erect and furnish an institution commensurate with our wants." The committee recommended that meanwhile a preparatory department could serve as an "Academic Institution for the entire youth of the Territory."

The basic document of the university in the 1850s, today, and probably for all time, is the charter itself, approved by Governor Ramsey on February 25, 1851, and given constitutional validity by Article VIII, section 4, of the constitution of Minnesota, adopted by the people six years later.[12] It may be of interest, against the background already sketched, to outline the provisions of the charter and to see what kind of institution the pioneers of 1851 planned. Viewed in the light of nearly a century, the charter reveals genuine educational vision and statesmanship on the part of its framers.[13]

These are the basic provisions of the charter: the name of the new institution — the University of Minnesota; its location — "at or near the falls of St. Anthony"; its object — to provide the inhabitants "with the means of acquiring a thorough knowledge of the various branches of literature, science and the arts"; its government — vested in a board of twelve regents elected by the legislature, the regents to constitute a "body corporate"; its attitude on sectarianism and religious viewpoint — "no sectarian instruction shall be allowed in such university," and "no religious tenets or opinions shall be required to entitle any person to be admitted as a student in said University; and no such tenets shall be required as a qualification for any professor, tutor, or officer of said University."

The charter granted large powers to the regents: to enact laws for the government of the university; to elect a chancellor who is ex officio president of the board; to appoint "professors and tutors" and such other officers as may be expedient and to determine their salaries; to remove any officer when the interests of the university so require; to regulate admission fees and charges for tuition with the proviso that as soon as the income of the university, in the judgment of the regents, permits, "tuition in all of the departments, shall be without charge to all students in the same who are residents of the Territory"; to secure a suitable site for the university and to proceed to erect buildings; to establish a preparatory department and to discontinue it when proper, after other departments have been established; to regulate the course of instruction and, "under advice of the professorships," prescribe books and authorities; to "confer such degrees and grant such diplomas as are usually conferred and granted by other universities"; to expend such portion of the university funds as the regents think expedient for buildings, apparatus, library, and a cabinet of natural history; and to select, manage, and control lands hereafter to be granted by Congress.

The act further declared that the proceeds from the federal land grants were to go to "a perpetual fund to be called the 'University Fund,'" the interest of which could be used for university support. It also set up a plan for the election of the regents—starting out with three classes, one for two years, one for four, and one for six, with biennial elections thereafter by joint sessions of the two branches of the legislature, four members to be elected at each session, for six-year terms.

'The charter included a clause declaring that the university should consist of five departments—science, literature, and the arts; law; medicine; the theory and practice of elementary instruction; and agriculture—and it specified that the immediate government of the several departments was to be entrusted to their respective faculties.'An interesting special provision is that authorizing the regents, if they think it expedient, to "receive into connection with the University any college within the Territory upon application of the board of trustees; and such college so received shall become a branch of the University and be subject to the visitation of the regents."

With a few minor additions,[14] the foregoing is the essence of the charter of 1851, basic to the establishment of an institution destined to become one of the great universities of the world.[15] Did the framers originate or borrow the ideas they incorporated in the charter?

That they should have drawn upon the experience of neighboring states seems only natural. Ideas as well as people moved westward, and cultural transfer plays a large role in the institutionalizing of American society. Minnesota turned to Michigan for many of the basic concepts of the university charter and for not a little of its phrasing. Thus the sections of the charter declaring the establishment of the university, describing its objects, setting forth the responsibilities of faculty and regents, naming its officers, fixing the corporate character of the institution, and defining some of the powers of the regents are either copied verbatim from the Michigan charter of 1837 or paraphrase that document, which also had a marked influence upon the charter of the University of Wisconsin.[16] One item in the Minnesota charter — that pertaining to religious tenets or opinions — seems to have been derived from Wisconsin or from an earlier source common to both, and a few minor provisions suggest that the Minnesota lawmakers had taken the trouble to read the University of Iowa act of 1846.

To proceed at this point to the state constitution of Minnesota, adopted by the people on October 13, 1857, is moving ahead of the immediate story, but the total picture will be clearer if attention is called at once to Article VIII, section 4, of that document:

The location of the University of Minnesota, as established by existing laws, is hereby confirmed, and said institution is hereby declared to be the University of the state of Minnesota. All the rights, immunities, franchises and endowments heretofore granted or conferred, are hereby perpetuated unto the said University, and all lands which may be granted hereafter by congress, or other donations for said University purposes, shall vest in the institution referred to in this section.[17]

Having taken one step in advance of the story, we may take yet another, and a longer one, to point out that it was the charter of February 25, 1851, in conjunction with section 4 of Article VIII of the constitution, that furnished the foundation of the university's case in 1928, when it challenged the attempted control of its finances by the state commission of administration and finance. The particular case involved only a minor sum of money, but the principle at stake was fundamental to the authority of the regents of the university. By sustaining the judgment of the Ramsey County district court, the state supreme court accepted the basic position that what the state constitution "perpetuated unto the said University" was the university as established and empowered by the charter of 1851, the university which, as Dr. Folwell says, was "doing business, if not keeping school" at the time the constitutional conventions were sitting.[18]

The charter of 1851 was the charter of the University of Minnesota as perpetuated in the constitution — valid in 1928 and for the future. The control of the university's finances could not be assumed by the state commission; it remained securely in the hands of the regents. One consequence of the decision was that the state was obliged to return to the system of election of regents by the legislature in joint session, as provided in the law of 1851 but as disregarded for sixty-eight years under later state laws. Incidentally it turned out that the university did not have a president as had been supposed, but a chancellor as specified in the provisions of the charter.

There was an immediate difficulty. The regents serving in 1928 had been appointed by the governor, not elected by joint session. This created a neat little tangle that was settled quite as neatly. The law of 1851 provided that if for any reason a vacancy in the board existed, it could be filled by the governor pending legislative election; so an ingenious attorney general, seventy-seven years after the charter was adopted, cut the Gordian knot by suggesting that the governor, within the provisions of the law of 1851, had in fact appointed regents to fill vacancies — and they could legally hold office until the next legislature elected a board under the terms of the original law.

To return to the situation in 1851, the action of the legislature in chartering the university seems to have caused no flurry of excitement in the newspapers of the time, though the *Minnesota Democrat* said that the "institution may be made the most popular and flourishing in the West, and become one of our proudest monuments of intellectual enterprise," and the *Minnesota Pioneer* commented chiefly about St. Anthony as "a quiet and delightful spot for an institution of learning." [19]

INFANCY AND HIGH HOPES

In the light of later events the early reports of the board of regents may make somewhat ironical reading, but this is an instance of wisdom after the event. The reports tell in a spirit of elation about progress made, and their optimism does not falter until after the blight of depression has struck the country. [20]

The legislature elected twelve regents on March 4, 1851, only a week after the charter had been approved. There was much ability on the board in men like Ramsey and Sibley; Atwater and B. B. Meeker, both former students at Yale; William R. Marshall, a hardware merchant who became governor after the Civil War; Franklin Steele, the St. Anthony pioneer lumberman; Socrates Nelson, a Stillwater businessman; and five other citizens of the territory. [21] These regents met for the first time on May 31, and by February 7, 1852, they were able to report considerable progress in their initial annual review.

A committee had already taken up with the Secretary of the Interior the question of selecting the lands granted by the federal government. It was decided to erect a building for the preparatory department, raising funds by private subscription for this purpose, with a limit of $2500. After examining various proffered sites, the board accepted one from Franklin

Steele near the center of the village of St. Anthony, about four acres including ground that had been intended for a public square plus some adjacent lots — the area now defined by Central and First avenues southeast and University Avenue and Second Street. The regents regarded it as "a most eligible situation on the bluff, just above the mills, fronting Main Street and the river, and commanding one of the most beautiful prospects in the Territory."

The building was actually put up — a wooden structure thirty by fifty feet in area, with a high basement and two stories. Elijah W. Merrill, a native of Conway, New Hampshire, and a Wesleyan College graduate, described in the regents' report as a "teacher of experience and ability," was chosen as principal of the preparatory department, which opened on November 26, 1851, with at least two rooms of the building ready for use. It announced a quarter of eleven weeks, with work in the "Common English branches" and the "Higher English branches," as well as in Greek, Latin, French, bookkeeping, and the higher mathematics.[22] The "Common English branches" consisted of grammar, spelling, reading, and arithmetic, whereas the "Higher English branches" included natural philosophy, chemistry, elocution, history, astronomy, and physiology. Tuition was four dollars for the common English branches, five dollars for the higher, and six for Greek, Latin, French, and other subjects — plus three dollars for fuel, sweeping, and other incidentals.

There were about forty students. A donation of six volumes of the *Annals* of Congress was received from the Smithsonian Institution, and some books and pamphlets were given by Sibley. These doubtless were the first gifts to the University of Minnesota library. Atwater, reporting for the regents, said that the institution "has commenced under the most flattering auspices, and promises to realize the most sanguine expectations of its friends." St. Anthony, he reported, was the proper location. The university needed the liberal support of citizens and also the "fostering care of the legislature." The report closes with these words: "Let the people of Minnesota extend to this school a generous patronage, not regarding it as a local, but a Territorial enterprise, and an institution will soon be built up which will be to Minnesota what Harvard and Yale are to New England, the cherished mother of her noblest sons."

As one follows through the reports from the first year to the Panic of 1857, one finds constant reflection of the sanguine hopes and optimism of that period, when the population of Minnesota rose to more than 150,000 and the movement toward statehood came to a climax. Not infrequently the secretary of the board grumbled about the necessity for a quorum of seven members to validate its business. At times members would travel the appalling distance of twenty or thirty miles to attend a meeting, only to find that a quorum was lacking by one or two and the journey had been officially futile. So, without success, the board urged a law either making attendance compulsory or reducing the number required for a quorum.

The preparatory school increased to an enrollment of 170 in one year and was carried through 1854–55 before it was discontinued. Merrill served as principal to the satisfaction of the board, which reported that his system of government was "mild yet firm." Some of the students who had taken work in the department went out as teachers, which seemed a justification of the legislative plans. In one year, when there were 85 students, 6 were enrolled in languages, 17 in algebra and geometry, 16 in physiology, 16 in bookkeeping, 29 in philosophy, and 6 in astronomy. What this astronomy was remains a mystery. At any rate, it is clear from the reports that there were no instruments or apparatus for use in the scientific courses. The library grew with occasional gifts, one a set of twenty-two volumes of the *London Encyclopedia*.[23]

Meanwhile several important developments took place. Much of the congressional land grant was located after the

Sioux lands were opened by the treaties of 1851, only some eleven to twelve thousand acres of the grant of 46,000 acres remaining to be chosen by early winter of 1858. The regents had entered both pine lands and rich farming lands through the land offices at Stillwater, Sauk Rapids, Winona, and Red Wing.

Even in the second year the regents were sensitive to the need of finding a better location than that in the immediate milling district, which was not thought "desirable for a seat of learning." Expansion would be necessary, and the little town had already closed around the first site. In the report for 1854–55, we learn that a new site had been chosen. It was that of the modern university, including what is today called the campus knoll. Starting out with twenty-five acres, bought for $6000, the regents now began to consider plans for a great new building on this favorable spot.

The report for the year 1856, written only a few months before the panic, is one of large plans and buoyant hopes. A huge four-story stone building, 57 by 81 feet, with extensions on each side 51 by 63 feet, had been contracted for at a cost of $49,600 and was to be ready eighteen months from September 6, 1856. It was expected to be "one of the most beautiful and convenient structures for educational purposes to be found in the western States." The canny and conservative Ramsey, in dissenting from this project for a great building, put his finger on its essential weakness. He made an effort to limit the building expenditure to $15,000 inasmuch as the board had "not offered any plan for the conducting of the University," but his motion was set aside. The practical Sibley joined Ramsey and two others in voting against the $49,600 proposal.

The great scheme, passed by a majority of one, was carried into effect. By the next year the Panic of 1857 had come and its effects were spreading, but the regents reported that "despite the stringency of the money market" the work had been pushed forward and would be completed on time. The building would contain 124 rooms, eight for lecture and recitation purposes, the remainder for dormitories. Under legislative authorization in 1856, bonds for $15,000 had been issued at twelve percent, secured by mortgaging "any lands now belonging or which may hereafter belong to the said University," and the institution, it was suggested, might even open its doors in 1858! [24]

But that was the end of the pioneer optimism and high hopes. A disastrous slump had come in business; banks failed; money was tight; land could not be sold and land values dropped away; the university was sinking deeper and deeper into debt; no realistic plans had been worked out for a college; and the opening of the university, so blithely anticipated for 1858, was still more than a decade in the future. Old Main, or rather its west wing and extension, did indeed stand on the campus, but it was a forlorn building that was soon boarded up, for many years a monument to the exuberance of pioneer planners who closed their ears to the cautious wisdom of an Alexander Ramsey.

It is easy, with the perspective of many decades, to charge the regents with folly, but it is only fair to remember that the board, in the surging, booming, speculative 1850s, did not anticipate the Panic of 1857, nor did it have prevision of the coming Civil and Sioux wars. As Dr. Folwell once asserted, the "whole territory was in a raging fever of speculation, with a maximum virulence about the Falls of St. Anthony." [25] But even bearing in mind the fervor of the time, the modern student finds it difficult to understand the projection of an ambitious building program with virtually no thought or planning for a teaching staff, a course of college studies, or a student body, except as the charter of 1851 envisaged a functioning institution.

STATEHOOD AND A SECOND LAND GRANT

As the clouds of panic hovered over Minnesota and the nation, many pioneer hopes were dimmed, but at least one did not lose its glow: the hope of statehood. The opening of new lands, the swift growth of population, and the building of towns and cities meant an end to the territorial status of Minnesota, panic or no panic.

When the congressional enabling act was passed in 1857, it included a provision, usual in such statehood measures, for setting apart seventy-two sections of land for a university, but this was not done in the customary phrase. The words written into the bill introduced by Henry M. Rice, who had succeeded Sibley as delegate to Congress in 1853, were "for the use and support of a state university," rather than merely for "a university." [26] The enabling acts of Michigan, Wisconsin, and Iowa used language clearly intended to confirm earlier territorial grants for universities, but Rice's phrase ultimately raised a serious question. Did it mean a new grant of seventy-two sections, in addition to the seventy-two sections reserved by the congressional act of 1851? Or was it merely a confirmation of the grant promised in 1851? [27]

Dr. Folwell believes that Congress, if it gave any thought to the phrase, probably assumed that it was in fact confirming the earlier grant to the territory; and that seems to have been the view generally held by the pioneers in Minnesota. [28]

One naturally turns to the discussions and debates of the Minnesota constitutional conventions in the summer of 1857 to learn what interpretation Minnesotans placed upon the language of the enabling act. The delegates, elected in June by popular vote, met in July to form a constitution. Republicans and Democrats, about equally matched in numbers, were both determined to control the convention. The result was an extraordinary spectacle. Chairmen from both the Republican and the Democratic groups rushed to the platform at the opening session and called the convention to order at the same time.

Neither group would recognize the other, and as a result the two groups organized separately. Thus Minnesota had two constitutional conventions, each declaring that it was *the* convention. Each adopted a constitution, and it was only at the last moment that a compromise committee managed to come together and agree upon one constitution.

Thus it happened that the University of Minnesota and its land grant were discussed by two constitutional conventions. In the Democratic convention, presided over by Sibley, not a word was said to indicate that anyone supposed the land grant of the enabling act to be a new grant, in addition to that of 1851. Attention was directed to confirming, through a constitutional provision, the permanent location of the university and to guarding its permanent funds and its character as established by its charter. The Democratic convention formulated the provision that finally emerged as Article VIII, section 4, of the states' constitution. One speaker did indeed assert that it was not necessary to have all future donations expended to the glory of the St. Anthony institution. Why not, he asked, endow a half dozen universities? But the convention did not agree with this idea. It confirmed the location established by existing laws, declared the institution to be "the University of the State of Minnesota," and guaranteed to it the land grant and future university donations.[29]

The debates in the Republican wing touching the university were lively and prolonged. They ranged from a proposal to elect the regents by popular vote to sharp exchanges on the questions of location and funds. Some members spoke of Winona, Owatonna, and Shakopee as possible sites. There were suggestions that the great building of the university had been put up mainly to prevent a possible removal of the institution from St. Anthony, and one speaker mentioned the enhancement of property values in St. Anthony that resulted from its having the university.[30]

But the spokesmen for keeping the university where it was,

"one and indivisible," and for maintaining its fund undivided were emphatic and effective. Fail to locate the university, said one speaker, and every town in Minnesota will bid for it and for a share in its fund. John W. North ridiculed the idea of a university "scattered around every neighborhood of our entire State" and sharply opposed moving it from St. Anthony. "Let it remain," he said, "so that it can acquire a character for stability and value." David Secombe, defining the object of a state university, said, "It is to encircle about one point, all the wisdom and all the intelligence that may be within the province of the State to encircle, and to send out and diffuse education through the whole State." Another speaker, opposing dispersion, scoffed at a "traveling locomotive University, upon wheels."

Only one delegate raised the question of a second land grant. This was H. A. Billings, who insisted that under the enabling act Congress proposed to give Minnesota a further grant of two townships. He drew a sharp distinction between the grant made in 1851 for the "University of the Territory" and that proposed in the enabling act for "a State University." North pointed out at once that Billings was "entirely mistaken." The act of 1851 had merely reserved lands from sale. That act and the enabling act, he said, "mean the same thing, and apply to the same land." To which Billings replied, "The gentleman says that Congress means something which they certainly do not say." [31]

The convention debates came to an end. The university section was agreed upon by the two conventions and adopted by the people of Minnesota as Article VIII, section 4, of the constitution. Meanwhile, however, the question raised by Billings was not permitted to rest. The idea of two grants bestirred the regents in 1860 to take action. At the urgent prompting of Dr. Neill, the chancellor, they requested Ramsey, now governor of the state, to take steps looking toward the selection of the land referred to in the enabling act — land for a "State University."

No allusion had been made in the enabling act to the earlier grant of 1851; the act seemed to be speaking specifically of a future state university; and Dr. Neill argued that "it was not the intention of Congress to turn over the debts and prospectively encumbered lands of an old and badly managed territorial institution, but to give the State that was to be, a grant for a State University, free from all connections with territorial organizations." Moved by such reasoning, the university, already the recipient of two townships of land, insisted that it had two more coming to it.[32]

This ingenious claim was prosecuted under one board after another for a decade, and an astute lawyer was employed to work on the case in Washington. After futile efforts to prevail upon the Secretary of the Interior to rule favorably on the claim, the case was taken to Congress itself, where, after much maneuvering, it managed to pass both the House and the Senate early in 1870. The ubiquitous Ramsey, territorial governor when the university was chartered, regent in the 1850s, and state governor when the board first made its claim, was now United States senator from Minnesota, and he played an influential part in persuading his colleagues to support the move. There is evidence that the Senate was not precisely enthusiastic, and one senator somewhat ruefully suggested that if Minnesota got more than her proper share, the error was at least "on the right side." [33]

PANIC, DEBT, AND RESCUE

The building of Old Main, coinciding with the Panic of 1857, created grave difficulty for the regents and the university despite the largesse of the federal government. The land grant of 1851 had not yet been converted into money, and the second grant did not materialize until more than a decade after the state was admitted to the Union. Some donations of money, it is true, had been made to the university near its outset, but at no time had there been appropriations or other income that could aid the institution in meeting the costs of a functioning college.

If in the prosperous years of the territory its citizens had banded together in some plan for immediate and continuing financial support of the university, it probably could have been got under way. We know that it was not impossible to start an actual college on the Minnesota frontier in the 1850s. This was demonstrated by Hamline University, chartered by the legislature in 1854. The businessmen of Red Wing, eager to have the institution in that Mississippi River town, donated a site for it, and by the beginning of 1855 it had a three-story building completed. Classes, which had begun the preceding autumn in the upper floor of a store building, were moved to the new structure, which "served as a dormitory, a library, and a chapel, as well as a recitation hall." This college at its outset received a gift valued at twenty-five thousand dollars from the Methodist bishop, Leonidas L. Hamline, whose name the college to this day bears. The school attracted students — seventy-three in its first year — and was conducted at Red Wing until 1869. Hamline, too, faced hard times after the panic, and its teachers probably were often paid in flour, potatoes, and wood rather than in money, but the college survived not only the panic but also the Civil War.[34]

Meanwhile, the University of Minnesota was embarrassed by an empty building and mounting debts. The board talked bravely about the possibility of opening the university's doors in 1858 and in fact attempted to resuscitate the preparatory department, appointed a new principal, and began classes, only to abandon them after a half year because the enrollment was pitifully small. The board also prevailed upon Edward D. Neill, an educator of ability and energy, to accept the chancellorship, but the building remained empty and Neill himself, when the war came, left to be a chaplain and soon thereafter one of President Lincoln's private secretaries.

As the financial situation of the university grew more desperate, the legislature, which already had authorized a $15,000 bond issue, opened the way, by an act of March 8, 1858, for an additional issue of $40,000 to be secured by lands belonging to or later to be acquired by the university.[35] In normal times these actions, backed by the grounds and building and by the 1851 land grant, might have saved the situation, but bonds carrying twelve percent interest are uncertain instruments for a university lacking regular income, and when they are issued in the midst of a national depression, the dangers are multiplied. It had been hoped that logs run down from university lands by way of the Rum River in 1857 would aid the university's finances, but unfortunately the Rum River belied its wet name and dried up in 1857. The stumpage did not come.

A legislative report on the university in 1860 found fault with its previous organization, the difficulties occasioned by the quorum rule, and the actions of the "enthusiasts" who had failed to heed Ramsey's counsel.[36] Minnesota had not had the wisdom to study the development of other state universities; a resolution in 1856 had proposed that Neill be sent to visit the universities of Wisconsin, Michigan, Ohio, and Virginia to learn of their policies and experiences, but this plan was not adopted.[37] The report noted that the "Universities of our Western States have generally excited but little interest among the friends of education" and pointed to substantial gifts to Hamline University and the Baldwin School — a precursor of Macalester College — as signs of the greater interest in denominational and private institutions.

It is interesting to learn, after reading this doleful allusion to donors, that when the legislature in 1860 passed a university reorganization act, it included a provision that any person who contributed not less than fifteen thousand dollars to endow a professorship should have the right to nominate not only trustees to care for the endowment, but also an individual to fill the professorship and a regent who would have "the same rights and privileges as those appointed in behalf of the State." But this move toward a greater university fund does not seem to have produced any donations.

The reorganization act of 1860, intended as a new charter, has a large sweep of detail, but its principal reform was with respect to the board of regents.[38] In contravention of the charter of 1851 as confirmed by the state constitution, it swept aside the joint legislative election of regents and provided for a board of eight members, to include the governor, lieutenant governor, university chancellor, and five persons to be appointed by the governor with the advice and consent of the senate. This act was approved on February 14, 1860, and the new board met on April 5, chose Ramsey as its president, and reelected Neill as chancellor. The board carried forward the probing of university affairs that had been begun by the legislative committee and was not gentle in its criticism of the former regents, who, it said, had been so "blinded by the glare of imaginary riches" that "they supposed that the University, like themselves, could never be embarrassed for want of money." [39]

Neither reorganization nor caustic criticism reduced the university's debt, and even a special act in 1862, giving the regents power to "arrange or compromise" the indebtedness and to sell "any or all" of the congressional lands, failed to improve matters.[40]

The turning point came when John Sargent Pillsbury was appointed a regent in 1863. This able son of New Hampshire, born in 1827, had already had a wide business experience before he came to St. Anthony in the mid-fifties as a hardware merchant. He lived near Old Main, and when in 1863 he was elected to the state senate, he made the affairs of the university his principal concern. He set to work to clear its debts and to retain for it as much of its federal land as he found humanly possible. He was determined not to let "the institution sink under debts and unpaid mortgages." [41] Much later he asserted that there was at one time danger that Old Main itself would be taken over by the state as an insane asylum and "only for the vigorous efforts of the regents" was this fate avoided.[42]

The most dramatic step Pillsbury took was to secure the passage in 1864 of a new reorganization act, which named three men as "sole regents of the University of Minnesota." They were Pillsbury himself, O. C. Merriman, a Minneapolis lawyer and businessman, and John Nicols, a St. Paul hardware merchant. These three men of business were given authority to sell a certain proportion of the university's lands, and Pillsbury is said to have visited personally all the creditors of the university, many of whom had purchased its bonds at fifteen to fifty cents on a dollar. He redeemed much of the indebtedness at one third of its face value, while meeting the earlier indebtedness, secured by Old Main and the university site, at face value. By 1867 the board could report that except for some six thousand dollars the debts had been paid, the building and site were saved, and thirty-two thousand acres of the 1851 federal grant still remained in the hands of the university. Pillsbury and his colleagues closed their report by expressing the opinion that "in view of all the circumstances of the case, a *beginning* ought now to be made." They said that many citizens had voiced "deep anxiety that immediate steps should be taken with a view to the early opening of a school of high grade at the University." [43]

Granting that times were improving in the post-Civil War period and that population was swarming into the state, with lands increasing in value, Pillsbury's achievement — and it was mainly his own work — was a splendid one. And it was no chance circumstance that the legislature in 1867 made its first appropriation to the university — fifteen thousand dollars for repairing the building and paying staff salaries for the school that was to be opened in the fall of that year. In fact the regents themselves had recommended an appropriation in support of a cause that they regarded as "of the highest importance to the educational interests of the people." [44]

Not a little lore has twined itself about Old Main in its barren and neglected years. Pillsbury, one of a committee of four that inspected the building in 1864, found it in a "sad condition and going to ruin." A family lived there, "pretending to have charge of it." Turkeys were kept in one of the basement rooms, hay in another, and wood in a third. In the main hall the floor "was nearly destroyed from the effects of splitting wood." [45] E. B. Johnson says that somewhat later the "doors were off their hinges" and that cattle, pasturing on the campus, wandered into the basement for "protection from the winter's storms." [46]

But now the change had come. A member of the board of regents visited "some of the colleges and preparatory schools in the East" to study ways of improving Old Main and to find teachers; Old Main was duly repaired; and on October 7, 1867, the preparatory school opened, with W. W. Washburn, a graduate of the University of Michigan, as principal. During the first year two other teachers assisted Washburn: Gabriel Campbell, also a graduate of Michigan, as instructor in Latin and German, and Ira Moore, who taught mathematics and the "English Branches." Seventy-two pupils were enrolled during 1867–68, and the next year the number rose to more than a hundred. Edward H. Twining, who had taught both at Yale and at Washington College in Pennsylvania, was appointed to teach natural science the second year, and an instructor in English, A. J. Richardson, was added for the fall term.

Old Main, plastered, papered, painted, and provided with blackboards and furniture, came to life. [47] The preparatory department issued a *Catalogue* in the summer of 1868 that gave information about the faculty, the courses of study, the students enrolled during the past year, and the cost of living in a room of Old Main. Such a room, with stove, bedstead, mattress, washstand, table, bookcase, and chairs, came to four dollars per term, and the price was reduced a dollar in the announcement for 1869–70. Tuition was free.[48]

"The night has passed and the morning has dawned at length," wrote the principal in 1868. In the "stately walls raised against the clear blue sky" and in the school's "one hundred souls thirsting for knowledge," Washburn saw the "prophecy of a glorious future."[49] Underlying his exuberance was the simple truth that he was preparing students for the first college class of the university. Many years later a student who entered the preparatory school in 1868 recalled his experiences and observations: Third Street "lined, morning and noon, with St. Anthony young folks lingering between home and college"; the "student cells" of Old Main; boys cooking for themselves, sawing wood, getting up at three in the morning to deliver newspapers, enjoying a twenty-minute recess in the morning class program, with jumping and boxing as favorite sports; the "study-bug" busy at Latin and other subjects; an ambitious boy "braced up" to try for the university — a big name for the institution of that time. The "prep" school was remembered as a "poor affair," but "most students were there for business."[50]

THE MORRILL ACT, GLENCOE, AND THE UNIVERSITY

In no aspect of university history does the gap between idea and achievement loom larger than in the field of agricultural education.

The charter of 1851 specified agriculture as one of the five departments proposed for the unborn university. In 1862 the federal Morrill Act, designed to aid every state in the Union in forwarding agricultural education, was a part of the law of the land; and as early as 1869 the university board of regents elected a "Professor of Agriculture." Notwithstanding these intimations of things to come, the actual start of agricultural education trailed the university charter by twenty-seven years at Minnesota.

Nevertheless the roots of the vast and fruitful growth of Minnesota agricultural education strike deep into the soil of the 1850s and 1860s. The idea itself goes straight back to the sponsors of the charter, but the main root is the Morrill Act, passed by Congress as early as 1858, vetoed by President Buchanan, repassed by Congress in 1862, and signed by President Lincoln. The impetus behind this beneficent law, which was sponsored by Justin S. Morrill of Vermont, came from "agricultural societies, farm journals and other advocates of vocation training for farmers and mechanics." [51] Its purpose appears in its title: "An Act donating public lands to the several States and Territories which may provide colleges for the benefit of agriculture and the mechanic arts." [52]

The provisions of the Morrill Act were mainly that any state or territory might receive thirty thousand acres of land, either "in place" or by land scrip, for each senator and representative to which it was entitled under the apportionment based upon the census of 1860 — a proviso that meant 120,000 acres for Minnesota. No mineral lands could be selected under this act; the investments accruing from the land sales were to constitute a perpetual fund; and the state must use the interest for the "endowment, support, and maintenance of at least one college where the leading object shall be, without excluding other scientific and classical studies, and including military tactics, to teach such branches of learning as are related to agriculture and the mechanic arts," to the end of promoting "the liberal and practical education of the industrial classes."

Though in general the North and the West supported this bill, Dr. Stephenson points out that there was some opposition to it in the West, even in Minnesota, and he cites the *St. Peter Tribune* as saying that the bill, if made into law, would "rob the West of millions of acres of public lands," that the older states would get most of the lands and the newer states not enough to put up a "respectable academy," even if they were willing to accept the money at all for the purpose of making berths "for a few seedy politicians." [53] The animus behind this vigorous opinion doubtless lay in the fact that under the terms of the law Pennsylvania, for example, would receive nearly nine hundred thousand acres of land, whereas Minnesota could claim only a little over one hundred thousand. But the general attitude seems to have been one of satisfaction that the law had passed.

One would suppose that as a matter of course the benefits of this generous federal action would have been steered, in Minnesota, straight to the university then struggling to transform itself from a paper institution into a functioning school, but the ways of history are often devious, and in this case a turn of events brought the state close to setting up a college of agriculture at Glencoe, in McLeod County, and pouring into it the proceeds of the 120,000 acres assured Minnesota under the act.[54]

The first move for an agricultural college at Glencoe was actually taken in 1858, four years before the Morrill Bill became a law. The pivot of the plan was John H. Stevens, a noted Minneapolis pioneer and one of the founders of the Minnesota state agricultural society. He was a farmer and stock raiser who in 1856 established a farm in McLeod County and was shortly thereafter elected to the legislature from that district. Dr. Folwell suggests that Stevens learned of Morrill's proposals, which were put before Congress in 1858. This appears to be conjecture, but it is a fact that in 1858 Stevens introduced an ambitious scheme into the legislature for the chartering of an agricultural college at Glencoe.

The bill became a law on March 10, 1858, and covered nearly every detail possible except an appropriation. The institution was to be governed by a board of twelve members selected by the state agricultural society. Its tuition was to be "forever free to pupils of this State." It was to conduct a long term from April to October and a short term from December to February, and its course of study was to include such subjects as "Animal and Vegetable Anatomy and Physiology," Veterinary Art, Chemistry, Natural Philosophy, and Mineralogy. Each student was to perform not less than three hours of manual labor a day.[55]

Stevens lost no time in raising money by popular subscription to buy a half section of land for the college, and on the eve of the Civil War he reported that ten thousand dollars had been subscribed for a building.[56] Unfortunately for the plan, the Civil War delayed the project, though the state in 1861 gave about five thousand acres of swamp land in McLeod County to the college.[57] And the grant offered in the Morrill Act of 1862 was accepted by Minnesota the following year, the state choosing to take land instead of scrip.

Matters then rested until near the close of the Civil War, when, in 1865, the backers of the Glencoe college secured an act from the state legislature approving the Glencoe site for an experimental farm and an agricultural college and declaring that the "design" of the college was to fulfill the conditions of the Morrill Act. A great many new details were added, such as the inclusion of additional college subjects — among them entomology, horticulture, and rural and household economy — and the setting up of a new "Agricultural College Board," which included the president of the agricultural society but provided for the election of four board members by the legislature. One of the principal provisions of the act was to allot to the Glencoe college the interest of all moneys derived from the sale of the Morrill Act lands; and the legislature also appropriated five thousand dollars for the college from the state treasury.[58]

The stage seemingly was set for the emergence of a real agricultural college at Glencoe, unconnected with the University of Minnesota. And yet the Glencoe supporters failed to turn the dream into actuality. Time passed by, and when in

1868 the university once more was reorganized, provision was made for an agricultural college as a part of the university and for the transfer of the Morrill benefits to the university. Perhaps, as Dr. Folwell suggests, the fact that Old Main could accommodate agricultural as well as other students had something to do with "smothering" Glencoe; but his most interesting explanation of the change in the drift of events is that John H. Stevens tired of Glencoe and returned to Minneapolis, where for many years he was "the most conspicuous citizen" of the community. He ceased to be a Glencoe promoter.

Other circumstances undoubtedly influenced the outcome: the plain fact that order was being created out of the chaos of university finances, the opening of a new preparatory school as an augur that college work was not far away, the argument of simple, good sense against two separate institutions, and the efforts of John S. Pillsbury, who was sharply opposed to presenting the Morrill funds to Glencoe. Pillsbury and his fellow regents in 1867 urged the legislature to add the Morrill grant to the university. They pointed out the value of one strong institution in preference to "two or more weak and sickly ones" which might never reach a standard higher than that of a "third-rate college." They also emphasized the advantages of an agricultural school within reach and "not separated and at a distance from the University." [59]

Their argument prevailed, and Glencoe disappeared from the college picture, no doubt comforted by the allocation of the swamp lands to Stevens Seminary at Glencoe.[60]

Thus the road was cleared for the agricultural college of the university, but it proved long and winding despite some fairly ambitious beginnings in the 1860s. As early as 1867 the regents bought ninety-six acres of land for an experimental farm "a quarter of a mile east from the University," and more land was soon added — steps doubtless influenced by the Morrill Act, which made provision for the setting up of experimental farms. When the university was opened in 1869, a professor of agriculture was appointed — D. A. Robertson, one of the founders of the state horticultural society — but, though he delivered a series of lectures on agriculture, few if any students enrolled in regular classes under him and he soon resigned. The lands for the experimental farm, purchased for $8500, were ultimately platted and sold in 1882 for $150,000. Then a new site was secured some three miles away, and this was the beginning of the modern university's St. Paul campus, where in 1888 the School of Agriculture opened.[61]

THE UNIVERSITY OPENS

When the regents presented their annual report to the legislature of 1868, the outlook for the university seemed bright. Most of the indebtedness piled up in the 1850s had been extinguished; Old Main had been repaired in 1867; the preparatory school had opened that autumn; Pillsbury and his two colleagues had accomplished the purposes for which they had been named sole regents; and they now proposed that the board should be reorganized.

Their recommendation was carried out in an act approved on February 18, 1868. This law, following a recommendation made by Pillsbury and his associates, provided for a board of nine regents, including the governor and the state superintendent of public instruction ex officio, with the other seven appointed by the governor, "by and with the advice and consent of the senate." Two of the regents thus appointed were to hold office for one year only, two for two years, and three for three years. Their successors were to be appointed for three-year terms.

The law stated that the university should establish five or more departments: elementary instruction; science, literature, and the arts; agriculture and the mechanic arts, including military tactics; law; and medicine. Among the powers authorized to the board of regents was that of electing a president — the name *chancellor* was abandoned — of the university. The idea of endowments for professorships, elaborated in the law of 1860, was also included in the new act, but in more conservative form. Any person or persons who contributed not less than fifteen thousand dollars was accorded the privilege of endowing a professorship, "the name and object of which shall be designated by the Board of Regents." [62]

This act set the stage for the opening of the university. The board as appointed by the governor included the three previous regents, Pillsbury, Nicols, and Merriman, with the addition of Sibley, R. S. Donaldson of Farmington, A. A. Harwood of Owatonna, and E. J. Thompson of Chatfield. William R. Marshall, one of the original regents of 1851, was now governor of the state and therefore served as a regent ex officio, as did Mark H. Dunnell, the superintendent of public instruction. Pillsbury was chosen president of the board.

When this board presented its first report, on December 22, 1868, it gave its attention largely to the preparatory department, then flourishing in its second year under the direction of Washburn with 109 pupils enrolled, including fifteen in a newly instituted agricultural course. The board reported that it would be necessary to open the university proper at the beginning of the next "college year" in order to meet the needs of classes completing their preparatory work and of students "applying for instruction in regular college studies." It was expected that the experimental farm would soon be in operation. Though the university's debts had been largely cleared away, land sales were still too few to provide an adequate operating budget. Nevertheless the board expressed the hope that a "lack of accessible funds" would not mar the "fair beginning of a career" that they believed would prove "an unending honor and a public beneficence" to Minnesota. [63]

The plans for opening college classes on September 15, 1869, were matured, but the first president, William Watts Folwell, arrived only in the nick of time — in fact, on the very day classes convened. The regents, thanks to the interest of a classmate of Folwell, an Episcopal minister in St. Anthony named George Leonard Chase, had learned of his qualifications and invited him to visit the university. They first elected him professor of mathematics, but this position he declined. Several other candidates were under consideration for the presidency, and it was not until August 23 that the board agreed to choose Folwell for that position. He at once accepted.

Folwell, then thirty-six years old, was versatile, resourceful in ideas, already rich in study and experience, and sharply interested in "certain long-cherished ideas about higher education," notably the idea that in a later time came to be known as the junior college. He was born on a farm in Romulus, New York, in 1833, and among sights familiar to him as a boy were bake-oven, smokehouse, leach tub, barn, and pigpen. Graduating from Hobart College in 1857 as valedictorian of his class, in the summer of 1860 he went to Europe, where he studied philology in the University of Berlin. Alert and curious, he interested himself, among other things, in the great German museums. On occasion he met notable scholars, among them Jakob Grimm, whom he described as the "father of the fathers of modern philology."

After his Berlin studies Folwell made the "grand tour," visiting Athens, Salamis, Marathon, Mycenae, Olympia, Delphi, Naples, Rome, Florence, Zurich, and other European cities. Watching a sunset from the Acropolis he wrote, "It is no wonder that the arts flourished under such a sky and in the midst of such scenery." But in the same letter, written to his mother, he voiced impatience that he had not yet launched his career. "Twenty eight! And nothing done," he exclaimed.

On his return to America he found the Civil War under way and promptly enlisted as an officer of engineers. He served for three and a half years in the Army of the Potomac, rising to the brevet rank of lieutenant colonel. After the war he first worked in the flour milling business and then, in 1868, took a position as professor of mathematics and civil engineering in Kenyon College, Ohio. Here the regents, looking for the first president of the University of Minnesota, found him.[64]

So, on September 15, Folwell and his wife and children arrived at St. Anthony, were bundled into a two-seated surrey, and rode to their temporary quarters. The daily paper a few days after his arrival carried an editorial pointing to the university as "the very Pharos or beacon light" of the Minnesota system of education. It urged "every lad in the State" ambitious for the future to "keep his eye steadily fixed on this noble institution of learning." [65]

Only two and a half months after his arrival, Folwell wrote his first report as president.[66] A freshman class of fourteen young men had enrolled, and there were 154 pupils in the preparatory department. Including the president and Robertson, the professor of agriculture, there were nine faculty members: Gabriel Campbell in moral and intellectual philosophy and German; Edward H. Twining in chemistry, natural sciences, and French; Versal J. Walker in Latin; Jabez Brooks in Greek; Aris B. Donaldson in rhetoric and English literature; Major General R. W. Johnson in military science; and Arthur Beardsley in mathematics and industrial drawing. President Folwell himself taught algebra and "elocution."

In his first report Folwell expressed the hope that soon the university would not be obliged to give preparatory training to so many of its students, that this basic task would be assumed by the high schools in the towns and cities of Minnesota — augur of an interest on his part that was destined to play a large role in the development of high schools in the state. He had in fact already recommended to the superintendent of public instruction a plan looking toward the advance of high school education.

Folwell had interested himself also in the matter of defining the powers of president and faculty in the government of the university and said, "The University Faculty should share both in the responsibility of the government and the conduct of it." Enlargement and rearrangement of Old Main were needed; the university grounds should be improved and decorated; the library must be built up; scientific and literary journals should be secured for the reading room; employment should be offered students on the university grounds and farm; a fireproof safe must be secured for university records; and a bell and a regulating clock were indispensable needs. These were some of the early considerations that engaged his attention. "The University of Minnesota may now at length be announced as on foot," he said.

The regents, presenting their report to the legislature, announced the election of Folwell and described him as "a gentleman of large and varied attainments." They too pointed to the library: the faculty had drawn up a list of books that would cost from two to three thousand dollars and were "absolutely indispensable." The first gift of any size to the university library consisted of some seventy volumes from the Minnesota Historical Society, a collection including *Peruvian Antiquities, Discoveries among the Ruins of Nineveh and Babylon,* and volume two of Davidson's *Virgil.*[67]

The regents also reported that more land had been added to the experimental farm and everything was in readiness for instruction in agriculture — in fact, that department would flourish "as soon as the farmers send us a sufficient number of their sons." Military training, required under the Morrill Act, had been given an impetus by supplies of arms, equipment, and cannon furnished by the state. The regents were worried about the roof of Old Main, built of tin and now "giving evidence of failure." It had withstood storms, said the regents, for upwards of twelve years.[68]

The regents did not detail an elaborate plan of university organization they had adopted in the spring of 1869, a plan Folwell says he did not learn of until sixty years later. Had he known of it, he says, he might not have proposed his junior college plan, might instead have been "content to let the institution run along in the old American way, leaving educational reforms to come along later." The regents' plan "contemplated two years of general cultural studies, to be followed by departmental courses selected by students." In agriculture and the mechanic arts, for example, the plan looked to two years of general training akin to that in the scientific program of the arts college, followed by two years of special studies in agriculture, mechanical engineering, mining and metallurgy, civil engineering, chemistry and mineralogy, natural history and geology. There were to be both resident and nonresident professors, the latter including, it is interesting to note, one for architecture. One of the regents' concepts has a distinctly modern ring: the university professor was not to give all his time to teaching — some part of each day was to be devoted to research.[69]

A PROPHET SPEAKS

One of the academic traditions of the university world is the inauguration of a president, amid pomp and circumstance, with an inaugural address as its climax. There was little academic pageantry, however, in old St. Anthony when William Watts Folwell delivered his inaugural address on December 22, 1869.[70]

The inauguration was held in a crowded room on the third floor of Old Main, the only building of the university, with John S. Pillsbury presiding. It came at the end of the first quarter of the first college year. The collegiate student body boasted only fourteen freshmen students, and the faculty, including the president, numbered only nine members. The address, moreover, was delivered not only in a frontier area but also in a pioneer and formative period of American state education and indeed of American higher education in general. Only two months earlier a new voice had been raised in the East when a man named Charles W. Eliot was inaugurated president of Harvard.

It is in this setting, local and national, that the educational

statesmanship of Folwell, viewed across the gulf of many decades, must be judged prophetic and realistic. He was no
dreamer of idle dreams. His spirit, as a later president said,
"was possessed with the future, not as a dream or a mirage,
but as a realizable reality." His address is one of the major
educational state papers of America and deserves a recognition
that has not yet been accorded it by the historians of higher
education.

Folwell's concept of a true university was a "federation of
schools . . . embracing potentially all subjects of human and
practical interest; teaching always with reference to principles; occupying ever an attitude of investigation; knowing
no favorite studies, at all times imbued with the scientific
spirit." That, he said, "is the University." Science, he believed,
is the "informing spirit which is to give life to the limbs and
elements of the University." The university is no "overgrown
college." The university professor is "first of all a teacher,"
but he is also "a scholar and an investigator," and "no mere
scientific showman."

Folwell interpreted the university in its relation to the needs
of society. In words not without point today, though uttered
only a few years after the close of the Civil War, he said that
Americans found themselves "mere empirics and journeymen
at handling the terrible social problems which the war, the
migration of races, and the sudden growth of great cities"
were thrusting upon them. "We need," he said, "to put a
solider basis of science not only under the technical arts and
learned professions but under commerce, government, and
social relations."

Advocating education in agriculture and the professions, he
also underlined the importance of the humanities, which,
he said, "enfold the nature of man, and his relations." As to
history, he declared that we "do not cling to the past in order
to reproduce it, but because we cannot spare its lessons. . . .
Unhappy will that nation be which cuts itself off from the

past. As well might a seaman throw overboard his compass and charts, and resolve to steer his ship by chalk marks on her taffrail." Language he saw as the "key and entrance" to history and literature, and he included ancient and modern languages, and "last, but not least, our own peerless, cosmopolitan English." His thought was never far from the people, and in "higher education, generous culture, scholarship, literature" he found forces that "inform, inspire, and elevate communities."

He challenged the value of study as discipline only, saying, "I would never compel a boy or girl to drudge and agonize over any study as a mere gymnastic." As to professional, and particularly agricultural, education, he counseled patience, reminding his audience that "Rome was not built in a day" and that such education, "a novel kind of academic work," could not be "brought to perfection in this new State, in any short period." The university, in his view, should be open to all "worthy comers." "It knows not male nor female, 'Barbarian, Scythian, bond nor free.'" The university was to be the "head and crown" of the school system, "sending her life-giving influence to its remotest fibres." He anticipated the modern junior college by advocating a plan that would keep young people in high schools or academies "until a point somewhere near the end of the sophomore year."

Folwell's mind flashed out to many potentialities far in advance of his own day. He asked for a museum of history, natural history, and art, not "as a curiosity shop," but as "the perfection and climax of object-teaching." All universities, he believed, ultimately would have departments of public health. He foresaw the need of training experts in legislation and the administration of public affairs. He called for a state geological survey, including botany and entomology. He envisioned research as one of the great functions of a university and gave an illustration that will interest particularly the scholars of horticulture who in our own day have developed the Haraldsen apple. He said that "if the expenditure of say $20,000 could result in discovering but one species of apple, sure to thrive in Minnesota, no one would call that money ill spent."

He also wanted a university observatory and prophesied that the time would come when the university astronomer, using the telegraph lines, would "drop a signal ball, daily at noon, atop of every court house and public building in the state." He put his finger on a great library as one of the paramount needs of the university. "Next to the instruction," he said, "the library is the great interest of the university." "To such a library as will some day exist here," he said, "can resort not only the scholar, and the learned author, but the historian, the statistician, the legislator, the editor, the manufacturer, and the inventor, to consult those works which are beyond reach of private means."

Throughout his address Folwell drove home the view that no university worthy of the name could be developed "without the interest, and co-operation of the *people* of this state." The university, he believed, was "not merely from the people, but for the people." At the time Folwell spoke the state had set aside only a few thousand dollars for the institution, but the young president looked to state support in terms of millions of dollars and boldly announced, "The state must endow the university, and if the state will have the university in its full proportions, let her first count the cost, and take the *million for her unit.*"

Folwell looked to the future. "Ours," he said, "is the hopeful toil of the sower, not the consummate fruition of the harvest." He had a sense of the fundamental nature of the educational pioneering in which he and his associates were engaged. "We found the American University," he declared, "with a double purpose; the increase of material wealth and comfort, and the culture and satisfaction of the spirit." How long his view was is indicated by a striking phrase: "We thank God for foundations now laid here which may endure to the end of the world, to the blessing and upbuilding of all the generations which shall follow ours."

Folwell liked to describe his junior college proposal as the "Minnesota Plan." Though officially adopted by the regents in 1870, this plan was too far ahead of its time for early realization, both because of the absence of any well-developed high school system and because of the weight of academic tradition. It existed on paper for some years, but it was in effect set aside by the regents in the very year of its adoption, when the faculty, by a majority of four to three, opposed it and the regents sustained the majority after a hearing in which the president argued the case at great length. Folwell himself, many years later, termed his own plan a "premature romance," [71] but he also recognized that education, a long generation after he made his proposal, was beginning to take the romance seriously. Willis Mason West, the historian, has said that Folwell's presentation of the junior college plan in his inaugural address was "the first public proposal of the kind in America." [72]

In the perspective of history it is fair to say that the real "Minnesota Plan" was not the junior college proposal, but rather the total modern conception of a state university that Folwell outlined in 1869. A contemporary newspaper described the inaugural address as "a masterly effort, which enchained the attention of the audience for more than an hour and a half." [73] Perhaps few realized that it would also enchain the attention of a much larger audience, unborn when its words were uttered.

Step by step the University of Minnesota has moved in the direction marked out by its first president. Of Folwell himself it may be said, looking back to his fifteen-year presidency, that he was more a prophet and originator of educational ideas than an administrator able to give "hands and feet" to the plans he conceived. One thing is certain: he challenged his own university, his state, and American education by formulating a comprehensive, modern charter of state university ideas and potential services. To have done this, and to have done it at the very outset of the University of Minnesota as a functioning institution, was no small achievement.

PAST IS PROLOGUE

That December day of 1869, when Folwell read his inaugural address, was at once a day of anticipation and a day when dreams, hopes, and plans came to fruition.

For eighteen years men had talked, planned, and worked to create a university. The pathway to its creation had been marked by charters, land grants, preparatory schools, an empty Old Main, bond issues, debts, panic, intricate financial tangles, frustration and disappointment, legislative reorganization, constitution making, town rivalries, Civil War, and an expansion of Minnesota's population from a scant six thousand to more than four hundred thousand. These and many other factors played their parts in the story, but the principal forces at work were ideas, men, and their will to bring into existence a functioning university, from Ramsey, Neill, and North to Pillsbury, Marshall, and Folwell. That will was achieved in 1869.

Eighteen years of effort, frustration, delay, and determination were the prologue to the opening of the university and the inaugural address of William Watts Folwell. The address he delivered in Old Main, with its ideas and vision oriented to a far future, was the prologue to the shaping of the University of Minnesota into one of the great universities of America and the world.

NOTES

[1] Wilfred Shaw, *The University of Michigan*, ch. 2 (New York, 1920); *Records of the University of Michigan, 1817–1837* (Ann Arbor, Michigan, 1935); C. W. Butterfield, *History of the University of Wisconsin from Its First Organization to 1879* (Madison, Wisconsin, 1879); *Session Laws of Iowa*, 1846, 188–89.

[2] President R. C. Hutchison of Lafayette College informs me in a letter dated February 13, 1948, that Ramsey was enrolled in that college in 1834–35,

was a member of the Franklin Literary Society and of the Phi Delta Theta fraternity, and in 1865 was awarded the honorary degree of Master of Arts.

³ Lotus D. Coffman, "Founders of the University of Minnesota," *Minnesota Alumni Weekly*, 31:411–12 (April 23, 1932).

⁴ *Journal of the House of Representatives*, 2nd Session, 1851, 33.

⁵ *Laws and Regulations Governing the University of Minnesota*, 75–77 (Minneapolis, 1920).

⁶ *Ibid.*, 1–2.

⁷ Le Duc's letter is in the Sibley Papers, Minnesota Historical Society, St. Paul.

⁸ On December 11, 1850, B. B. Meeker wrote Sibley about the Fort Snelling Military Reserve. "Go in for selling to the highest bidder," he wrote, "and get an appropriation of the money to endow and found there an University for the Territory." Samuel Thatcher, Jr., signed a petition dated December 20, 1850, requesting the sale of the military reserve at public auction, the chief part of the proceeds to be used for endowing and establishing a "University of learning." These documents are in the Sibley Papers.

⁹ Ramsey Papers, Minnesota Historical Society.

¹⁰ The role of Le Duc in the founding of the university has come to light through an examination of the unpublished correspondence of Sibley. Gideon Ives sketches Le Duc's career in the *Minnesota History Bulletin*, 3:57–65 (May 1919).

¹¹ *Journal of the House of Representatives*, 2nd Session, 69–71.

¹² *Session Laws of Minnesota*, 1851, ch. 3, p. 9; *Laws and Regulations Governing the University of Minnesota*, 202–6.

¹³ An early form of the bill "For an Act to Incorporate the University of Minnesota" has the following preamble: "Whereas, The cultivation of learning is one of the first dictates of enlightened patriotism, and indispensable to the success of free government; And Whereas in the establishment of a new State, intelligence should increase with its prosperity, and its wisdom be commensurate with its power; And Whereas, it is highly important to commence at an early day, the foundations of THE UNIVERSITY OF MINNESOTA, that it may grow with the increase of our population, and furnish the youth of our Territory the means of education . . ." A copy is in the state archives, preserved by the Minnesota Historical Society.

¹⁴ Such as the requirement of reports to the legislature, a clause declaring that seven members shall constitute a quorum of the board, and another stating that the legislature may at any time alter, amend, modify, or repeal the act.

¹⁵ Various dates have been suggested and used as marking the founding of the university, but in 1939 the board of regents officially and correctly designated February 25 as the date. The board's resolution states "That February 25, 1851, be and now is specified as the date of the founding of the University of Minnesota and shall be so stated on all occasions and in all instances that require an indication of the founding date." Board of Regents, *Minutes*, 1939–40, October 14, 1939, p. 149. Dr. Folwell, in an address delivered in 1924 on "Granting Our Charter," says simply that the university was established on February 25, 1851, "and it has never been disestablished." *Minnesota Alumni Weekly*, 23:336–38 (February 14, 1924).

¹⁶ The text of the Michigan charter is in *Session Laws of Michigan*, 1937, 102–6; see also Shaw, *University of Michigan*, 17–18.

[17] In quoting this section, I use the text as given by William Anderson in his *History of the Constitution of Minnesota*, 234, which differs in eight particulars from the text in the university's compilation entitled *Laws and Regulations Governing the University of Minnesota*, 206 — two differences in words (*unto* instead of *into* and *hereafter* instead of *hereinafter*) and six in punctuation and capitalization.

[18] William W. Folwell, *A History of Minnesota*, 4:126–34 (4 vols. St. Paul, 1922–30).

[19] *Minnesota Democrat*, March 18, 1851; *Minnesota Pioneer*, March 6, 1851.

[20] Typewritten copies of all the reports of the board of regents for the period from 1852 to 1860 are available in the archives division of the University of Minnesota library and in the office of the Dean of the Graduate School. These copies were prepared by E. B. Johnson in 1892. The reports are printed in the official documents of Minnesota for this period, and specific references to their printed form may be found in Esther Jerabek, *A Bibliography of Minnesota Territorial Documents*, 35 (St. Paul, 1936).

[21] The additional five regents were J. W. Furber, Henry M. Rice, C. K. Smith, A. Van Vorhes, and N. C. D. Taylor.

[22] See *St. Anthony Express*, November 15, 1851.

[23] This encyclopedia is mentioned in the *Second Annual Report of the Board of Regents*, dealing with affairs in 1852. The report indicated that the Smithsonian Institution had forwarded several volumes of its *Contributions* to St. Louis "subject to the order of the University." The secretary adds that these volumes "will probably come to hand on the opening of navigation in the spring."

[24] The territorial legislature on February 28, 1856, authorized the regents to issue bonds to the amount of $15,000 — $10,000 for building and $5000 to pay debts. *Laws and Regulations Governing the University of Minnesota*, 77–78.

[25] *Minnesota Alumni Weekly*, February 14, 1924.

[26] *Laws and Regulations Governing the University of Minnesota*, 2–3.

[27] A valuable discussion of "Federal Land Grants for the Support of Universities" constitutes chapter 3 of Matthias N. Orfield, *Federal Land Grants to the States with Special Reference to Minnesota* (Minneapolis, 1915). He also deals in detail with the "Early Finances of the University and the University Lands," pp. 245–55.

[28] Folwell discusses "The Double University Land Grant" in his *History of Minnesota*, 4:97–103.

[29] Discussion of the University of Minnesota may be found in *The Debates and Proceedings of the Minnesota Constitutional Convention* (Democratic), 454–60 (St. Paul, 1857) and *Debates and Proceedings of the Minnesota Constitutional Convention* (Republican), 477–503 (St. Paul, 1857).

[30] No evidence has been found to substantiate this statement, but the regents were doubtless aware of the fact that many communities in the 1850s had university and college ambitions. In the territorial legislature in 1857, for example, six colleges and universities, not to speak of a similar number of seminaries and academies, were incorporated. They included Fremont City University of Minnesota, Hastings University, Hobart University, Cedar Valley University, Lake University, and a college at Excelsior. *Session Laws of the Territory of Minnesota*, 8th Session, January 7, 1857.

[31] *Debates and Proceedings of the Minnesota Constitutional Convention* (Republican), 489.

[32] Dr. Neill's letter urging the second grant is printed in full in the *First Annual Report of the Board of Regents of the State University to the Legislature of Minnesota*, Session of 1861, 20–21 (St. Paul, 1861).

[33] Folwell, *History of Minnesota*, 4:97–103. The "right side" meant in this case federal support translated ultimately into money that played its part in building a permanent University Fund that by 1948 exceeded twenty million dollars. The wording of the enabling act, for which Rice was responsible, and the vigorous championing of the double claim by Neill in 1860 were crucial to the success of the cause.

[34] Hellen D. Asher, "A Frontier College of the Middle West: Hamline University, 1854–69," *Minnesota History*, 9:363–78 (December 1928).

[35] *Laws and Regulations Governing the University of Minnesota*, 78–79.

[36] *Report of the Standing Committees of the Senate and House of Representatives on the Subject of the University and University Lands* (St. Paul, 1860). The report is signed by David Heaton and J. F. Baldwin, members of the senate, and by Orange Walker, G. W. Greene, L. H. Garrard, and A. M. Hayes, members of the house. Dr. Neill states that it was written largely by himself. See *History of Minnesota*, 634 (4th ed. Minneapolis, 1882). This volume contains several interesting documents of early university history, including a letter of February 25, 1861, from Neill to Ramsey, in which Neill tendered his resignation as chancellor, pp. 642–43.

[37] *Board of Regents Report*, Session of 1861, 9.

[38] *Laws and Regulations Governing the University of Minnesota*, 206–11.

[39] *Board of Regents Report*, Session of 1861, 18. The university has the manuscript minutes of the board of regents beginning with the meeting held on April 5, 1860. The minutes in photostated form are in the archives division of the university library. The first volume, including 101 pages, runs from 1860 to 1868. The next volume, beginning after the reorganization of the university in 1868, runs to 1887.

[40] *Third Annual Report of the Board of Regents of the State University to the Legislature of Minnesota*, Session of 1863, 5 (St. Paul, 1863); *Laws of Minnesota*, 1862, Special, ch. 87, sec. 1.

[41] *Laws and Regulations Governing the University of Minnesota*, 211–15.

[42] John S. Pillsbury, *An Address Delivered before the Alumni of the University of Minnesota, June 1st, 1893, A Sketch of the Growth and Development of the University for the Thirty Years in Which He Has Been a Regent*, 22–23 (n.d., n.p.).

[43] *Annual Report of the Board of Regents of the State University to the Legislature of Minnesota*, Session of 1867, 3–7 (St. Paul, 1867). See also John B. Gilfillan, *University of Minnesota*, 26–27 (Austin, Minnesota, n.d.). Gilfillan's paper, delivered as an address before the Minnesota Historical Society in January 1906, is a useful review of the history of the university in its earlier years. An excellent interpretation of the early development of the university is given by Fred B. Snyder in his address, "The Beginning of the University," delivered on Founders' Day, April 21, 1932, and published in the *Minnesota Alumni Weekly*, 31:409 (April 23, 1932). Incisive characterizations of early leaders of the university are given in Guy Stanton Ford, "*The Making of the University: An Unorthodox Report*" (Minneapolis, 1940).

[44] *Board of Regents Report*, Session of 1867, 7.

[45] Pillsbury, *An Address*, 15–16.

[46] E. B. Johnson, ed., *Forty Years of the University of Minnesota*, 28 (Minneapolis, 1910).

[47] The affairs of the university during 1867 and 1868 are fully covered by the board of regents in the annual reports for those two years, published respectively in 1868 and 1869.

[48] University of Minnesota, *Catalogue of the Preparatory Department for the Year 1867–68* (St. Anthony, Minnesota, August 1868). A copy of this, the first catalogue of the University of Minnesota, is in the archives division of the university library.

[49] W. W. Washburn, "Report of Principal of the University of Minnesota," *Annual Report of the Board of Regents of the University of Minnesota, to the Governor of Minnesota, for the Year 1868*, 17–31 (St. Paul, 1869).

[50] W. S. Pardee, "Swaddling Days," *Minnesota Alumni Weekly*, 20:5 (March 24, 1921).

[51] See articles on "Land Grants for Education" and "Morrill Act" in *Dictionary of American History*, 3:236; 4:27 (New York, 1940).

[52] The text of the Morrill Act is in *Laws and Regulations Governing the University of Minnesota*, 5–9. See Earle D. Ross, *Democracy's College: The Land-Grant Movement in the Formative Stage* (Ames, Iowa, 1942).

[53] George M. Stephenson, *The Political History of the Public Lands from 1840 to 1862*, 244 (Boston, 1917).

[54] An excellent account of the beginnings of "The Agricultural College of Minnesota" is Folwell, *History of Minnesota*, 4:77–85, with full citation of sources used.

[55] *Minnesota General Laws*, 1858, 42–45.

[56] Darwin S. Hall and R. I. Holcombe, *History of the Minnesota State Agricultural Society*, 54, 65, 66 (St. Paul, 1910).

[57] This was a singularly wise decision, for the states that received scrip fared ill in ultimate benefits. The idea of scrip was that states which did not have within their own borders enough public land to meet the terms of the grant could take scrip and trade it for lands elsewhere. Scrip opened the gates to speculation. Illinois, using scrip, realized $319,494 from 480,000 acres, and Pennsylvania salvaged only $439,186 from 780,000 acres. Minnesota actually got less than a sixth as much land as Pennsylvania, but realized $563,183. Had Pennsylvania done as well, it would have received considerably more than three million dollars instead of less than a half million. Folwell, *History of Minnesota*, 4:82n; "Land Scrip," *Dictionary of American History*, 3:238.

[58] Folwell, *History of Minnesota*, 4:82–83; *Minnesota General Laws*, 1865, 26–31.

[59] *Board of Regents Report*, Session of 1868, 6; see also Pillsbury, *An Address*, 19–21; Folwell, *History of Minnesota*, 4:83–85.

[60] An act of March 6, 1868, established Stevens Seminary and endowed it with 4684 acres of swamp land.

[61] *Board of Regents Report for 1868*, 9; Johnson, *Forty Years of the University of Minnesota*, 30–31.

[62] For further provisions in the act of 1868, see its text as published in *Laws and Regulations Governing the University of Minnesota*, 215–20.

[63] *Board of Regents Report for 1868*, 14. An interesting broadside bearing

the title *Announcement for 1869* describes the three terms, or quarters, for the university year and sets forth the details of the classical and scientific courses planned for college work.

[64] This brief section is based mainly upon Solon J. Buck, ed., *William Watts Folwell, The Autobiography and Letters of a Pioneer of Culture* (Minneapolis, 1933).

[65] *Minneapolis Daily Tribune*, September 18, 1869.

[66] *Annual Report of the Board of Regents of the University of Minnesota, to the Governor of Minnesota, for the Fiscal Year Ending November 30, 1869,* 17-31.

[67] Theodore C. Blegen, "The Minnesota Historical Society and the University of Minnesota," *Minnesota History*, 23:1-10 (March 1942).

[68] *Board of Regents Report for Fiscal Year Ending November 30, 1869,* 5-14.

[69] Folwell, *History of Minnesota*, 4:60-65.

[70] *Addresses at the Inauguration of William W. Folwell as President of the University of Minnesota* (Minneapolis, 1870). Dr. Folwell's inaugural address is reprinted in his *University Addresses*, 1-76 (Minneapolis, 1909). Much interest is added because Dr. Folwell interlards many comments on the address as viewed by him with the perspective of forty years.

[71] *History of Minnesota*, 4:67.

[72] Johnson, *Forty Years of the University of Minnesota*, 37.

[73] *Minneapolis Daily Tribune*, December 24, 1869.

Westward
in a Covered Wagon

THE covered-wagon heroine has been honored in novels and poems, romance has been woven about her, and Hollywood has projected an aura of glamor about her. But when one turns to her own day-by-day record, the worn diary in which she herself told her story, the heroism, romance, and glamor, if present, are not given much emphasis.

Instead, one finds the homely detail of everyday living on the westward trail. No matter what the changing circumstances of wind and weather, health or sickness, joy or sorrow, food must be prepared, dishes washed, beds made, clothes washed. Such episodes fall into their place in the larger picture, with no dramatic or melodramatic exaggeration. On the other hand, the larger picture, with its vivid detail put in unpretentious language, is perhaps not less impressive than the pictures drawn by the novelists, poets, and makers of cinemas.

Here is a diary kept by a woman, Jane M. Grout, in 1873 on a covered-wagon journey from central Wisconsin to southwestern Minnesota. No love scenes by moonlight, no attacks by Indians, no intrigues, no shooting, no murder or violence, no lost treasures are described; the narrative is one of real life, real people, genuine events, and the story is the story of millions of Americans.

Competently Mrs. Grout does the job of providing as much comfort as possible for her family despite the handicaps of primitive pioneer travel. Not for her the conveniences of the modern housewife on wheels—the trailer equipped with refrigerator and gas range, the trailer camp supplied with laundry facilities. Instead, she reports that four days out on their journey she and her family camped near a house and she "Baked some beans and sponged bread"—and the next day she continues, "Camped for dinner near the house of Mr. Goodenough where I baked my bread that I sponged last night." One entry begins, "Arose about four o-clock but did not get started until seven." Such a delay is understandable in the light of another entry: "We arose in good season, cooked our breakfast by the road side. . . . After our usual work of dishwashing and packing we started off." And another: "Libbie and I went to washing and washed about nine hours before we could get through the pile of dirty clothes."

A certain quiet humor creeps into Mrs. Grout's account of the hardships and annoyances of the journey: "We slept nicely until about two o-clock when an ambitious whip-poor-will succeeded in waking us. The birds sang so among the trees we could sleep no more." Another morning, "We got up early and got started about half past six, cheered on by the music of the hungry mosquitoes." Again, "We . . . cooked our breakfast by the road side. The hogs showed their appreciation of victuals by taking a ball of butter out of my basket." At one stop they took dinner at the home of a cousin: "It seemed a luxury to have our dinner . . . cooked without ashes or sand in it."

That humor was an asset to the party is clear enough when one reads about laborious travel over roads made all but impassable by rains and through sloughs and across swollen streams and rivers. Near the close of the story Mrs. Grout comments dryly on the day's travel: "The sluey places were only wet not miry." Another time she tells that after more than five hours of work getting their wagons across the Little Sioux River, the ladies of the covered wagon "put on some old dresses and all went bathing, so that we had some sport as well as a good deal of work in this river."

As the diary proceeds detail is piled on detail — a runaway, illness and recovery after homely therapies, visits with friends and relatives, preaching services on Sundays, a musical evening enlivened by the strains of an accordion, impressions of the country that evoked the comment, "the farther we go the better I like it," and an occasional dissonant note, such as the diarist's remark after she and her friends had viewed a sod house: "We were none of us charmed."

After Mrs. Grout reached the end of the trail, she put the covered-wagon diary away and did not look at it again until fifty-four years had passed. Then she read it and added a few comments from the vantage point of more than half a century. What she said then is almost an epitome of America. She looked back proudly on the early beginnings of Luverne, Minnesota, the little village to which she went in 1873. And she contemplated serenely the handiwork of the pioneer generation, who had built "a beautiful thriving little Rail Road city and the entire broad prairie of beautiful Agricultural Rock County, dotted all over with fine houses and barns." She took note also of many neighboring villages and of the schools that were built in all of them. "Every family of our Emigrant train," she wrote, "has high school graduates and college graduates among their children and grandchildren."

JANE GROUT'S DIARY, 1873

Thursday May the 15th 1873. Left our old home about nine o-clock accompanied by Br. John. Sad at parting with old neighbors. Reaching Father Henton's at the next town we concluded to lighten our load by taking out the bureaux, one chest, and several farming tools, we then packed up again. Father Henton's folks having very kindly prepared dinner for us we partook and about one o-clock started on our journey again. We stopped at Rio to see some friends but did not find them at home. We reached Wyocena about five o-clock, where we parted with Br. John and Father Henton (who had accompanied his son), they returning home. We traveled about two miles farther where we found a nice camping ground and put up for the night. It seemed some like camp-meeting. We slept nicely until about two o-clock when an ambitious whip-poor-will succeeded in waking us. The birds sang so among the trees we could sleep no more.

We lost our canary bird before we reached Wyocena and John took the cage home to Jessie.

Friday May the 16th 1873. Arose early, prepared our break-fast. Family worship conducted by Sister Henton. Had a call from the lad who had provided us with the necessary accommodations for the night. We then moved on toward Portage. Just as we reached Portage Mrs. James (Henton's Sister) missed her pocket book containing twenty dollars. We all halted and Br. Henton took one horse and went back in search. Providentially he only had to go about half a mile before he found it in the road. In the midst of the city we found E. H. Bronson and family and Orvie Taylor waiting to join our company. We camped for dinner about a mile out of Portage. This afternoon our road has laid along the Wisconsin river. The river is dotted with rafts of lumber. The scenery quite varied and beautiful. Cherry trees in bloom. Commenced looking for a camping place about four o-clock, but traveled until seven before we could find hay and a barn to put up our teams. Camped about thirteen miles from Portage on the river. The wind blew quite hard while we were preparing supper and we looked for rain.

Saturday May 17th 1873. We did not get to rest very early last night, but slept nicely while we did sleep, all except E. H. B.'s family who had not got things very well arranged yet. We set our tables around the camp fire for breakfast and then had family worship. Scripture read by Orvie Taylor, prayer by G. Henton.

We started on our journey about eight o-clock. Reached Delton where the scenery is beautiful and winter greens plenty — a distance of about six miles. About ten o-clock stopped awhile in town. Drove out about two miles and camped for dinner, near an English family. Started out again about half past one. Drove out about three miles, when little Beauty (the pet dog) being out to play and run, was run over by the loaded team and died in a few minutes. The children all cried bitterly, and felt very sad all the afternoon. They carried him along to our camping ground and there buried him. We camped about four o-clock to prepare for sabbath. The men got some boards and crotches and built a table large enough for the whole company and then drove down some crotches for a fire place, and when our supper was ready and we surrounded the table one would think of campmeeting.

Sunday May 18th. We all breakfasted together, then cleared away our work and dressed ourselves and sat down for bible class. Then about half past twelve went about getting dinner. After which some of us climbed a bluff about 100 feet high to write some letters. I wrote one to Cousin Eunice. We were called down to prayer meeting, Mr. Bancroft the man with whom we stopped joining us.

At five o-clock we went to the school house near by to sabbath school. The school was not very large. The Supt. quite energetic and seemingly a good man. There was a bible class which we joined. E. H. B. was invited to take charge of it and did so. We came back to camp, took a lunch and went to bed.

Monday May 19th. We arose early, prepared our morning meal, packed up, bid our kind host Mr. Bancroft adieu and resumed our journey in good season. Did not see anything very beautiful until we had traveled near ten miles when we came to a beautiful spring near the road, stored up and water conducted into a large trough near the road. The country is very hilly and sandy. About this time it began to rain. We traveled about five miles in the rain passing many majestic looking bluffs reminding one of pictures of ancient ruins. We camped about twelve o-clock where we could get the horses under shelter and ourselves also out of the rain, and called for dinner. Accommodations very good. The rain did not cease, so we spent the afteroon very pleasantly at Mr. Davidson's. Some of us took supper with him and E. H. B.'s family. Orvie Taylor, Elsie and Mrs. James lodged in their house. Baked some beans and sponged bread.

Tuesday May 20th 1873. It rained most all night, but our family slept in our wagons and did not get wet any. We all took breakfast at Davidsons. Our bills quite light. No charge to E. H. B. because he was a minister. Reached Mauston before noon. Mailed some letters, bought some feed for the teams &c then drove out six miles and a half and camped for dinner near the house of Mr. Goodenough where I baked my bread that I sponged last night. We cooked our dinner by the road side washed up our dishes and packed up to start. Just then quite a company of Indians came up with ponies well loaded. My team was afraid of them and had to be led past. Both of our teams acted badly as we came along past the cars.

About nine miles from Mauston is a tastey looking village by the name of Lisbon, on the Lemonweir river, a sawmill doing considerable business. We drove out about five miles farther (passing a little place called Orange) and then finding good hay we camped for the night, at about half past five o-clock.

Wednesday May 21st. We arose in good season. Cooked our breakfast by the road side. The hogs showed their appreciation of victuals by taking a ball of butter out of my basket. Reading of scripture and prayer by Mrs. James. After our usual work of dishwashing and packing we started off. Hiram Trip's train passing just before for Augusta. After traveling out two or three miles we came to the junction (Camp Douglass) of the two rail roads M. & St. P. and West Wisc. near which are some of the most magnificent bluffs I have yet seen surrounded by pines. We passed near one I should think to be 150 feet high. Thadeus is abed in the wagon sick, was sick most of the night. The day is a beautiful one but the country through which we pass is poor. Now and then a tamarack swamp. The pines are small but now and then we find a decent farm with good buildings. We camped about twelve after driving over nine miles of sandy and rough roads. Found a well of soft water. Cooked dinner and did some washing.

Reached Tomah about five o-clock after riding some ways in a very hard rain. They run the wagons under the shed and put the horses in the barn at the Grant house. Walked out, all looked at the town in the evening.

May 22nd 1873. Thursday half past eight. We drove out a few miles and got breakfast and fed our teams. Before breakfast was quite done it commenced raining so we ate in our wagons and taking our family in the light travelling wagon started for Sparta a distance of twenty miles to visit brother Albert Ingalls. It rained very hard for about an hour and then cleared up. We passed the dividing ridge through which a tunnel eighty rods long is dug for the cars to pass through. Next of note was a little place by the name of Lafayatte in which was a steam saw mill. In the suburbs of Sparta was a little place called Angelos.

We reached brother's home about one o-clock, feeling sadly disappointed at finding him absent. We had an excellent visit with his wife and her brother Mr. Lockwood. About six o-clock our company drove up and camped near brothers on the green. In the evening Mrs. James, Mr. Lockwood, Fannie, Ammie and I took a stroll around the City. First we visited the Artesian well with a fountain situated in the Courthouse yard, then another Artesian well in the park. Sparta is beautiful.

May 23rd 1873. Friday. The morning was beautiful. Our Co. breakfasted early and started off for Lacross. We stayed behind to prolong our visit. I did some washing and cooked some beans to take on the road. After dinner we took our leave of brother's family and started on expecting to camp with our Co. tonight. We found the roads good and the country very pretty. Out about ten miles from Sparta to our left is a pretty little village by the name of Bangor nestled among the hills. Out three miles farther another village by the name of Salem on the rail road, very thrifty looking with three nice little churches. We overtook our Co. seven miles from Lacross. Went on a few miles farther and all camped on Black river, purposing to get an early start in the morning so as to cross the Mississippi in the first boat.

Saturday May 24th 1873. We were all awakened about four o-clock by G. H. Henton. Prepared ourselves as soon as possible and went into Lacross, a distance of about three miles. Stopped in town to get our mail and some bread. Rode five miles on the Mississippi, landed a few minutes after nine on the Minn. shore. Lacrescent is a little village not far from where we landed. We found the country very hilly after we left the river for about fifteen miles. We climbed one fearful hill, it seemed nearly a mile from the bottom to the top. In this region there was no wells. Cistern water scarce and at noon we had to buy water for our teams and for cooking. We were obliged to travel late at night before we could find water and hay and grain for our teams, but finally we got in with a Baptist man where the accommodations were good. A nice little grove back in his field, with a well near by. The young men brought out an accordeon and entertained us finely with music in the evening. We are so nicely situated for the sabbath we think it is a blessing from the hand of our Father.

Sabbath May the 25 1873. When we awoke this morning it was raining quite hard. We all lay quietly and sensibly and snoozed until the rain was over and then got up about eight o-clock. It cleared off and we had a beautiful day. In the afternoon we had a good prayer and conference meeting, sev-

eral of the neighbors coming in and taking part with us. We
then got our second meal and after that I wrote to Br. Milo's
folks and Br. Albert's folks. Thadeus wrote to Str. and Aunt J.
The company all wrote letters home. We then had family
worship and retired to our wagons, some to write a little more,
others to talk a little, others to sleep.

Monday 26th. Arose about four o-clock. Got ready to start
on our journey about seven. Passed some very pretty country
before noon, but no market very near. Came across a young
man who was out to Rock Co. last spring and made a claim
six miles south of Luverne. Bought some potatoes of him.
Camped about noon having traveled about fifteen miles. The
country we passed over in the afternoon was equally as good
as that in the A. M. except around a little village called Bush
creek which was very hilly and stony. When near this village
it began to rain and rained harder and harder until it almost
poured down, but it cleared off in a little while. We drove a
few miles farther and camped with a big farmer who had big
barns and good conveniences for keeping travelers. They were
very kind and accommodating to us. Their name is Patterson
and their farm six miles from St. Charles.

Tuesday 27th of May 1873. We rested well last night, all
slept in our wagons except Mrs. James and Libbie. We cooked
our breakfast in the house. Had family worship by our
wagons, reached St. Charles about ten o-clock and Mrs. Henton and Mrs. James left our train and took the cars for
Rochester to visit some friends. After we left St. C. we found
the deepest mud we have yet seen. Passed through a little village called Dover. Camped about twelve o-clock and cooked
dinner and I baked bread. It commenced raining about the
time we were ready to start and rained furiously. We found
the worst roads I ever saw, no exceptions. We passed one little
village this afternoon. The country is really beautiful through
which we have passed today. Got the privilege of camping in
a grove on the farm of a young man by the name of Pitcher.

It was a pretty place. We traveled about twenty-five miles today.

Wednesday May 28th 1873. Did not get a very early start this morning. Were up quite late last night cooking meat and sauce. Reached Rochester between nine and ten o-clock and mailed some letters, bought bread &c. G. H. Henton here left us, joined his family and went to visit his brother who lives out ten miles from Rochester. We met his brother after we left him. We find the roads very bad. Camped about half past eleven under a pretty line of willows. In the afternoon we found a beautiful country but bad roads as before. One curiosity between Rochester and Mantorville which is a big stone perhaps 15 feet high and no other stone to be seen anywhere. We also met with an accident. Got into a bad place in a slue and broke a whiffletree.

About ten miles from Rochester up on the prairie to our left stood a little village called Byron. Very good buildings around here surrounded by the white willow in almost every case. This is all the timber you will see in going from Rochester to Mantorville, a distance of seventeen miles, except when within three miles of Mantorville we came to a beautiful piece of oak timber in which we camped for night. Traveled about twenty miles.

Thursday May 29th 1873. Last night it rained terribly, but we all slept in our wagons and did not get wet. We did not get a very early start in the morning as it was very wet and some rainy. We reached Mantorville middle of forenoon while it was raining. Stopped and got some bread and enquired the way to Andrew Curtis' whose residence we reached about eleven o-clock, where we were all taken in and hospitably entertained. The weather was cold and we felt thankful to get in by the fire.

Cousin Esther in tears told us of her recent affliction in the loss of her darling little baby nine and a half months old. At times she receives it as from her Father's hand for her good, then again she murmurs and thinks it so hard. Soon comes in Cousin Ella Snyder with her two little ones who I have not seen since she was five years old. I did not know that she lived so near to Esther. Esther got us a good nice dinner. It seemed a luxury to have our dinner in the house and cooked without ashes or sand in it. Libbie and I washed considerable in the afternoon. It did not rain. Esther is anxious that we all stay over until Monday hoping the mud will be dried up. The report is that the slues ahead of us are impassable. Think we shall accept their invitation to stay over sabbath.

Friday May 30, 1873. Esther and Ella lodged us all in their houses except Orvie Taylor who slept in one of the wagons. We rested nicely. This morning we prepared and Esther and her husband, Ella, Libbie, Thadeus, Fannie and I and some of our little ones went over to Cousin Milton Green's about two miles. Had not seen Milton since he was fourteen years old. He is a large fleshy man, no traces of the boy Milton in his looks except when he laughs. He has a wife and three children. What changes twenty years make. Thadeus had taken cold and toward night was quite sick. About six oclock we all prepared to go back to Esther's, but Milton came in and said I must take off my things as Thadeus and I were not going. We stay and the others go back. Thadeus feels badly.

Saturday May 31, 1873. We had a good night's rest, breakfast at six and a quarter o-clock. Thadeus does not feel any better this morning. Cousin Milton made Thadeus a pair of whiffletrees and then took us back to Cousin Esther's. Thadeus then felt so bad that I went to work and gave him a good thorough sweat with hot corn. Br. E. H. B. treated him with quinine powders. We had promised a visit to an old acquaintance this afternoon, N. Grems, and Thadeus felt a little better and thought we had better go and leave him in the care of Grandma Curtis. Esther, Andrew and I went and had a pleasant visit with the old gentleman and his maiden daughter who seem to be very happy in each other's society. His farm is beautiful, the prairie and heavy timber meeting on it. A good house and splendid spring as ever graced a farm. When we returned we found T. P. better. Libbie and I ironed until quite late. Libbie and Elsie have been at work hard all day. Orvie took Fannie and Ida over to Uncle Nick's after we came back to stay all night. Charley Cowan came down from Owatonna this afternoon. I have not seen him before since he was about five years old.

Sunday June 1st 1873. This morning was warm and pleasant. Ammie and Johnie went to sabbath school. Thadeus felt some better and he and Eddie went to Mantorville to church and brought Mrs. Bata back with them. Uncle Nick Grems and Cornelia came over about noon to bring Ida and Fannie back and to see how Thadeus got along. Milton and wife also came over toward night as he felt alarmed about Thadeus last night. Mrs. Bata stayed all night. It has not been as quiet a sabbath as I could wish.

Monday June 2nd 1873. We arose in good season and although rainy made preparations to start on our journey. Our things were badly scattered so that it took us some time to get ready. Ella Snyder and Charley Cowan are going with us up to Owatonna. We bade adieu to our friends and started off. Traveling over very pretty country but the worst of roads as we soon reached places where there had been heavy showers. Traveled about ten miles and then camped for dinner. About the time we were ready to start it began to rain and the roads were very bad. We had to double our teams to get through the slues. E. H. B.'s team got stuck in a slue just before dinner. We camped quite early. Got our supper and I arranged so as to lodge Charley Cowan and Ella and her two children.

Tuesday June 3rd 1873. We had a very hard rain last night and it rained this morning so that we took a lunch in our wagons and did not try to cook breakfast. Old Rover feels so sober after laying out in the rain that we cannot get him to even wag his tail. It is the most lonesome and tedious day we have yet seen. We took a lunch for dinner and as it still rained we got the privilege of going into the house, we cooked our supper indoors. E. H. B. brought in his bed but the rest slept out in our wagons. Charley Cowan made up his mind to leave us and take the cars at Claremount a distance of five miles. I made biscuit for supper and after supper fried a mess of cake. Our hearts were made to rejoice about six o-clock by the king of day making his appearance.

Wednesday 4th of June 1873. I never felt more thankful to see the sunshine than I did this morning. We cooked our breakfast indoors, prepared ourselves and started off. The weather fine. The roads very bad. We reached Rice Lake a distance of about four miles and found Charley Cowan awaiting us to lighten our loads. He took off several trunks and passengers and although the roads were very bad we reached Cousin Charley's in Owatonna very comfortably at about five o-clock with no accident except one of our horses getting badly corked. Cousin Charley's wife was ready to receive us, and we tired, hungry and muddy were grateful for their kind hospitality. Soon Cousin Althera and husband who live near by came over to see us, and invited us over to visit her. Cousin Ella and children and Elsie went home with her to spend the night.

Thursday June 5. 1873. E. H. B.'s family, Orvie Taylor and our family breakfasted with Cousin Charley Cowan and then went over to Althera's to make a forenoon visit. Cousin Ella Snyder was there, we had a pleasant time. After dinner we took our leave of them and in company of two other cousins started for Aunt Jemima's who had cordially invited us. We had not got far from Owatonna before it began to rain and rained very very hard for about an hour, and the roads were awful. We reached and greeted our Uncle and Aunt about five o-clock. Found Aunt in very poor health but glad to see us.

Friday June 6th 1873. We arose at the call of breakfast and after prayers Libbie and I went to washing and washed about nine hours before we could get through the pile of dirty clothes. Elsie baked a large amount of bread, and she and Fannie ironed some.

Saturday June 7th 1873. After breakfast and prayers Libbie, Elsie and I went to ironing and did not get through until most night. Auntie and hired girl and Fannie tended to the work. The men got ready for threshing in the forenoon and in the afternoon finished up Uncle's threshing which was left on account of the Epizootic among the horses last fall. About five o-clock we were gladdened by the arrival of G. H. Henton's family who left our train at Rochester. They had much to tell us of their perils in mud and slues.

Sunday June 8th 1873. Last night it rained again very hard. We have had no rain for two days. This morning it is pleasant but the wind blows very hard. We got ready to go and hear Nelsen Liscomb preach. (An old acquaintance.) But were too late, and the neighbors invited E. H. B. to preach in some of their houses. It was decided that he should preach here at Uncle's at five o-clock. We had a good congregation and a good sermon. At the close prayer by T. P. and G. H. H. It seems more like Sunday to have preaching.

Monday June 9th 1873. It rained hard most all night and some this morning. We did not resume our journey until after dinner. Romey piloted us out several miles and carried some of our luggage. When out about eight miles from Uncle's and within one mile of a village named Wilton we met with a sad accident. Our heavy loaded team leading the way got into a very bad slue and got down. E. H. B. quickly unhitched his team from his wagon and went to the rescue, letting his team stand alone a few moments. They took fright at the floundering of our team in the slue and ran away. They ran some ways and then came back to the wagons, just hitting H. Henton's team and rushing past a buggy where Elsie was standing, knocked her over and ran over her. She got up alone, walked a few steps and then sank down again. We thought her hip or back broken. We took her up and put her on a bed in the wagon. Then she had a piercing pain in her side. We bathed her in strong camphor and thought to have a doctor see her at W. but before we reached there she felt so much better she would not have a Dr. We camped at Wilton and got her a bed in the hotel. We bathed her with Arnica and got her in bed feeling quite comfortable.

Tuesday June 10th. The morning is gloriously bright, the night moonlit and cool, well calculated for tired ones to rest and those thrown into nervous headache by yesterday's accident are healed. Elsie walked from the hotel over to the wagons before we got our breakfast ready. Feels sore and bad with quite a hard headache but is much better than it seemed possible she could be when we think of those horses running directly over her. God has seemed to care for us all through our journey.

We started off again about half past eight, traveling over a very level tract of country new because owned by speculators. We found many wet slues. Camped about noon, cooked dinner in a little house (paddie house) started again about two o-clock, getting out on a prairie all boundless except at a great distance off on one side a little crooked piece of timber. Here we came in contact with the Little Cobb river and soon after crossing E. H. B. got his horses down in a soft miry place and had to take them off and put them on the back end of the wagon and draw it out. E. H. B. left one chain and had to go back after it. After going a mile or so farther we crossed another stream along which were many mounds supposed to be an Indian burying place. We forded another stream. E. H. B. got stuck again toward night. We found bad slues. Camped about seven, in front of a man's house under some nice cotton woods of about nine years growth. We got a bed for Elsie in the house. She has felt pretty bad today.

June 11th Wednesday. Arose about four o-clock but we

did not get started until seven. Found the roads improving in
the beautiful sunshine which has blest us since Monday and
yet some very bad places. Today we see timber which follows
the Big Cob river. We do not see timber only along the rivers.
Camped about noon with a sabbath school Supt. of the M. E.
Church. Had a very nice place to set tables among the willows
and cooked dinner in the house. This camping place was about
two miles west of Minnesota Lake, a small village on the lake.

We found the roads worse in the afternoon having often to
double teams. Thadeus and H. Henton went off the road to
look at a cow they wished to buy and got into a bad slue with
the light wagon. Then toward night we crossed a nice high
prairie near Delevan and then a large marsh. G. H. Henton
got his team in badly and the others had work to get through.
It was so late we had to camp as soon as we came to a house.
The first house we came to was a Methodist preacher's. They
took Elsie in and did all they could for us. Their name was
Mock. E. H. B.'s left us this P. M. and went on to Winnebago
City to visit some friends.

Thursday June 12th 1873. This morning we cooked breakfast in the house with the minister's family and all went in to
attend prayers. We expect to renew our pleasant acquaintance
ere long as Br. Mock goes onto a claim near Worthington this
fall. As we got into our wagons and turned our horses to the
road we saw the cars for the first time this week. They were
passing through Delevan, a nice litle prairie town. Just before
noon Orvie got his team down in a slue. We have had to
double our teams several times. We were welcomed into a
Baptist minister's house to cook and eat our dinner on his
table.

After dinner we pushed on to Winnebago City finding several places we could not get through very easy. Winnebago is
a nice enterprizing looking place. Good buildings and in good
repair. We were made glad by letters from Brs. Eli and Cyrus
Henton at this place. Leaving W. City we passed through a

nice piece of timber in which lays the Blue Earth river which we crossed on a ferry boat. We camped with the ferryman near by. It rained very hard for an hour after we camped. Elsie took a bed in the house, and in the evening she fainted away and did not come to herself in some minutes. We thought her dead. But she came out of it and rested well all night.

Friday June 13th 1873. It is bright and pleasant this morning since the shower of last evening. Elsie feels better this morning, but is not very well. We did not get started until half past eight this morning, we took Mr. Case' daughter along with us a mile to school. We drove out a mile or two and came to the farm of one of our old neighbors, Capt. Huntington. We had to double up our teams twice before dinner and yet the roads have been better than heretofore. We camped and cooked dinner with a lady by the name of Vanbanklinburg. While we were eating E. H. B.'s folks drove up having left us at Winnebago.

Soon after we started out again one team got stuck in a slue. Since then it has been good roads a few rods and then a *comfortable* slue. We can see ponds on this prairie all around, more in this (Martin) county than in Faribault I think, but F. county is more miry. We traveled along by or near Elm creek about eight miles and then at night camped on the bank of it. The men turned the horses out to graze but in a little while they were frightened by a dog and ran off. The men had a *gay* time getting them again.

Saturday June 14th 1873. We got up early and got started about half past six, cheered on by the music of the hungry mosquitoes. In the forenoon we had very good roads. The sluey places were only wet not miry. We camped again at noon on the Elm creek, cooked our dinner in a kind lady's house whose husband was Justice. In the P. M. we traveled quite fast over good roads, until at night we came to a bad place where the water covered the ground. Our team got a little out of the road and got in. We have traveled all day out of sight of trees except along Elm creek. They are setting little slips around their sod houses. This afternoon we came to a sod house and all got out and went in to see how it looked. We were none of us charmed however, I think.

Orvie is quite sick, we feel considerably alarmed about him. It appeared very much like a hard storm and we camped near a small frame house which looks rare, for many miles surrounded as it is by little sod ones. We are thankful to get shelter and wood and milk and oats and all we *really* need out on this almost wild prairie tonight.

June 15th Sunday 1873. Orvie Taylor is better this morning. Also Elsie is doing well I think, but little Eddie Bronson is badly broken out with erysipelas and feels very bad. We see other Emigrants camped off at a distance for sabbath. Some of them have been over here and say they have no wood. We feel very thankful that we are so comfortably situated. The storm that threatened with such violence as to make us fear for our safety, was not permitted to reach us. Truly goodness and mercy have followed us. The family with which we are stopping are from Sweden. They are Christians. We went in this morning and had prayers in the house. They have no children of their own but a little adopted girl who is very smart and polite. We got a lunch for dinner and had a bible class and class meeting. Had some singing by the Swedes, cooked supper and then had some singing by our own company.

June 16th Monday 1873. Got up before four o-clock, cooked our breakfast in the house. Prayers conducted by G. H. Henton. We did not get started until seven and half o-clock. The country looks better as we advance, though not a tree to be seen of any size. We see more frame houses than sod. When within about five miles of Jackson we met the grasshoppers which are coming from the west where they have done much damage.

Just at the foot of a steep hill lies Jackson on the Des Moines river, a little sprightly looking village with a nice court house. We drove through the village and camped for dinner on the banks of the De. M. When out on the prairie again we could see three trains of Emigrants besides our own, one train of eleven teams. The country is very pretty, the roads are very good excepting some bad slues. We camped ten miles out of Jackson at what is called the ten mile house. Libbie has been very sick this P. M. Nellie's eyes are very bad. Orvie does not get well yet. Elsie is very faint and tired. Every night it is hard to keep her from fainting away some times.

Tuesday June 17th 1873. G. H. Henton called us up about three o-clock. We built a camp fire and cooked our breakfast. Prayer by T. P. Grout. We started off about half past six, reached the Little Sioux in an hour and did not get our teams all across until noon. We camped on the bank and got dinner and washed our dishes and then put on some old dresses and all went in bathing, so that we had some sport as well as a good deal of work in this river. A good number of teams crossed the river while we were camped. It is a difficult place. When out four miles from the river G. H. Henton learned that he had forgotten his chain and had to go back. We went on, leaving him the light wagon. We had several small streams to cross, and in crossing one R. P. broke his evener. While fixing up G. H. overtook. We drove until after sundown and then camped within two miles of Worthington. We did not build a fire but ate bread and milk for supper. We heard the whistle of the cars tonight again, it seemed like the voice of an old friend.

Wednesday June 18th 1873. Started out about seven o-clock. Soon reached Worthington, a lively village out on the wild prairie of two years growth. The wild grass growing right up around the houses. Our train stopped some time at Worthington to get supplies and as we sat in our wagons a gentleman came up to enquire about another emigrant train, who taught the Milford school in Jeff. Co. Wis. last winter. He said Alice Ingalls, my niece, went to school to him. I like the country around Worthington very much but the farther we go the better I like it. We camped for dinner fifteen miles from Worthington at the halfway house.

After dinner we traveled about four miles when we came to the Kanaranza, a beautiful stream with a hard pebble bottom, quite a treat after ploughing slues to ford it. After crossing the Kanaranza the country is perfectly beautiful. We found when out seven miles from the Kanaranza that G. H. had lost his dog. So we went back after it about two miles. Could hear from it but could not find it. The rest went on and we overtook them at Luverne. We crossed the Rock river in boats at Luverne but the teams came through without any trouble. We found Br. Eli, Jennie Grout and Abbie waiting for us on the other side to welcome us. *Our* family went on to Eli's, E. H. B.'s to Uncle William's, G. H. Hentons to Cyrus Henton's. We got to Luverne about sundown and did not get to Eli's until after dark. It seemed an awful long five miles. There we rested for the night. Our trail ended.

ADDENDA OF JUNE 18, 1927

On June 18, 1873, we ended our quest or trail at a place where a few energetic business men had taken up government land and platted out a town in village lots. Here we were welcomed and my husband was offered two of those lots if he would build on them and start a Sunday School. This he did, as he was a *Sunday School man*. As we had a Methodist Minister, Rev. E. H. Bronson and family in our Emigrant train, we soon started religious services in one of the little sod houses and soon organized a Society.

Just a few years and a church Edifice was planned. My husband was made chairman of the building committee and helped push it through.

It was not long before our Rev. E. H. Bronson was sent us from the M. E. Conference to serve our organization as Pastor. Educational interests were also given attention and a nice two story school building erected.

I am now eighty-seven years old and have seen Luverne — the end of our trail — grow into a beautiful thriving little Rail Road city and the entire broad prairie of beautiful Agricultural Rock County, dotted all over with fine houses and barns, surrounded by groves which have become useful for not only their lovely shade, but an *occasional* stick of timber. Also many thriving villages have grown up with their necessary high school buildings; which have been liberally patronized. Every family of our Emigrant train has high school graduates and college graduates among their children and grandchildren.

MRS. T. P. GROUT

On our wagon trip from Wisconsin over here to Minnesota I picked up a *Cast off Composition Book* and wrote each day — what we saw and did — for my own amusement and to tell my friends when I wrote to them — never thinking to keep the record all these years — but the younger members of our Emigrant train have asked for it, and have typed it to keep for themselves, even tho' it was not in very good condition.

My own daughter — who was then only five years old — can remember enough of the trip that she wants to reserve the Original for her own.

MRS. T. P. GROUT

Pioneers
of the Second Line

Hɪɢʜ honor has been paid in America to the pioneers of the successive wests that reached from the Atlantic to the Pacific – the pioneers who explored unknown land, turned untouched sod, built wilderness cabins, raised up cities, and blazed trails for coming generations. These conquerors of the frontier were "giants in the earth," and they have been so recognized by historians, poets, and novelists.

In recognizing the pioneer contribution we not only do what is just and proper, but also serve a need of our own day: the need of understanding the roots of American society nourished by the humus and the flowing springs of our civilization, the need of history and tradition to bind together past and future.

Yet in the cultivation of our common history, we have paid less heed to a second line of pioneers than we have to the first. The pioneer tradition was kept fresh and alive because, on the heels of the men of the land frontier, we had a second line of pioneers who explored frontiers of transition in American living and devised new ways of meeting the problems of a changing society.

One finds such pioneers in all the regions of America, but the Middle West seems to have been blessed in peculiar degree with folk of this stamp. They appear in virtually every field of advance – in medicine and public health, in conservation, in education, art and music, social legislation and public welfare, and other domains.

When Minnesota's forests of white pine were falling, Christopher Columbus Andrews, whose very name was prophetic, sounded, in advance of the thought of his own generation, a clear call for conservation. In 1869 President Grant chose this man, a Civil War officer, as United States Minister to Sweden and Norway. As he traveled about Sweden, Andrews noticed something curious and interesting: checkerboard patches of forest, with trees in different stages of growth. What did they mean? Simply that Sweden had solved the central problem of forest conservation with a scheme for cutting each year an amount of timber not exceeding the annual forest growth. A tree lover, this American saw in the Swedish plan the secret of perpetual forests.

When at the end of the Grant regime Andrews was retired from diplomacy, he became a preacher of planned conservation not only in his own state but throughout the country. Use and save the forests at one and the same time, he urged. Make them perennial, clothe wastelands, never let the annual harvest exceed the annual growth. His own crusade was reenforced by the efforts of the Minnesota Horticultural Society, which in the 1870s advocated tree planting and forest protection. This was social vision, social pioneering. To an unheeding generation the society drove home the truth that the forests were not inexhaustible. But progress was slow, and it was not until 1892 that a political party — the Populists — ventured to come out for genuine forest conservation.

In the 1890s calamity reenforced preaching. In the dry summer of 1894 a hurricane of fire roared down upon the Minnesota village of Hinckley and burned nearly two hundred people to death. Only nine days before that fire Andrews had delivered an address in Brooklyn entitled "The Prevention of Forest Fires." Preaching and calamity together led to the appointment of a chief fire warden and by successive steps to a forestry board, a forestry service, and a conservation commission. True conservation was under way. Society was catching up with its prophets.

The pioneer of public health did not bear the name of the discoverer of America, but no less than Andrews he had the pioneering spirit. Dr. Charles N. Hewitt succeeded in getting a state board of health established in Minnesota as early as 1872. He held the first professorship of public health in an American university, established in Minnesota in 1874. And in the mid-eighties he started a magazine called *Public Health*. For a quarter of a century he fought for public health reforms in the face of what Dr. William Watts Folwell has called "general ignorance, professional indifference, and legislative parsimony."

Being men of "hope and forward-looking minds," the Doctors Mayo and their pioneer father turned a "little town on the edge of nowhere" into "one of the world's greatest medical centers." They were of the breed of the second line of pioneers, these frontier surgeons who pioneered medical cooperation in solving the problems of disease and of a vast medical practice, graduate education in clinical medicine, the integration of experiment with experiment, scientific communication, and hospital and medical administration based upon the concept of service to people.

In the domain of public charities, of caring for the sick and unfortunate and the mental and moral cripples of modern society, a Minnesota village minister named Hastings H. Hart, beginning in 1883, laid the foundations for today's state government Divisions of Social Welfare and Public Institutions and pioneered an enlightened approach to one of the most perplexing of human problems. Similarly in the 1880s and 1890s LeGrand Powers pioneered the field of state intervention in behalf of better conditions for labor and industry, calling as early as 1891 for a law that Minnesota actually passed twenty-three years later — a workmen's compensation act. Not infrequently one finds, in tracing the course of social progress, a lag of from twenty to thirty years between original idea and popular acceptance and practice.

In the 1890s a university professor, Theophilus L. Haecker, drawing inspiration from the cooperative efforts of Danish immigrants, was an early advocate in Minnesota and the Middle West of the agricultural cooperative movement which has become so notable a phase of the economic and social life of state and region.

A third-party political leader, the volatile and eloquent Ignatius Donnelly, led in the 1870s the Granger struggle for state regulation of railways, advocated in the 1880s such a daring and radical reform as the establishment of a state railroad and warehouse commission, and to the end of his life, notwithstanding defeat and frustration, pioneered in political thinking. Occasionally he went beyond the boundaries even of later acceptance, but in the main he crusaded for reforms that time has shifted from the category of the radical to that of the conservative.

These men and others of their kind were, like Ibsen's Brand, in league with the future. Out of their thinking and planning came many of the effective institutions and practices of contemporary life. Sometimes they were not understood or appreciated by their contemporaries, but later decades have recognized in them trail blazers of modern assumptions and a new age.

In this company of pioneers of the second line appears an American landscape architect named Horace William Shaler Cleveland, whose ideas and career invite somewhat more detailed analysis and comment. He was a national figure, for he served as a pioneering architect of landscape and of parks and playgrounds not only in Minneapolis and St. Paul, which he liked to refer to as the "United Cities," but in the Middle West generally, the East, and the South. His designs are written permanently into Roger Williams Park in Providence, the grounds around Natural Bridge in Virginia, and the Jekyll Island winter resort in Georgia.

Everywhere Cleveland preached and practiced doctrines that were in league with our own day. He detested tawdry display and "blind adherence to geometric rules." To him landscape gardening was no merely decorative art, but an "adaptation of natural features to the necessities of human occupation" and use. The destruction of natural beauty and its replacement by artificial beauty seemed to him to be a denial both of taste and of common sense. And he saw the importance of planning and carrying out plans early, while man, as he said, "is moulding the earth's surface to the needs of civilization."

What Cleveland proposed was design "in harmony with the character of the situation," beauty resulting from "the convenient and graceful adaptation of the natural features to the objects of its creation." If he had a sense of mission, it was because he understood that unless the original design achieved such harmony, subsequent decoration could never recapture the beauty lost from the beginning.

Cleveland was a nineteenth-century figure, spanning in his life the period from James Madison and the War of 1812 to William McKinley and the eve of the twentieth century. One can be very certain that no small part of his education stemmed from his parents, New Englanders of deep culture, the father a sea captain and writer, the mother a gentle woman with an abiding interest in schools and schooling. Early education in a classical school presided over by Jared Sparks, historian and later president of Harvard, left marked influences upon Cleveland, as did association, through a kinsman, with Longfellow, Charles Sumner, and other luminaries of Boston who liked to congregate in a society that bore the enigmatic name "Five of Clubs."

But if the boy grew into a man sensitive to all aspects of natural beauty, as he did, it is possible that the beauty of his home community in Massachusetts played a considerable part. Here, in the vicinity of his birthplace, as Cleveland later wrote, the Nashua wound "through the rich meadows as of old." Here "the grand old elms, for which the valley is famous," waved "their gracefully drooping arms." And here "the rounded forms of Wachuset and Watatoc, and the more distant and picturesque outline of the Grand Monadnoc" were "pencilled against the evening sky."

Add to all this a stay in Cuba while his father served as vice-consul there, with a taste of life on a coffee plantation. Add, further, studies in civil engineering, some years of farming, and professional association with such distinguished landscape architects as R. Morris Copeland and Frederick Law Olmsted, and we begin to understand the emergence of this landscape pioneer of wide vision.

Cleveland's connection with the West goes back to as early a date as 1834, when at the age of twenty he visited St. Louis, but it was not until four years after the Civil War that he removed to the West, settling in Chicago. There, in partnership with W. M. R. French, the distinguished civil engineer, he wrote his ideas into Washington and South parks and Drexel Boulevard and into numerous private and public landscape projects elsewhere in Illinois, in Nebraska, where he designed the Omaha park system, in Indiana, where he laid out the Brookside area of Indianapolis, and in Michigan, Kansas, Wisconsin, and Iowa.

Though many think of Cleveland as a Minnesotan, he did not actually move to that state to live until 1886, when he was seventy-two years old. Yet his identification with St. Paul and Minneapolis antedated his residence there by fourteen years, for it was as early as 1872 that he presented a park and boulevard plan to the Common Council of St. Paul. He called for parks at Lakes Como and Phalen, both within the city area, for the preservation of a city lookout upon the Mississippi, for the use of a commanding hill for state buildings in the future, the laying out of spacious radiating avenues, the building of a great, direct interurban street, and the planning of a river boulevard connecting the two cities of St. Paul and Minneapolis, which he foresaw must become virtually one city with time. In accordance with his philosophy, he warned against the spending of money on "artificial decorations" beyond the wants of that time, but he underlined the duty of transmitting to the future "God's gift" of beauty which had been lavished upon the town.

If Cleveland's recommendations of 1872 do not seem remarkable to modern ears, let it be remembered that they were made more than three quarters of a century ago. There was then no public appreciation of parks comparable with that of our day. St. Paul did indeed acquire Como Park one year after Cleveland made his recommendation, but there was much opposition to this forward-looking move, including a public petition against it; and one alderman viewed it as an advantage only to the rich, who could visit the park in carriages.

Minneapolis in 1864 refused an offer of twenty acres in what is now the heart of its southtown, but then was regarded as out in the country. Two years later the Mill City rejected an opportunity to buy all of Nicollet Island, in the Mississippi above the Falls of St. Anthony, for a relatively small sum; and in the 1870s it refused an offer of two hundred and fifty acres around beautiful Lake Harriet for fifty thousand dollars.

Cleveland spoke to a generation that did not see with his own vision what great cities the Twin Cities would become and what a boon parks, wide and beautiful avenues, and convenient playgrounds would prove to them in the future. As he saw the matter, "the wealth of the world" could not buy what he regarded as a "heritage of beauty" to be treasured forever, and that heritage might be lost through failure to act. In one of his letters in the 1870s he uses the phrase: "What we might have done had we taken time by the forelock!"

As his ideas took root in Minnesota, he himself came to feel the attraction of the Twin Cities, and in the 1880s he chose to make his home there; but even before he did so he had been called to advise Minneapolis on parks and boulevards. He was selected by Charles M. Loring, who has been called the "apostle of parks and playgrounds" in Minnesota, but there is evidence that Cleveland and his ideas played no small part in inspiring Loring to advocate a Minneapolis board of park commissioners and to accept its presidency when it was established in 1883. Not the least of Loring's distinctions lay in his choosing as wise and expert an adviser as Cleveland.

The outstanding contribution of the landscape architect in this period was his unremitting advocacy and designing of connecting parkways between the "United Cities," particularly great riverside boulevards and parkways along the Mississippi. In these plans and projects he got stalwart support from Loring and from Joseph A. Wheelock, civic leader of St. Paul, who said of a twin river boulevard, each side duplicating the charms of the other, "There will be nothing like it, or approaching it in beauty, in any other American city."

These men rose above intercity rivalry. To Cleveland the very possibility that such rivalry might stand in the way of the achievement of his dream evoked strong language. If either city along the river failed to "preserve like a jewel in a costly setting" the riverside with its natural features, the citizens of the future, he said, would "bemoan with bitter objurgations the lack of spirit which suffered its counterpart to be destroyed" and "point with scorn at the dismal scene across the river."

To younger men impatient of results that could not be realized until a seemingly remote time, he pointed out that he himself remembered days when cows were pastured on what was now Boston's "beautiful Common and Public Garden."

To the end of his life he held true to his basic principle that "the landscape gardener has no other duty than to serve as the high priest of Nature." He could scarcely find words severe enough for those who would resort "to artificial means of decoration" for the Mississippi itself in its course through the "United Cities." Those "who can see no beauty in Nature," he declared, "till they have washed her face and combed her hair and put her in stays — should be hurled headlong from the precipice whose features they would thus desecrate."

To Cleveland, as indeed to all the pioneers of the second line, one may appropriately apply the famous inscription honoring the builder of St. Paul's: *Si monumentum vis, circumspice.*

North Star Perspective

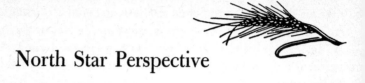

Time is relative, and the people of the Middle West do not accept as fixed and final the connotations, limited to Europe, of such terms as *ancient, medieval,* and *modern.* In the almost incredibly rapid pace of American life such terms are not incongruous in interpreting the backgrounds of states that boast a century of organized political history but actually appear on the historical scene three centuries or more ago. In the perspective of North Star State history, for example, three ages are discernible for which the hallowed tags of Europe may be used, if one so wishes, with entire appropriateness. The first is the age of explorer and fur trader. The second is that of settlement, the age of the pioneer. And the third is the age of Minnesota's growing up — its advance from youth to maturity.

These ages form a true sequence, but no sharp line can be drawn between them. One merges with another, and their problems overlap. The virgin timber of the north woods is gone, but all the iron ore, even that of highest grade, has not yet been dug out of the red-tinted earth and shipped to the steel mills.

In transportation, transition and overlapping are constant. The gallant and picturesque steamboats that graced the Mississippi of old are gone, the railroad system created by giants in the earth like James J. Hill was nearly complete by 1900, and recent decades have seen the development of a vast and intricate highway system. But the prosaic barge is on the scene, each year more streamlined automobiles are omnipresent, trains are like some fantastic dream of only a generation ago, the sky is full of airplanes, and transportation is constantly writing chapters in an unfinished book.

Many large, even imponderable, forces have moved through our history. One is the influence of the physical environment, which ties the present to a prehistoric past dim even in its outlines. The slow-moving glaciers vanished in a bygone age, but their prints are everywhere, in lakes and hills and soil. The iron deposits were laid down in geological time, but dug out by power-driven shovels, they help to explain the Range cities of today, the advance of American industry, aspects of modern education, and some of the cosmopolitan elements in the population of the Upper Midwest.

Man may not do much about the weather, as Mark Twain once intimated, but the climate does much to man. It was the climate that helped to stock Minnesota with muskrat, beaver, and other fur-bearing animals that attracted the French, the English, and the Americans like an irresistible magnet. When the white man came, he used the water highways that time had carved out of the terrain, and time's highways, from south, east, and north, serve our people in modern days of steel fleets on inland seas and of dams and barges on the Father of Waters no less than they did in days of canoes, side-wheelers, and decimated forests fashioned into rafts.

Another long-range factor in our history has been the rubbing of civilization upon the Indian culture. We learned much from the red man in our conquest of the wilderness, but we profoundly changed his way of life as our weapons, utensils, and ideas tore the fabric of his society.

When Radisson arrived in the seventeenth century, he found a people of the late Stone Age living in the north country. But it was not only Radisson and his fellow "Caesars of the wilderness" who challenged the native Sioux of Minnesota. The challenge came also from Algonkian Indians migrating westward — Chippewa who claimed woods and rivers and lakes, Chippewa with powder and shot to enforce their claim. By the middle of the eighteenth century they had pushed the Sioux back into the prairie country, and their stubborn invasion underlay a hatred between the two tribes that was one of the persistent problems of the pioneers.

What a sorry sequel this native chapter of history has! Ramona with a Minnesota setting! We gave the Indians fleeting prosperity, but we broke their old economy. Our implements and trade meant revolution: they disrupted the old balance between population and food supply. The Indian helped us in an international business that reached out to the far markets of Europe and Asia, but the help was a prelude of sad music — a prelude to misery, intemperance, and disease for the red man, overwhelmed by a rolling tide of white population, pushed back and restricted, a forlorn victim of the march of American power.

Errors of the past are now being counterbalanced; the Indians are advancing in the arts of a civilization they did not elect. And meanwhile we cherish their legends, such as that of the maiden who flung herself to death from Maiden Rock on Lake Pepin; their words live in phrases like *Indian summer*, the *pipe of peace*, and *Great Spirit*; Americans use, every day, inventions and adaptations of nature that these children of nature perfected; and they have left a lore of song with an art all its own, as illustrated in these lines from the Sioux:

> The owls hooting softly, the owls hooting low,
> In the passing of the night, the owls hooting low,
> In the gray dawn of the morning, the owls hooting low,
> To whom are they calling, I wish I could know.

Our early age is cosmopolitan, with a succession of French, British, and American control, and the region's harvest of sleek furs explains in large part its place in international politics. The French were long in the land. From Jean Nicolet's day onward they dreamed of finding the Pacific and reaching

Marco Polo's Cathay, but the dream remained a dream, and finally they bowed to the tough-fibered British. Louisiana, including western Minnesota, came under the Spanish flag, and the Upper Midwest on the east side of the great river became British in the 1760s. But if the French regime ended, French influence lingered, for the sons of France brought their language to the northern woods; French chansons were sung on our rivers wherever Frenchmen paddled their canoes; they sprinkled names lavishly on our map; and a French flavor remained in the atmosphere of the North Star State long after the day of the fleur de lis had passed. A century ago, when Minnesota's first newspaper appeared, it sometimes ran a special column in French for readers who could not understand English.

Once the British, a stubborn people, got their hands on Minnesota, they held it with characteristic stubbornness, and for a generation after the American Revolution this region was under the Union Jack. This was the era of the search for the Northwest Passage under Rogers and Carver, and of Peter Pond, the phonetic speller. A new day came in the fur trade, freed of the arbitrary restrictions the French imposed upon it. After the Revolution, the powerful Northwest Company, trading out of Canada, dotted Minnesota with fur-trading posts, chief among them the stockaded post at Grand Portage on the Superior shore. This was the meeting place of East and West in the late eighteenth century, with sleek canoes bringing men and goods out from Montreal and traders and voyageurs and furs in from the wilderness.

Neither the peace of 1783 nor the Louisiana Purchase thirty-five years later shook the British grip on the empire of beaver and muskrat, and it was not until after the War of 1812 that the Americans really took over the Minnesota country.

The foundation factor in Minnesota was the extension of

American civilization to this region and the founding of an American pioneer commonwealth. The British trading posts were merely isles of civilization; the major advance came in the American period. It was consolidated by traders, soldiers, and missionaries, but primarily by settlers — and it was permanent.

Its nucleus was the famous fort established in 1819 at the fork of the Mississippi and Minnesota rivers, first called Fort St. Anthony and then Fort Snelling, built on a site selected fourteen years earlier by Lieutenant Pike, and designed as part of a general plan for frontier defense. One must interpret Fort Snelling in terms, not of gun and sword, but of ax and plow, for it became primarily, not a war center, but the center for the penetration of the region by settlers.

Fort Snelling figured in the history of exploration from Cass to Schoolcraft and Nicollet, and when the steamboat *Virginia*, the *Clermont* of the Upper Mississippi, made its pioneer voyage from St. Louis in 1823, its goal was Fort Snelling. Near the fort, as we have seen, Henry Hastings Sibley, in days of "Early Candlelight," established his headquarters as the agent of the great American Fur Company. To the fort came President Monroe's emissary, Lawrence Taliaferro, who for two decades showed the country that there could be an honest Indian agent. And Fort Snelling was the objective of those caravans of squeaking, large-wheeled carts that followed the Red River trails. It was a center also for the zealous missionaries seeking to convert the Indians to Christianity.

Most important of all, the pioneer settlements of Minnesota clustered beneath the walls of Fort Snelling. If typical Minnesota figures in the 1820s and 1830s were soldiers, fur traders, and missionaries, it remains true that farmers and lumbermen were coming upon the scene. And when in 1837 the government purchased the triangle of land between the St. Croix and the Mississippi, the settlers' advance gathered momentum. But it was the organization of Minnesota Territory in 1849 and the land cession treaties of 1851 that signaled the first real boom in settlement.

The extension of civilization to Minnesota meant much more than a rush of land-hungry people. It meant that farm lands were occupied, towns and cities laid out, back regions filled up. These things, of course. But it also meant streams of social and cultural influences flowing from the East and from Europe. How many and varied the people were! Enterprising Americans from New York, New England, and the Old Northwest; stalwart emigrants from the Scandinavian countries, Germany, the British Isles; and after a while, pulled by farm, lumber camp, mill, mine, and factory, Finns and Poles and Czechs and other nationalities that gave Minnesota's population a cosmopolitan flavor matching that of its earlier history. Minnesota blossomed out as a state in which two thirds of the population was of European blood of the first and second generations. We often think of the pioneer age as an age of institutional beginnings, but many of these beginnings were really transplantations — transfers of culture, institutions, techniques.

A visitor in 1849 was so impressed by the bustle and change and noise and growth of Minnesota that he said "it looks as though Aladdin were here with his wonderful lamp." Territorial government was established and set into motion. Laws were passed; courts organized; local government started; political parties formed. Churches, Catholic and Protestant, were planted, business and social activities multiplied, and a cultural life of surprisingly high level took form. When Ramsey and his associates formed the Minnesota Historical Society, someone exclaimed, "History in a land of yesterday!"

Men were aware that they were building foundations for a great state to come. They worked hard, looked to the future, were independent and self-confident in an unspecialized society, dreamed dreams but were always practical in doing the day's job, were democratic and tolerant, with the door of opportunity open to all, and they planted a pioneering tradition for their successors. This was the spirit, this the temper, of Minnesota as it ran its nine-year territorial course through buoyant boom and panic and depression to statehood in 1858.

Frontier society enjoyed cultural and institutional traffic over bridges with the East, but it was essentially a dynamic society. Old customs and practices were modified by life on the frontier — by its breezy give-and-take, the wide expanse of the country and its newness, the swift change of a territory in which towns sprang up almost literally overnight, and the wide opportunity that offered rich rewards to enterprise.

The equality of the American frontier was potent in shaping a pioneer democratic individualistic society, and it is no chance that that society was expansive and deeply concerned with booming and exploitation. The saga of exploitation includes the lumber industry, which took and used our white pine forests; pioneer farming, which made wheat king; and town building, in which hot speculation and inflation usually were halted by the cold hand of hard times. Modern America sometimes is a hard and cynical critic of the pioneers for their failure to conserve, but it is only fair to remember that they followed the standards of their own time and place. If posterity has paid a price for the pioneers' ruthlessness, we must not forget the great gains in their building of a commonwealth. Nor should we forget the frontier ordeals they met with courage — the ordeals of hardship and panic and disappointment, of prairie fire and blizzard and lonesomeness, of civil war and bloody Indian outbreak.

Here then are two great ages — those of the fur trader and of the pioneer — and they are the background of the third age, that in which the pioneer commonwealth grew up and became modern. Here too one can point to large forces that played into the processes of time and change.

One can now see what the central trend was from Civil War

times to our own day. We changed from a youthful, agrarian, and individualistic society to an adult, integrated, machine-age society, with interdependence assuming major importance. In underlining basic forces at work in the building of Minnesota, however, we must not forget the influence of individuals — of character and personality. Leadership made its impact through pioneer planners like Ramsey and Sibley; industrial captains like James J. Hill and Frederick Weyerhaeuser; educational prophets like Edward D. Neill and William Watts Folwell; political captains like Ignatius Donnelly, Knute Nelson, John Lind, John A. Johnson, Frank B. Kellogg, and Floyd B. Olson; cultural leaders like John S. Pillsbury, Cass Gilbert, Maria Sanford, Oscar Firkins, O. E. Rölvaag, Sinclair Lewis, George E. Vincent; medical and dental men like the Doctors Mayo, Dr. Hewitt, and Dr. Alfred Owre; inspired spiritual leaders like Archbishop Ireland, Bishop Whipple, Georg Sverdrup, and Erik Norelius; and many others in a long and distinguished roll. They have imprinted upon the state's personality a legacy of character, saltiness, and achievement.

But that personality owes even more to thousands upon thousands of unnamed people: the wilderness Marthas who sustained the men of the frontier, the farmers and workers who did the jobs of their day quietly and efficiently, the men of trades and professions and business and enterprise, the men and women of faith and of dreams, the builders of homes and of the web of our social life, the sustaining folk at the roots of our existence.

It is from the people that much of the Minnesota personality has been expressed in such institutions, traditions, and practices as the Norwegian St. Olaf Choir and the sacred songs of hundreds of congregations, the *sokol* of the Bohemians, the *kantele* and *sauna* of the Finns, the Swedish singing societies and Institute of Arts and smorgasbord, the Danish cooperatives and folk high schools, the German *Turners*, the Minneapolis Symphony Orchestra, the sport of skiing, the Minneapolis Institute of Arts, churches and schools and clubs, even our creative literature and arts.

One mark of Minnesota's coming of age is the passing of the frontier. Many forces pushed it beyond the state's boundaries, not least the building of a statewide network of railways. Another was the swarming of people, a tide that increased the population from 200,000 in 1865 to more than 1,300,000 in 1890 — twenty-five years in which the tide swept out over the Red River Valley. Yet another was the basic transition we have described in farming — the transition from exploitive one-crop use of the soil to diversification and scientific methods. That was part of Minnesota's emergence from childhood to adult status.

Still another factor in bringing on the modern age was the rise of industry, the smoke of industrial chimneys, the whir of industrial wheels, the hum of water power. We had a vast business expansion. A mighty flour industry made Minneapolis the "Mill City" and kept abreast of progress in technology so astutely that it won national and world industrial leadership. Lumber enjoyed its golden age and then, after the era of the mythical Paul Bunyan, adapted itself to become a "forest products" industry, alert to the demands of tree farming, conservation, and diversified use.

Seven iron men began to disturb the sleep of the ancient giant Mesabi sprawled in the northern earth, and a majestic iron ore industry developed, with the opened pits of Mesabi lying between the Vermilion Range on the north and the Cuyuna Range on the southwest.

Another giant, labor, shook its limbs and lengthened its stride. The half-dozen unions organized in the 1860s were hard hit by the Panic of 1873, but worker sentiment led to a state federation of labor in 1890, and by 1914 more than four hundred organized labor groups were active in Minnesota.

And towns and cities grew strong, many of them, like Austin, Rochester, and Red Wing, specializing so well that the world, in proof of the Emersonian doctrine, beat paths to their doors. In the Twin Cities a vibrant industrial, financial, and cultural metropolitan center emerged, with a supporting hinterland that stretched far beyond the boundaries of Minnesota, creating an economic state given concrete form when the ninth federal reserve banking district was established.

With the passing of the frontier and the rise of modern industry came a transition in modern social and cultural conditions that touched Minnesota life everywhere. Old institutions continued into the new age, but often their meanings changed as points of view changed, and many new institutions not known to the pioneers sprang up. Education blossomed, expanded, and specialized to serve the needs of the new day, with a great state university, colleges, high schools, and grade schools all playing large roles in both the training of leadership and the democratization of culture.

In music, art, and literature Minnesota began to stand more sturdily on its own feet, producing sculpture, painting, poetry, histories, and novels that contributed to the main stream of American creative effort — incidentally giving the country, in the 1920s, a Nobel Prize winner who found his material in the Main Street of Gopher Prairie and a Norwegian-American author who interpreted with originality and power the saga of *Giants in the Earth.*

A sense of social responsibility went along with increasing maturity. The woman's movement made notable advances. One began to hear new concepts voiced and translated into action: conservation, cooperation, public health, state parks, organized recreation and sport. The cooperative movement, statewide in its support, gave Minnesota a position of national leadership in that important field. State government expanded in scope until it reached and touched the interests of every man at nearly every point. Along a thousand fronts society grappled with the problems of modern living as invention and industry and professional specialization changed that living from simplicity to complexity.

All this does not mean that we created Utopia, though many a Minnesota dreamer, like the brilliant Donnelly, dared to draw blueprints of such a state. But the common sense of Minnesota's citizenship was aware of shadows and unsolved problems, and complacency was not permitted to go unchallenged. Politics tended to lag behind economic and social change and need, but often exhibited ferment and agitation, stimulated both by aggressive leadership in old parties and by the challenges of intermittent agrarian and labor reform movements which made Minnesota in some sense a center for what historians have called the "agrarian crusade."

Perhaps the dreamers of Utopia are less important in the advance of the people than the men and women of research whose patient work beyond established frontiers points the way to better living and better use of the resources of nature in a society far more complex than that of our ancestors. The researchers are in a special sense the pioneers of the modern day. They work in laboratory and in library, in field and in hospital, tackling fundamental problems of knowledge and understanding and the application of discovery to human use. The University of Minnesota is one of the focal points for their researches. Through its constituent colleges and an overall Graduate School, they pass the torch of research skill and training to others.

The scientists of agriculture have ushered in a new day for the farmer, with hybrid corn, a new breed of hog, fights against animal and plant diseases, and scientific approaches to farming along a hundred fronts. Researchers in metals have gone far in the advance toward the use of taconite as the high-grade iron ores near depletion. The men of medicine, working out from a firm base in the sciences that underlie their science, have forwarded understanding, control, and treatment of a wide range of diseases. Chemical and engineering researches have solved hundreds of specific problems that seemed almost insoluble only a generation ago. And alongside the scientists are the people who are exploring the meanings and actualities of things in social, economic, cultural, and intellectual areas, deepening human understanding by their work.

Old frontiers have disappeared, but frontiers of learning no less challenging are a part of the modern scene, with health and happiness and knowledge as the rewards of pioneering.

Ingenuity, technical skill, and enterprise have also marked business and professional leadership in the region. The modern scene bears witness to the quality of that leadership in the remarkable advances of bus and rail transportation, of merchandizing, of business organization, of food processing, and of manufacture in general, with systematic research the modern guide to change.

We often speak of the pioneer ordeal and sometimes forget that there was much happiness and joy among the pioneers, zest in living, and faith that sustained people in hours of trial and suffering. Conversely, if in viewing the modern age we sometimes emphasize too strongly the comforts created by modern technology, we do well to recall that modern Minnesota has had its ordeals too, including two world wars to which its youth marched away with a devotion and patriotism matching that of the pioneer generation, and including also panic and distress and the dislocations of a fast-moving industrial era.

All honor to the pioneers, but let us honor also the courage of their descendants in working out problems more complex than those of the pioneer age. Vision and patriotism and earnestness still mark our people, who are aware of the need for tough fiber as they face an unpredictable future.

How difficult it is to interpret the history of a people! Among the many and diverse forces that have been at work, how easy to miss some of the master clues! Surely the generating power of the frontier has marked our life. Surely the industrial revolution of modern times and the advancing specialization of society have influenced our ways. But even these forces, great as they have been, do not furnish the full answer, for we must never forget that Minnesota is a part, not only of section and of nation, but of the world, which has steadily grown smaller, if more complex.

At any time in the past, the fact that Minnesota has had lines of interaction with the world has offered clues to events and characteristics in our history, but no one living today would deny that this truth has been driven home to us in modern times more forcibly than in earlier days. We have been called isolationists, but a son of Minnesota has been a leading American voice in calling for world cooperation and control to insure justice and peace, and his voice bears the undertones of the good sense of the people for whom he has been a spokesman.

One of the unforgettable charms of Minnesota is that though it has come of age, there is still a touch of the wilderness of vanished years about it. We seldom hear the thump of Sioux drums or the wail of Chippewa songs, but who among us has not viewed winding northern rivers as primitive as they were a century or more ago? Tucked away in the land are lonely lakes seldom seen by human eyes. In northern woods one can still discern trails made by French voyageurs long years ago. In deep forests one can still find the rare orchid called *moccasin*, which is the state flower. And one does not have to go to the forests to catch glimpses of the sleek gopher, who supplies the state's nickname.

The Falls of Minnehaha still "flash and gleam among the oak-trees, laugh and leap into the valley," and people still find solace "by the waters of Minnetonka." From the Canadian border to the Iowa line, from the Wisconsin boundary to the Red River Valley, Minnesota offers to human eyes a beauty of nature marked by almost infinite variety — graceful valleys and noble hills, waving prairies, mysterious woods, meandering rivers and streams, red earth that can be transformed into steel, thousands of lakes of alluring beauty, flowers and birds and fish and water and sky and sun, even winter snows and ice. Aquatennials and winter carnivals merely dramatize these natural splendors for a nation that sends its tourists to Minnesota summer and winter.

As valid as the interpretation by historian is that by poet, and Arthur Upson somehow gets the fragrance and authentic atmosphere of the North Star State into that stanza of "Minnesota, Hail to Thee" in which he sings of the "stream that bends to sea," of "the pine that seeks the blue," of "woods and waters fair," of "prairies waving far," and of sons that are "strong and true."

This Minnesota, like America, is not just land and people and institutions. These it is, but more, for they are bound together and given meaning by a past that stretches through the three ages of fur trader, pioneer, and maturity to the ever-shifting line of the present. No retrospect can furnish final answers to the question of where we are and whither we are tending, but it can supply a foundation for strength and steadiness as Minnesota, like all America, faces the future — a foundation in awareness and understanding of the meaning of its own history across the span of passing centuries.

Acknowledgments

A few of the chapters in this book have been rewritten from articles published previously. In some instances these were footnoted, and readers who are interested in tracing the information in the reprinted papers to its lair may wish to consult the earlier versions.

UNDER NORTHERN STARS. This article was prepared as an address for the fifteenth state historical convention held under the auspices of the Minnesota Historical Society, at Roseau, Minnesota, on June 19, 1937. It appeared under the title "Fort St. Charles and the Northwest Angle" in *Minnesota History,* 18:231–48 (September 1937).

PIONEER OF CULTURE. I edited this document, from the hand of Henry Hastings Sibley, for publication in *Minnesota History,* 15:382–94 (December 1934).

THE BOOMING OF GOPHER PRAIRIE. Much of the material in this paper formed part of an address given in International Falls, Minnesota, before the League of Minnesota Municipalities on June 9, 1938. It was published in *Minnesota Municipalities,* 23:277–81 (August 1938). I have incorporated into the paper certain parts, also, of an article entitled "Some Sources for St. Croix Valley History," which appeared in *Minnesota History,* 17:385–95 (December 1936).

PIONEERS OF THE SECOND LINE. Some of the ideas in this paper are drawn from a talk I gave in Rochester, Minnesota, on October 23, 1940, on the occasion of the twenty-fifth anniversary of the establishment of the Mayo Foundation for Medical Education and Research. The account of Cleveland is based

ACKNOWLEDGMENTS

upon an address I gave in Minneapolis on October 17, 1948, at the dedication of a memorial marker in commemoration of Cleveland. It was published in pamphlet form by the St. Anthony Park Area Historical Association under the title *Horace William Shaler Cleveland: Pioneer American Landscape Architect*.

NORTH STAR PERSPECTIVE. An abbreviated version of this chapter was presented in the *Farmer* for April 2, 1949, under the title "Minnesota — One Hundred Years." The chapter draws upon material in an essay on "The Scope of Minnesota History," which forms the introduction to my *Minnesota: Its History and Its People*, published by the University of Minnesota Press in 1937.

For the privilege of utilizing these papers in the present book, with extensive revision, I am grateful to *Minnesota History*, *Minnesota Municipalities*, the *Farmer*, and the St. Anthony Park Area Historical Association.

CHANNELS TO THE LAND. Some years ago Bertha L. Heilbron, now editor of *Minnesota History*, and I planned a volume of stories dealing with the trail blazers of the Northwest. To form a considerable portion of "Channels to the Land," I have revised and rewritten chapters originally drafted for that work. These papers have profited by much expert editorial and historical criticism from Miss Heilbron, and I wish to express my most grateful thanks for her aid.

WESTWARD IN A COVERED WAGON. The original of Jane Grout's diary is preserved in the manuscript collection of the Minnesota Historical Society, St. Paul. I am indebted to the Society for its use in this volume and particularly to Myrtle Bloemers, Gertrude Ackermann, and Dr. Grace Lee Nute for the transcription. For the convenience of readers I have capitalized words at the beginnings of sentences, omitted repetitions of words, and made some other slight changes that in no way affect the meaning of the diary.

Mr. Benjamin F. Rogers, Jr., a graduate student in history, gave me excellent aid late in the preparation of this book by collecting material for me on the role of the farmer in the history of Minnesota. This material has been very helpful to me in writing my chapter on "The Land Takers."

The paper entitled "A State University Is Born" was prepared for presentation before my Dining Club at the University of Minnesota.

In the general revision of the manuscript and the preparation of the index, I have been aided very competently by my editorial assistant, Mrs. Zephyra Shepherd, to whom I am deeply grateful.

Finally, let me express my sincere appreciation of the superb work done by the staff of the University of Minnesota Press in the editing and designing of the book.

T. C. B.

Index

INDEX

Kelley, George W., 127

Kelley, Oliver H., 121

Labor, 219, 234

Lakes: Michigan, 15–16, 18, 21, 42; Champlain, 17; Ontario, 17; Huron, 17, 42; Superior, 19, 39, 51, 61; Erie, 42; Pepin, 44, 50, 228; Lake of the Woods, 61–62, 73; Julia, 87; Itasca, 89

Larson, Agnes, quoted, 142

La Vérendrye, Jean Baptiste, 63, 67–68, 73

La Vérendrye, Pierre, Sieur de, 62–73

League of Minnesota Municipalities, 135

Le Duc, W. G., 112, 154–55

Le Sueur, Pierre Charles, 51–54

Lewis, Sinclair, 233, 235

Liquor, on the frontier, 118; Puritanism, 141–42; temperance, 145–46

Long, Stephen H., 87

Loring, Charles M., 224

Louisiana, under France, 30, 38, 51

Lumbering, 142–43

Macalester College, 155, 171

Mackinac Island, 31, 48, 56–57, 63, 75, 80

MacLeish, Archibald, quoted, 3

Mandan Indians, described, 69

Map making, 17, 31, 35, 58, 74, 87, 88; on birch bark, 62; Peter Pond, 84

Marquette, Jacques, 31–35

Marshall, William R., 153, 161, 181

Maynard, Theodore, quoted, 4

Mayo, Dr. Charles H., 219, 233

Mayo, Dr. William J., 219, 233

Mayo, Dr. William W., 219, 233

Medicine and illness, 8, 117, 206, 209–10, 213, 217; Indian, 45; vaccination, 88, 90–91; education in, 219; Drs. Mayo, 219, 233; research, 236

Meeker, B. B., 161, 191 n. 8

Mendota, 96, 97

Merrill, E. W., 162, 163

Mesabi range, 234

Mesaiger, Father, Jesuit, 63

Middle West: discovered, 14–19; described, 20; under France, 30, 51; claimed by Du Lhut, 38; Charlevoix's report, 55–56; Treaty of 1783, 85; agriculture, 111–27

Mille Lacs, 38–39, 44, 46

Mining, copper, 51, 53; iron, 66; Mesabi, 226, 227, 234, 236

Minneapolis, 40, 45; Mill City, 120, 234; beginnings, 130–31; park system, 220, 222–24; growth, 235

Minnesota: exploration, 74–78, 86–90; Territory, 97–98, 151–52, 156–57; boom, 98, 128–30, 165, 231, 232; education, 98, 143–44, 151–95, 235; described, 99, 102; agriculture, 111–27; politics, 131–32, 147–48, 166–68; founding of towns, 131–34; Sioux uprising, 134; early social life, 141–42; lumbering, 142–43; university, 151–95; statehood, 166–69, 231; mining, 226, 227, 234, 236; machine-age society, 233

Minnesota Historical Society, 68, 99, 231

Minnesota Horticultural Society, 180, 218

Minnesota Pioneer, quoted, 161

Minnesota River, 52, 76

Mission of St. Michael the Archangel, 58

Missionaries, 37, 144–45; Marquette, 31–35; Hennepin, 36–47; Guignas and De Gonnor, 56–59; Mesaiger, 63; Aulneau, 66; Boutwell, W. T., 88, 114, 117, 144

Montreal, 26, 37, 56, 63, 68

Morals, 97, 130, 140–41

Morrill Act, 175–79

Morrison, William, 91

Music, 30, 44, 51, 147, 203, 213, 217–18, 228, 233; of voyageurs, 68, 229; of war, 80; ballads, 111, 113, 118

Neill, Edward D., 146, 152–72 *passim*

New England, in Upper Midwest, 79–84, 123, 130, 137–50, 152–53, 155, 220–25

New France, 17, 21, 31, 41, 74

Niagara Falls, described, 41–42

Nicolet, Jean, 14–19

Nininger (Minnesota), 129

Nisbeth, Hugo, quoted, 115

North, John W., 152, 155–56, 168

Northrop, Cyrus, 144, 150

Northwest Angle, 61–62

Northwest Company, 84

Northwest Passage, 15, 25, 69–70, 75, 77–78

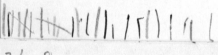